Society, Power, and Land in Northeastern Zimbabwe, ca. 1560–1960

NEW AFRICAN HISTORIES

SERIES EDITORS: ALLEN ISAACMAN, DEREK R. PETERSON, CARINA RAY, AND JACOB DLAMINI

David William Cohen and E. S. Atieno Odhiambo, *The Risks of Knowledge*
Belinda Bozzoli, *Theatres of Struggle and the End of Apartheid*
Gary Kynoch, *We Are Fighting the World*
Stephanie Newell, *The Forger's Tale*
Jacob A. Tropp, *Natures of Colonial Change*
Jan Bender Shetler, *Imagining Serengeti*
Cheikh Anta Babou, *Fighting the Greater Jihad*
Marc Epprecht, *Heterosexual Africa?*
Marissa J. Moorman, *Intonations*
Karen E. Flint, *Healing Traditions*
Derek R. Peterson and Giacomo Macola, editors, *Recasting the Past*
Moses E. Ochonu, *Colonial Meltdown*
Emily S. Burrill, Richard L. Roberts, and Elizabeth Thornberry, editors, *Domestic Violence and the Law in Colonial and Postcolonial Africa*
Daniel R. Magaziner, *The Law and the Prophets*
Emily Lynn Osborn, *Our New Husbands Are Here*
Robert Trent Vinson, *The Americans Are Coming!*
James R. Brennan, *Taifa*
Benjamin N. Lawrance and Richard L. Roberts, editors, *Trafficking in Slavery's Wake*
David M. Gordon, *Invisible Agents*
Allen F. Isaacman and Barbara S. Isaacman, *Dams, Displacement, and the Delusion of Development*
Stephanie Newell, *The Power to Name*
Gibril R. Cole, *The Krio of West Africa*
Matthew M. Heaton, *Black Skin, White Coats*
Meredith Terretta, *Nation of Outlaws, State of Violence*
Paolo Israel, *In Step with the Times*
Michelle R. Moyd, *Violent Intermediaries*
Abosede A. George, *Making Modern Girls*
Alicia C. Decker, *In Idi Amin's Shadow*
Rachel Jean-Baptiste, *Conjugal Rights*
Shobana Shankar, *Who Shall Enter Paradise?*
Emily S. Burrill, *States of Marriage*
Todd Cleveland, *Diamonds in the Rough*
Carina E. Ray, *Crossing the Color Line*
Sarah Van Beurden, *Authentically African*
Giacomo Macola, *The Gun in Central Africa*
Lynn Schler, *Nation on Board*
Julie MacArthur, *Cartography and the Political Imagination*
Abou B. Bamba, *African Miracle, African Mirage*
Daniel Magaziner, *The Art of Life in South Africa*
Paul Ocobock, *An Uncertain Age*
Keren Weitzberg, *We Do Not Have Borders*
Nuno Domingos, *Football and Colonialism*
Jeffrey S. Ahlman, *Living with Nkrumahism*
Bianca Murillo, *Market Encounters*
Laura Fair, *Reel Pleasures*
Thomas F. McDow, *Buying Time*
Jon Soske, *Internal Frontiers*
Elizabeth W. Giorgis, *Modernist Art in Ethiopia*
Matthew V. Bender, *Water Brings No Harm*
David Morton, *Age of Concrete*
Marissa J. Moorman, *Powerful Frequencies*
Ndubueze L. Mbah, *Emergent Masculinities*
Judith A. Byfield, *The Great Upheaval*
Patricia Hayes and Gary Minkley, editors, *Ambivalent*
Mari K. Webel, *The Politics of Disease Control*
Kara Moskowitz, *Seeing Like a Citizen*
Jacob Dlamini, *Safari Nation*
Alice Wiemers, *Village Work*
Cheikh Anta Babou, *The Muridiyya on the Move*
Laura Ann Twagira, *Embodied Engineering*
Marissa Mika, *Africanizing Oncology*
Holly Hanson, *To Speak and Be Heard*
Paul S. Landau, *Spear*
Saheed Aderinto, *Animality and Colonial Subjecthood in Africa*
Katherine Bruce-Lockhart, *Carceral Afterlives*
Natasha Erlank, *Convening Black Intimacy in Early Twentieth-Century South Africa*
Morgan J. Robinson, *A Language for the World*
Faeeza Ballim, *Apartheid's Leviathan*
Nicole Eggers, *Unruly Ideas*
Mark W. Deets, *A Country of Defiance*
Patrick William Otim, *Acholi Intellectuals*
Ademide Adelusi-Adeluyi, *Imagine Lagos*
Daniel Magaziner, *Available Light*
Admire Mseba, *Society, Power, and Land in Northeastern Zimbabwe, ca. 1560–1960*

Society, Power, and Land in Northeastern Zimbabwe, ca. 1560–1960

Admire Mseba

OHIO UNIVERSITY PRESS
ATHENS, OHIO

Ohio University Press, Athens, Ohio 45701
ohioswallow.com

Printed in the United States of America
Ohio University Press books are printed on acid-free paper ∞ ™

Library of Congress Cataloging-in-Publication Data
Names: Mseba, Admire, author.
Title: Society, power, and land in northeastern Zimbabwe, ca. 1560–1960 / Admire Mseba.
Other titles: New African histories series.
Description: Athens : Ohio University Press, 2024. | Series: New African histories | Includes bibliographical references and index.
Identifiers: LCCN 2024022868 | ISBN 9780821425893 (paperback) | ISBN 9780821425886 (hardcover) | ISBN 9780821425909 (pdf)
Subjects: LCSH: Land reform—Zimbabwe—History. | Land tenure—Zimbabwe—History. | Zimbabwe—Colonial influence.
Classification: LCC HD1333.Z55 M74 2024 | DDC 333.316891—dc23/eng/20240520
LC record available at https://lccn.loc.gov/2024022868

Contents

Illustrations

MAPS

FIGURES

TABLES

Preface

In Zimbabwe, as in many former settler colonies, issues of land and power raise the specter of racialized injustice and anticolonial resistance. When, in July 2000, the Zimbabwe African National Union (Patriotic Front) (ZANU [PF]) government commenced its Fast Track Land Reform Programme, it called the exercise the Third Chimurenga,—the third war of liberation. In its view, as in those of many others, this was, in linear fashion, Zimbabweans' third struggle against colonial domination. In the First Chimurenga, waged between 1896 and 1897, Zimbabweans had fought against the imposition of British colonial rule on their land. Although this *chimurenga* ended in defeat, so the narrative went, it inspired the Second Chimurenga, successfully waged in the 1960s and 1970s to rid the country of British colonialism. The Second Chimurenga had brought political independence. The Third Chimurenga sought to bring economic independence. Regaining lost lands was central to this. Indeed, in the 2000 parliamentary elections, the ruling party's main campaign slogan was "Land is the economy. The economy is land." Eight years later, in 2008, the party ran with the slogan "Our Land, Our Sovereignty."

In these words, the ZANU (PF) government invoked the liberation struggle to legitimate its land reform policy. It also firmly inserted land at the center of power and national politics. It did so because it understood the centrality of land in the Zimbabwean struggles against colonialism. The version of history that the ruling party invoked was a simplified one. Historians have offered more complex versions.[1] The contours of this history are as follows: the British South Africa Company occupied the Zimbabwean plateau in 1890 with the hope of exploiting the region's mineral resources. Finding these resources to be poorer than it had assumed, the regime quickly turned to the new colony's land resources. Over several decades, the colonial state dispossessed Africans of their land, parceling it to the colony's settler population. The avariciousness of the colonial state and its settler constituency was confirmed by the Land Apportionment Act (1930). This piece of legislation institutionalized racial segregation in land allocation, reserving fully half of the colony's land, which was also best suited for agriculture, to the colony's tiny white settler population. The act assigned 25 percent of the colony's landmass, consisting of mostly poor and marginal land, to the African population as native reserves, underscoring its architects' racist beliefs that Africans belonged to "tribes" through which they could access the resource. This tribe was presided over by "tribal" chiefs. Under the Land Apportionment Act, a tiny proportion of the remaining 25 percent of the territory's land was assigned to better-off Africans as Native Purchase Areas while the rest was retained by the state either as unassigned land or as national parks.[2]

The implementation of the Land Apportionment Act in the middle decades of the twentieth century, accompanied by a host of discriminatory policies, squeezed even the most enterprising African at a time when the tide of anticolonial struggles was increasing. Dispossessed of their lands and clasped by the brutal hands of the colonial state and the colonial capitalist economy, Africans swelled the ranks of African nationalists calling for the end of colonial rule.[3]

The passage and implementation of another draconian piece of colonial land legislation, the Native Land Husbandry Act (1951), made the nationalists' message particularly cogent. Enacted in part to create a group of landless Africans who could cheaply fulfill the labor needs of the colonial capitalist economy and in part to cure the contradictions of racist colonial land policies—supposedly the need to address land degradation and improve production in the overcrowded native reserves—without taking an inch of the land assigned to white settlers, the act exemplified the callousness of the colonial state toward its African subjects. Its implementation entailed forced cattle culling (an attack on people's property and wealth), forced contour ridging (a huge demand on already stretched African labor), and the restructuring of patterns of landholding, including the assigning of a family's land to its male heads, which denied women and young male labor migrants the possibility of ever owning land in the reserves. All this generated immense resentment among the colony's Africans. So intense was the resentment that it drove the colonial state to reconsider this policy even before the 1950s decade was over.

Refusing to recognize its culpability in fomenting African opposition to the Native Land Husbandry Act in particular and colonial rule more broadly, the Rhodesian state blamed all this on African nationalists. Rather than addressing the grievances over land that the Africans presented, the colonial state delegitimized—as inauthentic representatives of Africans—the nationalists who were amplifying the call for the equitable distribution of the resource. Instead, it pointed to chiefs as the legitimate African leaders. But this was never a sincere recognition of the power of chiefs. Instead, it was a contorted, racist attempt to simultaneously use chiefs as a counterweight to African nationalists and as a buffer between the central state and its increasingly restless subjects.[4] Apart from the political calculus behind it, the whole policy was premised on the idea that Africans were so primitive that they had not only opposed the modernity of the Native Land Husbandry Act but also deserved to be ruled through their "traditional" institutions, the chiefs. Soon, the colonial state renamed the reserves tribal trust lands.

Because this move by the colonial state failed to address African grievances over land, it did not silence the African voices calling for independence and the equitable sharing of land. What the turn toward community development—the colonial policy that replaced the Native Land Husbandry Act—did was to leave chiefs in an invidious position. Long tasked with implementing hated colonial policies, chiefs became the local face of the colonial state. Save for a few—Chief Rekayi Tangwena is a good example—they were viewed by their subjects as stooges of the colonial state and were incredibly unpopular.

The colonial stooges label was one that chiefs found hard to shake off. It influenced their relations with the leadership of the nationalist movement and the guerrillas who executed the war of independence in the 1960s and 1970s. Ultimately, Zimbabwe's anticolonial fighters sidelined chiefs in favor of spirit mediums.[5] After independence in 1980, the nationalists, Zimbabwe's postcolonial rulers, continued their sidelining of chiefs for a decade. The ZANU (PF) government deployed party functionaries through the village and ward development committees (VIDCOs and WADCOs) to serve as important counterpoints to chiefs in land matters in the former reserves—by then renamed communal areas. Not until the 1990s did the postcolonial state restore some of the chiefs' powers. Since then, the state has incorporated chiefs in its scheme of rural rule mainly because these leaders are a vital cog in the ruling party's voter mobilization machinery.

This story of colonialism, race, land, liberation, and chiefly power is well known and much discussed by Zimbabweans themselves. Indeed, scholars of Zimbabwe have done much to show us how colonial experiences shaped the postcolonial realities.[6] My purpose in this book is to show how the dynamics of ancient times, alongside the systems put in place by Zimbabwe's colonial rulers, set out the terms on which contemporary struggles over land are conducted.

Acknowledgments

This book has been long in the making. In the more than ten years that I have taken to complete it, I have accumulated immense debts to institutions and individuals. I can never repay all of them but want to thank the institutions and individuals who helped me along the way. I also want to apologize in advance for those whom I will certainly forget to mention by name.

I conducted the bulk of the research for this study in 2012 and 2013. I could not have done that without the fellowships and grants from the Department of History, the Graduate College, and the Executive Council for Graduate and Professional Studies at the University of Iowa. As a holder of a very generous postdoctoral research fellowship at the International Studies Group (ISG) at the University of the Free State, I transformed the manuscript from its earlier form as a dissertation. I want to thank the ISG for funding subsequent research trips to Zimbabwe in 2016 and 2017. I also want to thank the American Council of Learned Societies for the African Humanities Postdoctoral Fellowship award (2018–19). This yearlong fellowship allowed me to focus on completing the first draft of the manuscript. When the COVID-19 pandemic prevented me from traveling to Zimbabwe to undertake additional research in 2020, my then two departments—the Department of Black Studies and the Department of History at the University of Missouri–Columbia—stepped in to finance the hiring of a research assistant. I am thankful to my then two chairs, April C. Langley and Catherine Rymph, for facilitating this.

Institutions funded my research and writing, but the intellectual project would have foundered without the support of teachers and colleagues. If readers find something meaningful in this book, it is because of the effort of those who taught me to become a historian. Jim Giblin directed the dissertation upon which this book is based. He has remained a source of support, advice, and wisdom over the years. I can never thank him enough. Members of my dissertation committee—Jeffrey L. Cox, Michel Gobat, Catherine

Komisaruk, and Edward Miner—suggested ways in which I could transform the dissertation into the book, and for this I am very grateful.

Ian Phimister took me in when I was a wearied, freshly minted PhD and created the best conditions for me to recover and revise the dissertation into a book manuscript. I am thankful to Ian for the mentorship over the years. At the ISG, he created the most comfortable environment that any scholar would wish for. He supported my follow-up research trips to Zimbabwe. He also supported my attendance at conferences and seminars where I presented drafts of this book. Ian also read and commented on parts of the manuscript. Allen Isaacman read several drafts of this book and remained very patient with me. I am very grateful to him and his co–series editors—Jean Allman, Derek Peterson, Carina Ray, and Jacob Dlamini—for their insights as I revised the manuscript. I am equally grateful to Ohio University Press's two anonymous readers for their very insightful comments. At Ohio University Press, I am grateful to Gillian Berchowitz, Ricky Huard, Beth Pratt, Tyler Balli, and freelance copy editor Sally Boyington for their immense help as I worked on the book.

I also want to thank the staff at the institutions where I conducted research for this book. I appreciate the help I received from the archivists at the National Archives of Zimbabwe. I extend my thanks to Livingstone Muchefa, Tafadzwa Chigodora, George Bishi, Alfred Chikomba, Kudakwashe Mavingire, and all the other members of staff for their help over the years. Father Steven Buckland and the late Father Anthony Bex granted me access to the Jesuit Archives in Harare and for this I say thank you. I have received help from librarians at the University of Iowa Library, the Sasol Library at the University of the Free State, the Ellis Library at the University of Missouri–Columbia, and more recently the University of Southern California Libraries. I want to thank them all.

I am especially grateful to my oral informants in Zimbabwe. Without the stories that they told me, reconstructing the narrative of land and power in the precolonial period would have been difficult. Many of them left their important businesses to attend to my questions about matters of the past. Accessing interviewees often depended on the generosity of colleagues. Esther Chipashu connected me to spirit mediums. She took a personal interest in the research, accompanying me when I visited some of the mediums. In fact, without her, I might not have been able to access most of the mediums. Happy Marufu and Nathaniel Chimhete helped me with their cars when I needed them most. Primrose Nyamhute rescued the research when the COVID-19 pandemic prevented me from traveling to Zimbabwe in 2020. I am grateful to her and her husband, Oscar Sigauke, for all the help in collecting the vocabularies in Nyanga. Fortune Puthi, Joyce Tembo, and Remaketsi Mbedzi helped me with Kalanga, Nambya, and Venda vocabulary. For this I am very thankful to them. I am equally grateful to Madlozi Moyo, a longtime colleague, who frequently clarified Kalanga words for me. I also want to thank Margaret Chipara for help in translating parts of António Alberto de Andrade's *Relações de Moçambique Setecentista* from Portuguese to English for me.

I presented draft chapters of this book at seminars at the University of Basel, the University of Bologna, and the University of Zimbabwe as well as meetings of the Southern African Historical Society, the Historical Society of South Africa, and the African Studies Association. I appreciate the feedback that I received from colleagues at these meetings. I want to thank Julia Tischler and Benjamin Brühwiler for arranging my presentation in Basel and Arrigo Pallotti for facilitating my presentation at the University of Bologna. The University of Zimbabwe has been my intellectual home for over two decades. I am thankful to past and present members of the then Economic History and History Departments for their feedback in seminars. My teachers in the then Department of Economic History—Joseph P. Mtisi, Victor E. M. Machingaidze, and the late Government Phiri—paved the road that I traveled in my formative years as a historian. I will forever cherish their mentorship. I especially want to thank Joseph Mujere, with whom I have discussed some of the ideas in this book. Without the help of Rebecca Grollemund, my former colleague at the University of Missouri–Columbia, my attempts to incorporate linguistic evidence in the book would have completely failed. I also want to thank Raevin Jimenez, to whom I turned when I first attempted to use linguistic data to reconstruct the early history of northeastern Zimbabwe. Her suggestions prevented me from completely going astray. As I revised the book, I benefited from the support of my colleagues in the Departments of Black Studies and History at the University of Missouri–Columbia. I finalized the book with the collegial support of my colleagues in the Van Hunnick Department of History at the University of Southern California. To Graeme Wynn, thank you for saving me from myself.

Parts of chapters 2 and 3 appear as "Narratives, Rituals and Political Imaginations: The Social and Political World of the Vashona of Northeastern Zimbabwe from the Sixteenth to the Nineteenth Centuries" in the *Journal of Southern African Studies* 46, no. 1 (2020). I want to thank *JSAS* for permission to incorporate this material in the book. I also want to thank the National Archives of Zimbabwe for the permission to use copies of Master Farmer and Master of Tillage certificates in this book. I thank Sekai Kashamba for drawing the maps for me.

This book would not have been possible without the support of my family. My parents, the late Reverend Elisha Nemanga Mseba and Tellia Nemanga, my siblings, Nomsa (may your soul rest in peace), Japhta, Zivaishe (may your soul rest in peace), Harris, Happias, Alford (may your soul rest in peace), Abinel, Afios, and their families have been pillars of material and moral support over the years. Precious and Admire Chikomborero have lived with this work in Iowa City, Cedar Falls, Uzumba, Harare, Bloemfontein, Columbia, and Los Angeles and have not complained once. Aiden Mukudzeishe arrived when the manuscript was close to being finished, and he has been a source of welcome distraction. I cannot thank the three of you enough. I dedicate this book to you and to the memory of my father, who passed away a week before I commenced the research upon which the bulk of this book is based. I remain solely responsible for the errors and shortcomings in it.

Abbreviations

BSAC	British South Africa Company
BSAP	British South Africa Police
FTLRP	Fast Track Land Reform Programme
NAD	Native Affairs Department
NAZ	National Archives of Zimbabwe
NLHA	Native Land Husbandry Act
(PF) ZAPU	(Patriotic Front) Zimbabwe African People's Union
ZANU (PF)	Zimbabwe African National Union (Patriotic Front)

Introduction

Power and the Deep History of Zimbabwe's Land Question

In September 2002, President Robert Mugabe of Zimbabwe framed the country's land question as a fundamental issue that "pitted the black majority who are the right-holders, and therefore primary stakeholders, to our land against an obdurate and internationally well-connected racial minority, largely of British descent and brought in and sustained by British colonialism."[1] At the time, the country was engaged in the Fast Track Land Reform Programme (FTLRP), intended to redistribute land once held by white commercial farmers to the country's Black indigenous peoples. By 2010, scholars were assessing the results of this exercise. Even the most favorable evaluations observed that "the land reform exercise focused on racialized imbalances of highly skewed landholdings and discriminatory land tenure systems" and failed to address gender disparities.[2] "Women, [especially 'ordinary' women] were always at the end of the queue in . . . [land] allocations and other benefits."[3]

The FTLRP's failure to address gender (and other) inequalities was a direct consequence of the way in which Zimbabwe's land question has been framed. Successive settler colonial states dispossessed indigenous Zimbabweans of their land and distributed it to white settlers. These regimes also corralled the indigenous population in poor, diseased, semiarid, and wretched places that they called native reserves.[4] Race loomed large, but the way colonialism was experienced was also shaped by other regimes of power. Gender was one of them.[5] It was not the only one. Other forms of power were rooted in kinship, seniority, and status. Mugabe's framing of Zimbabwe's land question recognized the colonial racialized land inequalities. It failed to recognize that colonialism entrenched many long-standing regimes of power and that together they shaped access to land (and other resources). His articulation of the land question was not incorrect. It was incomplete.

This book examines the relations between land and power (in its many guises) in the northeastern part of the Zimbabwean plateau (see map 0.1), to illuminate a long, tangled, and substantially neglected history of struggles over land in the centuries that preceded colonial rule. It argues that the unequal distribution of land in Zimbabwe was substantially shaped by the imbrication of colonial policies with these struggles. This, then, is an account of the roles and actions of kinspeople, subject peoples, healers, spirit mediums, and ruling elites in creating a web of relations and associated sociopolitical structures that colonial authorities sought to govern without fully understanding. *Society, Power, and Land* is a study of the "plural articulations" of power, its mediation, and its influence on how land was claimed, controlled, and accessed in northeastern Zimbabwe in the centuries before 1960.[6]

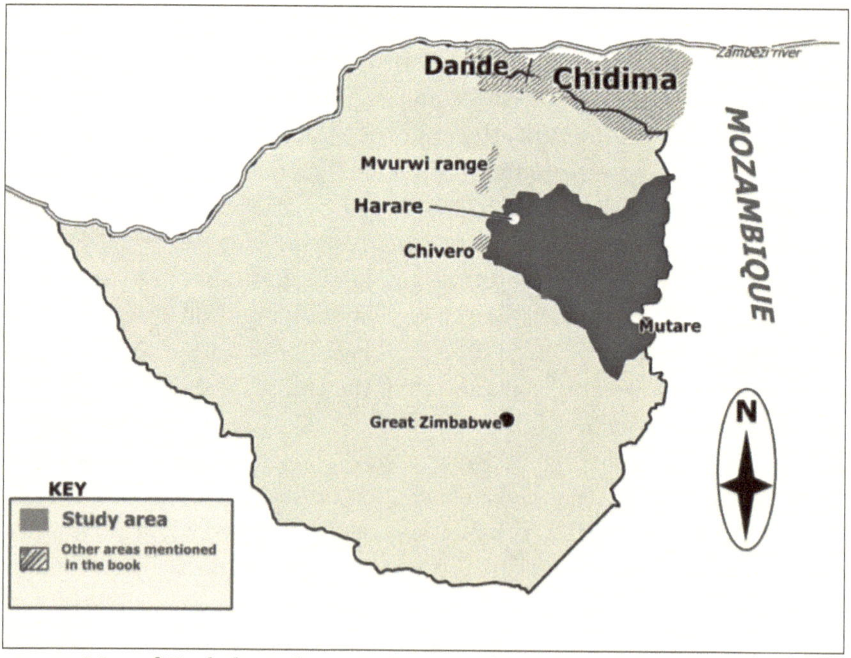

MAP 0.1. Map of Zimbabwe showing the area of study. Map drawn by Sekai Kashamba.

The book's central argument is that unequal power relations rooted in kinship, gender, generation, and status have influenced patterns of access to, and control of, good, productive land among the farming men and women of northeastern Zimbabwe since at least the sixteenth century. Land, the book further argues, was also central to the making of political power. In the sixteenth century, ruling lineages wove narratives locating their power in their relations with their subjects and with the land. From the seventeenth century onward, many other dynasties legitimated their authority over land and people by seeking closer association with the Zimbabwean plateau's larger polities. Concurrently, an ability to ensure the land's fecundity, and thus the collective well-being of its inhabitants, became important in the making, and moderation, of the power of ruling elites. In all of this, no single group (neither rulers nor spirit mediums and healers) was able to consolidate power. At the time of colonial conquest in 1890, land was unequally distributed and authority was circumscribed. The imposition of colonial rule and the uneven incorporation of Africans into the colonial economy affected the relations of power and the social dynamics of landholding in contradictory ways. Colonial policies assigned land to male heads of the households, deepening their power at the expense of women and junior men. However, wage labor sometimes allowed junior men to accumulate resources formerly controlled by their seniors and assert their own autonomy.[7] At the same time, differentiated access to wages and markets enabled new forms of accumulation, social differentiation, and landed inequalities. To restate the argument: power shaped patterns of access to land. Control of land legitimated the power of ruling elites. But this power was moderated by the actions of those whose craft was understood by society to ensure the fertility of the land and general collective well-being. These included spirit mediums and healers.

Power operated in many forms in the area that became northeastern Zimbabwe. On one plane, access to resources allowed "male elders, chiefly lineages, and other privileged groups to exercise hegemony over the rank and file of children, junior males, nubile women," and outsiders.[8] This form of power, I argue, allowed those in powerful positions to access better-quality land than the subordinate groups that existed alongside them. It also allowed the powerful to exclude those without power, particularly women who married into existing networks of kin and other non-kin who were mostly outsiders.

Power also operated on a second plane, incorporating "beliefs about nature and the universe."[9] In particular, ideas about fertility, collective well-being, and their sources were important in claiming and contesting power.

The veracity accorded such ideas legitimated chiefs' powers and spawned institutions that mediated the authority of these leaders.[10] Ultimately, the ways in which all this played out depended on many other factors. As chapter 4 demonstrates, for example, in the colonial period the ability of spirit mediums to moderate the power of chiefs was undermined by the colonial state's efforts to reduce their authority. At the same time, the colonial state challenged the cosmological basis of chiefly power by denying their ability to "cool" land heated by antisocial, even criminal, acts such as incest and murder.

POWER RELATIONS, LAND, AND AUTHORITY

Kinship gender, generation, wealth, and status have long been understood to be important to the life of Africans. Together, they shaped the ways in which people related to one another and to the land.[11] Precisely how they did so remains obscure because our understanding of questions of land and power has been drawn from narratives that developed out of colonial administrative expedience.[12] Colored by fantasies about "tribal" Africa held by colonial officials and early ethnographers, these narratives coupled African access to land with membership of "tribes."[13] They also envisioned people who lived in essentially egalitarian communities.

Anthropologist Jon F. Holleman encapsulated this egalitarian vision. In his view, "communal tenure"—ownership of land by virtue of being a member of the "tribe"—in indigenous Rhodesia meant "that because the land and its resources belong to the community, every full member of this community has an inalienable right to a reasonable share according to his requirements. For this reason this right is secure as is a person's membership of the community." Elaborating, Holleman explained that "in customary law, the permanence and inviolability of the land rights of individuals are not conceived, as is ownership in most Western law, as a relationship to a specific holding in perpetuity, but as a perpetual relationship with any such unencumbered portion of the land of the community as may be available for individualized occupation whenever required from time to time." This, he concluded, gave each member of the community a vested right to share the land.[14] Holleman was correct in pointing out that African conceptions of land rights differed from, but were no less legitimate than, those of European settlers. Yet he never questioned the idea of the tribe itself or addressed the ways in which social and power relations within such a community mediated claims to land.

The "tribe" that Holleman envisioned was assumed to be an extension of a kinship group, and for much of the early and mid-twentieth century, colonial officials and social anthropologists located relations in such a group in descent, traced through the patriline (and the matriline for matrilineal societies).[15] However, since the 1960s, many other anthropologists have questioned "the over-emphasis in the anthropology of Africa on unilateral descent groups at the expense of other social units, such as component households, houses, and networks based on bilateral or cognatic (through both mother and father) and affinal (marriage) links."[16] This thinking is perhaps best captured in Marshall Sahlins's relatively recent formulation: "What Kinship Is—Culture; What Kinship Is Not—Biology."[17] In Sahlins's view, central to the idea of kinship was "the mutuality of being," which can be "constituted . . . by procreation, social construction, or some combination of these."[18] This, in many ways, is what happened among the peoples of northeastern Zimbabwe. They constructed new networks through marriage and utilized both paternal and maternal relations to access land. But for them, this was because kinships were more than groups of "people who . . . [were] intrinsic to one another's existence—thus mutual persons," as Sahlins put it; rather, kinspeople had their fair share of conflicts and hierarchies.[19]

If marriage allowed families and communities to accept and settle outsiders who became their sons- and daughters-in-law, it also structured relations and afforded idioms through which power could be articulated and contested in very gendered ways.[20] Ordinarily, upon marriage, women moved to live with the families of their husbands, where they could face discrimination and exclusion.[21] Thus, gendered inequalities were baked into the kinship cake. While gender differentiated women's experiences from those of men, seniority, understood here in terms of both generation and age, and status could potentially handicap ordinary men's and women's claims to land. What is more, kinship was also exclusionary because, while it united kin, allowing those who belonged to access resources, including land, it divided kinspeople from non-kin and denied outsiders similar access.[22]

Kinship, gender, and generation underlined hierarchies within societies long before the archaeological record reveals inequalities rooted in wealth and status in the terminal centuries of the first millennium. As chapters 4 and 5 show, these axes of differentiation were reinforced by colonial rule. Only by examining the ways in which relations rooted in kinship, gender, generation, and status mediated the rhythms of life can we, then, understand how power regulated access to productive resources in the most intimate settings of African societies in the deep past: households and kinship groups. However, the appearance of these varied forms of power in the sources is quite uneven, forcing us to sometimes discuss them together and often at different moments throughout the period covered in this book.

Associated with the notion of communal land tenure was the idea that land was abundant in precolonial Africa, whereas labor and capital were scarce.[23] The result, several studies argued in what came to be known as the wealth in people thesis, was that political and social control "tended to be over people rather than over land" and "neither individuals nor kin groups bother[ed] to lay specific claims to large tracts of territory."[24] According to Terence Ranger, writing about Makoni District in northeastern Zimbabwe, in precolonial times "men were much more concerned with contestations over other goods than they were in seeking to control productive land. Chiefs, headmen, and their leading followers contested for women and cattle above all, and though the women obtained by raiding and in war were employed in cultivation, these contestations took up much male energy."[25] The indifference to land is said to have ended with the advent of colonial rule. In the colonial period, unoccupied land became subject to highly specific rights because of rapid population growth and the intervention of colonial officials in land matters.[26] Further impetus to control land was driven by the production of cash crops or by the exploitation of land for commercial purposes.[27]

Both the idea of wealth in people and the argument that land was unimportant to the organization of social, economic, and political life among precolonial Africans were not without limitations. As Jane Guyer pointed out three decades ago, "the idea of 'wealth in people' is underspecified, in that the systematic dynamic implied is a simple accumulative one: more wives, more children, more clients, more alliances, more patrimony and so on. Neither the changing constituents of wealth (including both things and people) nor the way in which people were variously valued in relation to each other and to things . . . [was] incorporated into the theory."[28] Guyer implored us to not "lose sight of wealth in things" even as she insisted on locating this in "[i]ts relationship to wealth—in—people."[29] Among those "things" that Africans valued as wealth in the precolonial period were knowledge, household goods, and land.[30]

Indeed, more-recent scholarship has rejected the "dominant paradigm of precolonial Africa's free surplus land—indifference to territoriality and absence of property, as well as the inalienability of land."[31] Or as Mariana Candido recently asked, if the idea that control over people was important while that of land was not is true, then why did coastal peoples and nearby rulers in west-central Africa "register land in the seventeenth and eighteenth centuries?"[32] The point is that these communities understood land to be important and scarce.[33] They were not alone. Carola Lentz's study among the Dagara and Sisala communities of West Africa shows that these communities possessed an acute sense of landownership in precolonial times. Lentz's informants connected claims to land with ideas of autochthony—being the original inhabitants. "Struggles over land rights and their transmission," she explains, "were punctuated by narratives of migration, settlement and first possession."[34] "First-comer narratives," Lentz elaborates, "locate the origin of legitimate property not in any social contract, but in the encounter between man and nature, or to be precise, man and earth deities."[35]

Society, Power and Land contributes to these efforts by looking closely at differences in soil quality at various scales. So we see, in chapter 1, that the thirteenth-century inhabitants of northeastern Zimbabwe understood that land possessed different qualities. Climatic, geomorphological, and environmental factors contributed to variations in soil quality and, in some areas, to the prevalence of disease-carrying insects, which people factored into their decisions about where to live and farm. Good farmland was relatively scarce, and not everyone accessed it in equal measure. Even when more land was available, the everyday realities of unequal power relations led to uneven access to the resource.

In contrast to Lentz's findings that claims to land were rooted in first-comer narratives, in northeastern Zimbabwe, these claims were based on narratives told by allochthons. The origin traditions that ruling families tell in this region celebrate an immigrant clan or dynastic founder who settled land already inhabited by people lacking the ability to make fire, or who ate their meat raw, or cultivators without knowledge of hunting—in short, people who were "uncivilized"—to legitimate the founder's assumption of power and claims to a particular territory or landed domain. Alternatively, they claim that dynastic founders were granted chiefship and territory by the Varozvi—elites of the Rozvi state. These claims underscored the point that claims to land—read as territory—were rooted in political relations between subject peoples and their rulers on the one hand and rulers of smaller states and those of bigger ones on the other.

Because land was political, rulers and their families spent much creative energy in legitimating both power and territorial claims. Gerald Mazarire's studies on another part of the Zimbabwean plateau have enriched our understanding of how this played out in the eighteenth and nineteenth centuries. Among the Karanga polities of south-central Zimbabwe, Mazarire argues, notions of territoriality were pivotal to the making of political authority.[36] These, he explains, centered on the *gadzingo,* the "local socio-political centres controlling the regions occupied by these newcomers."[37] These spaces, Mazarire elaborates, "had to be kept fertile, defended and associated with specific ruling families. . . . [They] were the residence of ruling chiefs, the burial grounds of their ancestors, their strongholds and places of refuge in times of trouble. They were sacred places of ancestral veneration and fertility rituals which found resonance and relevance in the hinterlands they controlled."[38] According to Mazarire, the *gadzingo* system was a local adaptation of a supraterritorial system, the Mwari "cult" utilized by the Rozvi. This "cult" was centered on a network of shrines located in the granite hills of the Matopos in the southwestern parts of the Zimbabwean plateau. To the shrines, the indigenous inhabitants of the southern Zimbabwean plateau sent messengers bearing gifts to ask Mwari/Mlimo for good rains and for protection against pestilence and disease. Local adaptations of this institution, Mazarire argues, enabled eighteenth- and nineteenth-century Karanga dynasties to deconstruct it to make it relevant at the local level by elevating individual ancestors associated with ruling clans to be the guarantors of fertility in the whole polity. "This founding mythology," he concludes, "legitimated the new rulers."[39] Put in slightly different words, as the embodiment of political and ritual power, the *gadzingo* served to centralize authority in the territories claimed and ruled by Karanga ruling dynasties.

The value of Mazarire's analysis lies in its attempt to understand how late eighteenth- and nineteenth-century Karanga dynasties created their own local power bases by combining political and ritual power. Its limits lie in its focus on the creative efforts at monopolizing power by ruling lineages, which deflects attention from the ways in which these efforts could be undermined from without. As shown in the first three chapters of this book, the capacity of chiefly lineages to centralize ritual and political power was always open to challenge from other actors. By the beginning of the second millennium CE, the most powerful of the ritual actors and institutions were supraterritorial. The Mwari "cult" dominated the southern and southwestern parts of the Zimbabwean plateau for centuries. The messengers and the adepts of Mwari, known locally as *manyusa, mbonga,* or *mazihosana,* constituted a network of ritual actors with authority that transcended territorial boundaries. The institution's influence persisted even as local chiefs adapted to it (through the *gadzingo*), and new political systems, such as the Ndebele state, emerged.[40] Other institutions also included the *mhondoro* spirit mediums, which dominated in the northern parts of the Zimbabwean plateau.[41] Moreover, in many parts of the Zimbabwean plateau, the northeast included, ruling lineages were migrants who wrestled political authority from the firstcomers. These firstcomers retained ritual authority over land. This authority rivalled the political power of the immigrants because it crucially guaranteed the fertility of the land, a key factor in farming men's and women's continued support of their rulers.

Although students of African history have generally neglected the question of land and authority before the advent of colonial rule, they understand that land was central to the efforts of colonial (and postcolonial) states to extend their authority to rural populations.[42] Writing more than four decades ago, Murray Steele stressed that Southern Rhodesia's colonial administrators persistently resisted the system of indirect rule that colonial states practiced in tropical Africa.[43] Southern Rhodesia, in Steele's view, practiced direct rule, a system that weakened rather than strengthened the power of chiefs. The Southern Rhodesia colonial state did not return some modicum of power to chiefs until the 1930s; even then, this was to help the increasingly deskbound native commissioners perform their duties.

Many years later, Mahmood Mamdani questioned the underlying assumptions of this claim.[44] Everywhere in Africa, Mamdani insisted, colonial states formulated modes of indirect rule that not only distinguished settlers (citizens) from natives (subjects) through race but also differentiated Africans along "tribal" lines. In this scheme of rule, African access to land depended on both the politics of race and the African's membership in a "tribe." Mamdani stressed that the "tribe" to which the colonial state consigned African access to land was dominated by native chiefs and headmen. When the colonial state allowed these leaders to administer African "customary law," Mamdani suggested, they effectively established a decentralized despotism. This formulation strongly resembles earlier arguments about the invention of tradition and the creation of customary law, which claimed that colonial states and African chiefs invented what passed as "tradition" and "customary" law in the twentieth century.[45] Once codified, so the argument went, this version of "customary" law froze debates about custom and centralized power in the hands of African chiefs and male elders.

Later studies disputed these claims. Terence Ranger even reconsidered his earlier insistence that "custom" was frozen as tradition was invented, noting that "however codified and static colonial tradition was intended to be, it could never end there."[46] Similarly, Sara Berry argued that the codification of customary authority did not resolve debates over what constituted custom; she pointed out that colonial states possessed limited capacity to exercise hegemonic power as the invention of tradition implied.[47] Other scholars have posited that "when colonial authorities sought to appropriate tradition . . . they became subject to a discourse of which they had little knowledge or control."[48] Further, colonial policies, particularly those that the state pursued in the name of development from the 1930s to the 1950s (and again in the 1980s), created an authoritarian state dominated by technocrats whose power rivalled and in many ways undermined the authority of customary leaders.[49]

The picture emerging from northeastern Zimbabwe between 1890 and 1960 broadly confirms the idea that colonial interventions neither centralized power in the hands of chiefs nor froze debates over custom, authority, and land. As chapter 4 shows, the contradictory actions of the colonial state strengthened and weakened the power of chiefs, sometimes simultaneously. In the aftermath of the 1896–97 Chimurenga uprisings, the colonial state attacked spirit mediums and other religious figures—the mediating institutions of precolonial times—by accusing them of leading the uprisings and fomenting discontent among Africans. At the same time, it propped up chiefs—imagined to be the custodians of African lands—while introducing competing authority over land and new legal regimes, which created ambiguities that allowed some subjects to challenge the power of the chiefs.[50]

My intent here is not simply to confirm that authority in colonial northeastern Zimbabwe was long contested. Focusing on how colonial states (and their functionaries) used control over land to exercise power over people unnecessarily limits our gaze to a fraction of those who participated in the politics of land. I seek to bring the people who were touched by such initiatives into conversations about land and power. I do this in chapter 6 by showing how some people in northeastern Zimbabwe used narratives of tradition and custom—the very tools of indirect rule—to legitimate their own claims to land. These strategies were perhaps most successful during the early decades of colonial rule. From the 1930s onward, the colonial state became increasingly critical of customary leaders and gradually shifted toward institutionalized racial segregation and technocratic authoritarianism. In the latter scheme of rule, agricultural experts imposed agrarian policies in the name of science and development and evicted African landholders whose claims to land rested largely on the argument that this was the land of their ancestors. This fueled inequality and social conflict at the household and community levels. In short, colonial policies not only enabled large-scale racialized dispossession of African lands but also profoundly affected social relations and patterns of access to land among indigenous Africans. They further deepened gendered and generational inequalities, disadvantaging women and young men.

PLACE, PEOPLE, AND TIME

The story of land and power told in these pages played out in the upper reaches of the Manyame, Mazowe, Ruenya, and Save Rivers—hereafter called the central watershed—and the eastern highlands of the Zimbabwean plateau (see map 0.2). Occasionally and where necessary, the study references

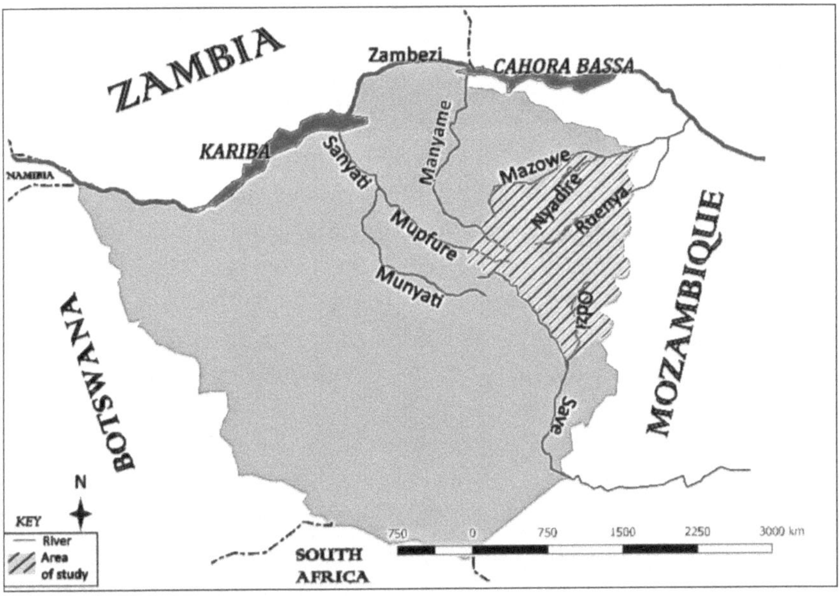

MAP 0.2. Hydrological map showing the central watershed and the area of study. Map drawn by Sekai Kashamba.

adjacent areas to the central watershed and the eastern highlands. By the sixteenth century, this area, like the rest of the Zimbabwean plateau, was home to linguistically and culturally related farming peoples. Most spoke dialects of Central Shona that we now call Zezuru, Manyika, and Korekore. Those in its far northeasternmost parts, in the Nyanga highlands, spoke the Nyanga dialect of Eastern Shona, often collapsed with Manyika but now understood to be a stand-alone dialect with closest ties to Ndau.[51] Some of these people of the Nyanga highlands spoke Nyanja-Sena languages.

Newcomers applied the name Shona, Zezuru, Manyika, Korekore, and Nyanga to both the language and/or dialects and the people who spoke them in the late nineteenth and early twentieth centuries. Those who called themselves Manyika before the twentieth century belonged to a specific polity, the Manyika kingdom ruled by the Mutasa dynasty, and the appropriation of this term to refer to the people of the eastern highlands more broadly only occurred in the context of labor migration and missionary dictionary-making in the twentieth century.[52] I use these terms here not as historical identities for the people who lived on the Zimbabwean plateau before the nineteenth century but as a shorthand to refer to people who clearly spoke distinct dialects of a common language and whose linguistic descendants have now appropriated these terms.[53] As is true for many unwritten languages, the names of languages ancestral to modern Shona languages are unknown.[54]

By the sixteenth century, the people of northeastern Zimbabwe identified themselves with the territories that they occupied. Not all of these territories were conterminous with chieftainships, although all people lived under chiefs and alongside powerful polities. These chieftainships varied in size.[55] At the beginning of the twentieth century, the central watershed and the eastern highlands consisted of the colonial districts of Goromonzi, Marandellas, Makoni, Umtali, Inyanga (originally a part of Umtali District), and Mrewa.

This study focuses on this region for numerous reasons. The complex physical geography of this area offered its inhabitants different opportunities and challenges. The eastern highlands receive more rainfall and are better suited for agriculture and herding than any other parts of the Zimbabwean plateau.[56] By the thirteenth century, people living in parts of the Nyanga highlands began terracing their lands and irrigating their fields.[57] These actions throw doubt on the received wisdom that land was plentiful in precolonial Africa, that shifting cultivation was the norm, and that everyone would access the resource in equal measure.

In contrast, lands to the west and southwest of the rugged eastern highlands are relatively flat and open (see figures 1.2 and 1.3). Granite kopjes

FIGURE 0.1. Zimunya landscape in the eastern highlands. Photograph by author.

FIGURE 0.2. Makoni landscape near Rusape. Photograph by author.

with "broken and castellated summits" are common, but soils derived from granite are "poor and shallow."[58] Here, too, the most favorable farming lands were not equally available. An anecdote recorded in the Chinamhora oral traditions suggests that when the Shawasha chiefs settled in their current territory, in the eighteenth century, they encountered people who claimed, like them, to be of the Soko (monkey) totem.[59] This group (called the Chirimudewe—inhabitants of the wetlands) occupied the marginal wetlands of this area. "Asked why they stayed in the wetlands [*mudeve*] . . . they said they were put there by those who claimed to be chiefs."[60] With the Shawasha conquest of the area, the Chirimudewe were resettled on higher ground and rechristened Chakaoma (that which is dry) because they belonged to the Soko totem.[61]

This story alludes to a very important point: the link between belonging, kinship, and access to good agricultural land. Before the Chinamhora clan's conquest of Chishawasha, members of the Chirimudewe clan were outsiders in an area ruled by members of Gunguwo's clan and were consigned to marginal agricultural lands where malaria might have been endemic. When the Chinamhora clan conquered Chishawasha, it ensured that those, like the Chirimudewe clan, who could be incorporated into the broader category of kin on the basis of their totem had access to good agricultural land. This intersection of social identities and access to land characterizes the history that I tell here.

In the centuries after their settlement of the region, the people of northeastern Zimbabwe came to realize that there were years of good rains and years of drought. They also came to believe that the fecundity of their land depended in some degree upon their creative efforts in interceding with spirits that controlled the rains. This brought questions of land and agricultural production into the social world of ancestors, elders, and firstcomers.

This book begins with an examination of northeastern Zimbabwe peoples' understandings of land's different qualities, social difference, and the making and moderation of authority over land and people between the fourth century, when the first farmers arrived on the Zimbabwean plateau, and the sixteenth century, when several important chieftainships appear for the first time in the written record.[62] Its main focus, though, is on the nexus between power and land beginning in the mid-sixteenth century, when claims to a landed domain became central to how chiefly lineages asserted their autonomy and legitimated their power. This took two forms. Some ruling lineages accounted for their land and power through their relations with the autochthonous peoples that became their subjects. Others justified their power through links with the Rozvi state, the most powerful polity on the Zimbabwean plateau between the 1690s and the 1830s. The power of the chief was never all-encompassing, however, because those who performed rituals to ensure the fertility of the land—the spirit mediums—had a potent capacity to rival the luminosity of chiefs, so long as its exercise bore the expected fruit.

The book ends in 1960. By that time, race had structured relations between European settlers and Africans for seven decades. It would continue to do so in the years that followed. However, the colonial interventions that together with kinship, gender, generation, and status influenced relations of land and power among Africans since 1890 had come full circle. Initially the colonial state couched its interventions in the language of custom. Later it intruded in African lives in the name of science and modernization. These logics were "two sides of one coin that flipped back and forth."[63] As chapter 4 shows, from the 1890s to the 1930s, colonial native policy was mostly couched in the language of custom and was meant to shore up the power of chiefs and the patriarchal power of African male elders. As discussed in chapter 5, subsequent policies of technical interventions throughout the 1940s and 1950s were packaged in the language of science and development. These policies held potential to undermine chiefly powers while strengthening the patriarchal power of male heads of household through whom the colonial state assigned land to Africans.

The colonial state's policy of community development mooted in the late 1950s and implemented in the 1960s and 1970s recalled the state's earlier attempts to interfere in African lives in the language of custom and to strengthen the power of chiefs.[64] It stressed the importance of custom in how Africans related to one another and to the land.[65] This reassertion of "custom" in matters of land and authority further undermined what little respect most colonial-era chiefs had retained. This is because despite its framing, this policy had very little to do with African customs. Rather, it was "meant to deal with the state's crisis of legitimacy triggered by the implementation of the Native Land Husbandry Act (NLHA) of 1951, and the political threat posed by the threat African nationalism."[66] Through it, the colonial state tasked chiefs (not white colonial officials as before) with enforcing the very high modernist policies—including those rooted in the Native Land Husbandry Act—that Africans were rejecting. The hope was that they would be the target of any resistance, acting, in this capacity, as a buffer between the colonial state and its disgruntled African subjects. For many chiefs, this is what happened. They were hated as enforcers of unpopular colonial laws.

This position influenced chiefs' relations with African nationalists and postcolonial Zimbabwe's future rulers. Throughout the late 1960s and the 1970s, when the anticolonial struggle gathered momentum, and the first decade of independence, Zimbabwe's nationalists sidelined chiefs in favor of, first, spirit mediums and, second, party functionaries. The relations between chiefs, their subjects, and Zimbabwe's nationalists-cum-postcolonial leaders and the policies that underwrote them since the 1960s lend themselves well to studies of the legacies of late colonialism and the postcolonial politics of land and authority—and these have been plenty.[67] For this study, which concerns itself with the rather neglected questions of land and power in the precolonial past and their imbrications with colonial policies, it is apposite that we stop in 1960, when the colonial state began its last dance with "custom," supposedly, if deceptively, rooted in precolonial practices—a dance that would inform chiefs' relations with the postcolonial state.

SOURCES

This study draws on a variety of sources, including archaeological evidence. Collectively, fragments of pots, bones, furnaces, tools, buildings, and other materials capture the social, economic, and political lives of the people who, for millennia, have called northeastern Zimbabwe home. They also help us to construct the chronologies told in the first chapter. From the seventh century on, archaeology also provides evidence of power, wealth, and social stratification. This took the form of stone-built capitals, accumulated exotic goods, and bone accumulations that pointed to elite consumption practices.[68] Beyond revealing, in unambiguous terms, differences in wealth and power, early settlements illuminate our understanding of ruling families' attempts to centralize political and ritual authority and to implicate land in their projects of rule. These settlements became centers of ritual practices meant to ensure the fertility of the land. Further, beginning in the thirteenth century, some of the communities in the Nyanga highlands turned to intensive agriculture, indicating their understanding that good, quality, productive land was scarce and raising questions about plenitude of land in precolonial Africa.

Archaeology, like other sources, has its limitations. It has often focused on the large, well-known sites, such as Mapungubwe, Great Zimbabwe, and Khami.[69] Documenting the lives of ordinary people who lived outside these larger settlements becomes a challenge. Over the past thirty years, several archaeologists have looked beyond these large sites, but much of their work has focused on the Shashi Limpopo valley or the Nyanga highlands. These are also niche environments: the highlands, an unforgiving topography; the Shashi Limpopo valley, an area of poor rainfall. The central watershed lies between these two extremes.

To get a sense of existing social hierarchies and the ways in which the people of northeastern Zimbabwe understood the land's different qualities, *Society, Power, and Land* draws on linguistic evidence. For more than a half century, scholars have developed a robust way of telling histories of early African societies from this source.[70] Their studies remind us that related languages evolve from a common ancestor, a protolanguage, and the word and its history are central to understanding the evidence that languages provide. As languages evolve, words are incorporated into them in three ways: they are inherited from an ancestral language; they are products of internal innovation; or they are loanwords, borrowed from other languages. "Each of these possible origins yields historical data."[71] Inherited words indicate that people speaking daughter languages were familiar with the things named or described by particular words before these languages evolved from their ancestral language.[72] It is from this kind of evidence that we can say the people speaking the language ancestral to modern-day Shona languages were mixed farmers. They inherited most words for farming and herding. Internal innovations tell us "something substantive about change in culture and society."[73] Thus, the flourishing of new words relating to soil types and to different parts of the landscape after the separation of proto-Shona into its daughter dialects discussed in chapter 1 indicates a fundamental change in the ways the peoples of the Zimbabwean plateau related to the land. By the time proto–East Central and proto–Central Shona speakers innovated with these words, they were paying much greater attention to the land than their linguistic ancestors had done.[74] Likewise, loanwords reveal cultural, economic, and social exchanges between speakers of different languages.[75] Not very many loan words relating to land appear to have entered proto-Shona and its daughter languages, although speakers of these languages might have borrowed words for other aspects of their agricultural economy, including sheep.[76]

Identifying the historical nuggets embedded in inherited words, internal innovations, and loanwords requires mapping out both the sequence through which daughter languages now available to us evolved from the ancestor language and the word histories themselves. The first task entails sorting languages into smaller groups by counting their shared cognates—the words that might have slight variations in their form and sound but were inherited from the ancestor language.[77] This process has its own limitations, including the fact that words may appear similar even if they were not inherited from the ancestor language. To overcome this, a second step is necessary: establishing whether the words identified as cognates follow a pattern of regular sound change.[78] This is because when sounds in words in related languages change, they tend "to affect all cases of the sound in question."[79] Those words that share a regular pattern of sound change, therefore, are cognates. This process helps us to recognize the word's own history—whether or not it is inherited, an internal innovation, or a loanword.

Scholars believe that those languages whose rates of cognition are highest diverged most recently. Conversely, those languages whose rates are lower will have diverged in the more distant past. Appendix 1 shows the sequence that Shona languages followed when I applied this method to the languages in this group alongside those in their closest cousins, Nyanja-Sena, Makuwa-Lomwe, and Ronga-Venda.[80] It especially shows that the three dialects spoken by the people of northeastern Zimbabwe in the sixteenth century and after—Zezuru, Manyika, and Korekore—had recently evolved from their proto–Central Shona ancestor. These three dialects also share many of the words relating to different landscapes and soil types, indicating, as noted above, that by the time they emerged, their speakers recognized and even preferred specific lands.

Linguistic evidence has its own limitations. While mapping out the sequence by which the languages evolved is possible, this does not give us calendar dates.[81] Glottochronology—the method by which some scholars estimate the dates by which related languages separated, on the understanding that languages replace approximately 20 percent of their core lexicon over a thousand-year period—divides scholarly opinion.[82] Its critics reject it on the grounds that the rate of change is not constant. Others argue that glottochronology provides only rough time spans, which can be confirmed from datable archaeological materials.[83] Indeed, by correlating the linguistic stratigraphy unearthed through the method I describe above with the archaeological evidence, I offer, in very broad terms, a suggestion about the point in time when the people of northeastern Zimbabwe began to pay greater attention to land's different qualities.

An additional challenge to working with Shona languages is that among contiguous dialects, a high degree of internal borrowing skewed their rates of cognition.[84] Significantly, although languages constantly incorporate new changes, their divergence, which helps scholars to build a linguistic stratigraphy, becomes quite visible after a lengthy period. Consequently, we can sketch only very broad chronologies, something reflected in the first chapter, which covers a period of over a millennium.

Archaeological and linguistic evidence was crucial to my understanding of the social and ecological world of the farming communities in northeastern Zimbabwe to the sixteenth century. Traditions of migration, settlement, and state-making told by members of local chiefly lineages help us to discern the relationship between land and political power, as discussed in chapters 2 and 3. In a set of polities that predated the rise of the Rozvi state in the 1690s in Manyika, Maungwe, and Bocha, ruling dynasties fashioned stories that portrayed their founders as heroic figures who settled and established their power base on land previously inhabited by people who lacked recognizable governance structures and the basics of civilized living, such as fire. Once civilized, these people became the subjects of the dynastic founders. Following the emergence of the Rozvi state in the late seventeenth century, some dynasties began to legitimate themselves by insisting that their power over land and people was bestowed on them by Rozvi elites.

In northeastern Zimbabwe, as in other parts of eastern and southern Africa, traditions told by chiefs and their families rationalized the territorial claims of ruling lineages.[85] To understand the multiple regimes of land and authority beyond what the rulers wanted us to know, I turned to traditions told by healers, spirit mediums, and many other individuals who did not belong to ruling families. Their narratives counterweight those of chiefs and the families that supplied them. Only by paying attention to the contradictions in the traditions told by elites and commoners, rulers and ritual actors, are we able to discern competing interpretations of the past by people who occupied different positions in the social ladder.[86]

I collected many of these stories myself. I also relied on stories that others recorded and textualized. Two sources of recorded oral narratives especially allowed us to transcend the narrow interests of a ruling elite. One of these sources is Jason Takafa Machiwenyika's "History and Customs of the Manyika."[87] Although Machiwenyika belonged to the Mandeya section of the Manyika dynasty and his manuscript carries many dynastic oral traditions, it also includes others that range from agricultural to social practices, including marriage and healing. The second source is a collection of oral histories recorded, transcribed, and deposited at the National Archives of Zimbabwe by the institution's then oral archivist, Dawson Munjeri, in the late 1970s and early 1980s. These cover several aspects of life in late nineteenth- and early twentieth-century northeastern Zimbabwe.

A drawback of these two sources is their relatively narrow geographical coverage. Machiwenyika's manuscript covers Manyika and, to some extent, Bocha, Jindwi, and Maungwe. Munjeri's interviews were conducted within a hundred kilometers of Harare. Most of his interviewees were older males, who reproduced the gender biases of their generation. To address these limitations, my fieldwork focused on religious figures and women.[88] My combined reading of oral traditions from ruling dynasties alongside those told to me by spirit mediums and commoners was particularly productive. It revealed the kind of contestations over power that accounted for their fashioning in the first place.

What is more, oral traditions contain many myths and new additions by the tellers. They, like any other sources, are social artifacts.[89] They contain information about the past but may be influenced by the environment in which they are told. The challenge that historians have always confronted is how to distinguish the historical data from the mythical aspects and the later additions in oral traditions. As a generation of historians has pointed out, overcoming this challenge requires us to untangle the tradition not as a single myth but as a work of art with several components: clichés or core images, episodes, and even personal reminiscences.[90] Episodes are the additions that the storytellers make as they engage their audience (including the historian), while reminiscences refer to the narrator's personal memories.[91] Neither may be central in telling histories of the deep past because they belong to the world of the teller. However, clichés or core images are retained even as the narrators bring in new information to reconstruct their stories. Scholars of oral traditions concur that "it is these core images that hold the key to the historical interpretation."[92] Chapter 2 draws on these clichés to show how ruling families in northeastern Zimbabwe claimed land and authority.

Oral traditions also especially lack temporal specificity. For example, while traditions mention dynastic founders and their successors—often but not always in chronological order—they rarely state the specific dates when the founder established the polity and each ruler presided over its affairs. At times, the founders are mythical figures who, in fact, represent more than one ruler.[93] To overcome this problem, this study complemented oral sources with written documents. This complementary use of oral and written sources, for example, established that Manyika existed as a political entity in the sixteenth century, because Portuguese documents dating to this period mention the territory and its Chikanga rulers.

Written documents pertaining to Zimbabwe date back to the sixteenth century, when literate Portuguese peoples began to interact with the peoples of the plateau. Collectively, these documents give an image of life in many parts of northern and northeastern Zimbabwe that helped me address, in chapter 2, the dynamics of power within and among different polities into the mid-nineteenth century. Thereafter, travelogues produced by other European travelers, whose numbers increased in the later part of the nineteenth century, constitute an important source for the shifts in settlements and the powers held by female rulers discussed in chapter 3. Both sets of documents also contain nuggets relating to the religious lives of the Africans and aid understanding of the relations between collective well-being and the moderation of political power.

The documents produced by the Portuguese and the late nineteenth-century European travelers varied greatly in value. They were produced by outsiders, many of whom had sparse knowledge of the societies they described. The Portuguese, in particular, were heavily invested in finding the region's mineral wealth and more interested in describing conditions of trade than in capturing the social lives of Africans. Reflecting the political template that they brought from Portugal, the Portuguese writers also identified the Zimbabwean plateau's two largest states, first the Mutapa and Butwa, and after the demise of the latter, the Mutapa and the Rozvi as kingdoms and the rest of the region's polities as chieftainships subordinated to these kingdoms.[94] Consequently, they embellished the powers of the rulers of the Mutapa and Rozvi states, placing their polities on a higher political pedestal than those of their neighbors. In the process they helped to create the legend of Rozvi and Mutapa power untangled in chapter 2.

The volume of written materials increased exponentially in the colonial period. Missionaries working in African areas in this period undertook the enterprise of dictionary-making, recording words that are useful in reconstructing the linguistic stratigraphy of Shona languages and in telling the histories of the people who spoke these languages. Alongside colonial officials, and some educated Africans, they also recorded, from local informants, oral traditions that have been indispensable to the story I tell here.[95] These local informants were, in Diana Jeater's words, "clearly the experts."[96] However, they were also mostly men, and most of them were associated with chiefly families. Such informants provide narratives that strengthened their position, reinforcing the power of male chiefs and elderly men.[97] For studies of land and power such as this one, this is both bane and boon: bane because it is largely silent on the views of those whom chiefs and elders sought to control; boon because it allows us to read the logics of power behind the elders' oral narratives. These were used not just internally in dynastic struggles for a chieftainship but also to claim land. It is, indeed, through this kind of reading of the oral narratives that I construct the history of territorial claims and power presented in chapters 2 and 3.

The problem of representation inherent in the textualized traditions discussed above is magnified in the colonial archive. This archive, which provides most of the sources used in chapters 4, 5, and 6, was produced during the course of the day-to-day colonial administrative work. Consequently, these documents mostly capture the views of colonial officials. Even when Africans appear in these documents, their appearances are mediated by colonial power. Yet the colonial archive also reveals the diverse interests of the people who inhabited the colonial state. These interests influenced African encounters with colonial officials and settlers. As chapter 6 shows, the conflicting interests coming out of the contradictory mandates of the Native Affairs and Lands Departments sometimes informed settler and African negotiations over tenancy and "squatting."

ARCHITECTURE OF THE BOOK

This history of power and land is told in half a dozen chapters. The first draws on archaeological and linguistic evidence to map out understandings of land's different qualities and the relations of power that governed the rhythms of life and access to resources among the people of northeastern Zimbabwe between the fourth century and the mid-sixteenth century. Generally these people are understood to have lived in fairly egalitarian communities.[98] But these societies had their own hierarchies, and unequal power relations regulated their rhythms of lives. Although early Zimbabweans apparently paid far less attention to the different qualities of their land than their linguistic descendants would do, things changed after about 800 CE. From then on, social hierarchies became more visible than before, at least in the archaeological record, and the people of the Zimbabwean plateau began to pay a lot more attention to differences in the land than they had done earlier. This chapter lays a foundation for the main argument of this book. It identifies inequalities—in social standing among households and communities, and in the utility of soils and lands in particular locales. Beginning in the thirteenth century, farmers occupying the Nyanga highlands clearly preferred soils that had inherent fertility in localities that received enough rain to sustain their agricultural enterprises. However, these areas were finite. Not everybody could access basic resources in equal measure. Exclusions rooted in status differentiated people's access to good agricultural lands. At the same time, the chapter notes that new polities, and with them new ways of legitimating power, as well as new ritual institutions emerged in or soon after the eighth century.

Chapter 2 draws on oral traditions and Portuguese documents to explore how ruling lineages in small polities in northeastern Zimbabwe legitimated their claims to land and authority in the presence of very powerful kingdoms in the 270 years after 1560. It advances the idea that land was important to politics, but power was not uncontested. When the founding patriarchs of the region's chiefly dynasties assumed their positions, they identified themselves as outsiders in places where belonging underwrote access to land. They joined networks of kinship by marrying into the families of firstcomer elites. But this only gave them access to land, not power. Consequently, ambitious immigrants invoked ideas of civilization to justify authority over people and territory. Their lineages also constructed images of founders who tamed the land by killing dreaded animals and thus making it habitable, on the presupposition that those who tamed the land had the right to rule. Many others claimed land by seeking closer identification with the Rozvi state. Once established, these ruling lineages expanded their territorial claims by settling members of their lineages in frontier areas. But chiefly powers were never absolute. Although the chiefs' authority rested on their abilities to ensure the fertility of the land and the welfare of their subjects, this was not always in their hands. Rituals that ensured collective well-being and political cohesion were often performed by people who did not belong to the lineages of chiefs. Even when the rituals were performed by members of a ruling lineage, these were not the chiefs but individuals who occupied a separate position as spirit mediums. These and other ritual actors possessed power that rivalled that of chiefs. Significantly, the appeal of the most powerful mediums often transcended the boundaries of a chieftainship.

Chapter 3 traces change and continuity in the politics of land and power after the collapse of the last powerful Shona kingdom, the Rozvi state, in the 1830s. It ends with the British occupation of parts of the Zimbabwean plateau in 1890. Here the argument is that land was political not only because the authority of chiefs rested on a claim to territory but also because the prevailing political climate affected where people were able to live and farm. In these six decades, there were marked shifts in the sites of fields and settlements of northeastern Zimbabwe that were shaped by relations between Shona speakers and others and influenced where people were able to live and farm. The Rozvi and those associated with them sought to sustain a claim to their landed domain, even as members of the Rozvi ruling houses lost their own lands to the Ndebele state. Several of these people ended up in the upper Save River basin, where they insisted that their ancestors had always appointed chiefs and apportioned land. At the same time, the chiefs in Manyika, Bocha, and other parts of northeastern Zimbabwe entrenched the practice of appointing female members of their lineages as ward rulers, in an attempt to secure their power, thus complicating the link between patriarchal chiefly power and control of territory. Still, power remained subject to contestation, by male rivals to the incumbent chiefs and by religious actors with transterritorial appeal who continued to hold sway in many parts of northeastern Zimbabwe.

Chapter 4 discusses the nexus between colonial imaginaries of African power, landholding, and authority, and African access to land in the first three decades or so of colonial rule. These imaginaries, it shows, were meant to shore up the powers of "customary" authorities—the hierarchy of chiefs, headmen, and kraalheads—and male heads of households, while suppressing the activities of religious figures whom the colonial state accused of leading the 1896–97 uprisings. The chapter's main argument is that the colonial state's efforts to suppress the activities of spirit mediums and other ritual actors—the mediating institutions of the precolonial era—and to prop up "customary" authorities, failed to centralize power over land and people in the hands of chiefs. The colonial state introduced policies that were, for the most part, contradictory, creating ambiguities that simultaneously undermined chiefs' power or allowed it to be contested. As in the precolonial period, then, authority over land remained contested.

Chapter 4 also examines how the imposition of colonial rule and the creation of reserves—the wretched pieces of land that the colonial state set aside for exclusive occupation by local Africans—affected the language and social geography of African landholding in these newly established spaces. The colonial state, together with some African elites, constructed an image of Africans as cultural, not economic, beings. The chapter teases out the implications of the claim that Africans accessed land as members of communities, usually "tribes," by showing that although many Africans used ideas of belonging to claim land, they conceived this in terms that were broader than the colonial category of "tribe." Africans' participation in the colonial economy also carried them beyond the confines to which the language of "tribe" sought to restrict them.

Chapter 5 discusses the shifts in colonial policies toward African farming and agrarian practices from the 1920s to the 1950s and shows how they affected questions of land and authority in the reserves. It highlights contradictions in the colonial state's attempts to strengthen the power of the chiefs while simultaneously denying them judicial authority. By the time the colonial state granted judicial powers to chiefs in the late 1930s, it was also undertaking agrarian measures that privileged the work of a technical bureaucracy over that of "customary authorities." Colonial agrarian policies also deepened gendered and generational inequalities in landholding by prohibiting, in the name of conservation, the cultivation of areas where women historically accessed land outside the tentacles of patriarchy, and by assigning all household plots to male heads of families.

Chapter 6 examines the fate of tens of thousands of Africans who, until their forced evictions in the post–Second World War period, remained on alienated land. It documents these people's experiences on settler farms as well as their journeys to the reserves following their forced relocations in the 1940s and 1950s. It emphasizes the entanglement of African struggles for land not only with the interests of colonial agrarian capital but also with colonial ideas of native policy and development—the colonial state's vision of maintaining authority over Africans—and intra-African conflicts. These factors mediated access to land along racial lines. But above all they deeply affected relations among Africans. In this way the chapter stresses the multiple structures of power that informed how Africans accessed land and related to one another.

The book ends with a short postscript. This briefly captures the book's main arguments. It reiterates the point that unequal power relations informed patterns of access to productive land while land, or territory, was itself important to the making of authority in the five centuries covered in these pages. This, it shows, remained the case in the period after 1960, but the space for citizens to limit the authority of their leaders is closing steadily. The chapter therefore makes an urgent call for the reopening of this space in hope of achieving the quest for equity envisioned in postcolonial land reforms.

1 ⁓ Knowing the Land, Marking Social Hierarchies, and Legitimating Claims to Land and Power

FROM THE first, proto-Shona-speaking farmers, who came to the Zimbabwean plateau in the fourth century, understood that land varied in quality.[1] They also afforded elevated status to successful farmers, expert hunters, potters, ironsmiths, and ritual and political leaders in their communities. This chapter maps out these people's understandings of land and its potential up to the mid-sixteenth century, when the chieftainships under which they lived began to catch the attention of literate outsiders. It also traces the networks of relations and power that governed the rhythms of life among these farmers. Social difference, I argue was rooted in gender, seniority, kinship, and disparities in wealth. Well entrenched by the end of the first millennium, these hierarchies ultimately informed patterns of access to resources, including land. By the thirteenth century, some of the cattle-rich peoples of northeastern Zimbabwe were turning to intensive agriculture, terracing hillsides, and growing crops under irrigation while their poorer neighbors occupied marginal lowlands with poorer soils.[2] Across the Zimbabwean plateau more generally, there arose from the terminal centuries of the first millennium political elites who distinguished themselves from their subjects by enconcing themselves in stone-walled settlements, often, but not always, located on hilltops. Their actions imbricated land and power. But this power was never complete. Accompanying the political transformations was the emergence of new ritual institutions, particularly the *mhondoro* (spirit mediums), whose craft was understood to be integral to the maintenance of the fecundity of the land and general collective well-being. The powers of many of these mediums and the spirits that they channeled (both known as *mhondoro*) often transcended the boundaries of a polity and moderated those of chiefs.

KNOWING THE LAND, MAKING LIVELIHOODS

When the earliest farmer-herders arrived on the Zimbabwean plateau in the fourth century of the Common Era, they found an environment that was broadly similar to the savanna woodland/grassland (**-jìkà*) that was known to their linguistic ancestors.[3] They called this landscape *nyika* (country or territory), suggesting that these were the environments in which to settle and pursue many familiar activities, including hunting; the collection of wild fruits, vegetables, mushrooms, and honey; livestock herding; cereal cultivation; iron production and smithing; and pottery making.[4]

Understanding the weather patterns and ecologies of the plateau was important to these farmers. They soon learned that weather patterns on the plateau differed from those that their Savanna and Mashariki Bantu linguistic ancestors had known. In settling the Savanna woodlands and the Great Lakes region east of the equatorial rain forest, these people had encountered three seasons, which they named **-limo, *-tíkà,* and **-saano.*[5] Deriving from **-lim-*, an older Bantu root for "to cultivate," the **-limo* season was "a time of rain."[6] **-Limo* marked the time after the first rains, when planting began. It lasted from October to December and was followed by **-tíkà,* the longer rainy season between February–March and May–June.[7] **-Saano,* the third season, lasted roughly from June to September. It was dry and relatively cool.[8] On the plateau there was no clear break between the October–December and March–May rainy seasons, and the incomers dropped **-tíkà* from their vocabulary.[9]

Recognizing landscapes similar to those known to their proto-Bantu, Savanna, and Mashariki Bantu linguistic forebears, these early farmers retained **-cángó* (forests) and **-tondo* (thickets) to name wild, and sometimes threatening, environments that required taming before they could be turned into homesteads and fields. The early farmers of northeastern Zimbabwe also recognized **-toolo* (bog, muddy landscapes), which, together with **-tòpè* (mud), they distinguished from **-bú* (soil). At the same time, these farmers recognized **dòngó* (clay soil), which, though difficult to work, may have been valued for its water-retention qualities.

In mountainous Nyanga, the earliest farmers seem to have preferred the lowlands, but elsewhere sources of water were important in determining settlement locations.[10] Annual rainfall declined across much of southern Africa for five centuries after 500 BCE, then increased to a maximum about 400 CE. Thereafter, precipitation totals declined for four hundred years.[11] Thus, the earliest farming communities in northeastern Zimbabwe sank their roots in a period of declining rainfall. In these circumstances, it made sense to settle near rivers and to exploit alluvial soils for farming. Rivers provided water for humans and animals, both domestic and wild. For people whose subsistence depended on food production and food collection, such locales were, therefore, strategic.

The early farmers of northeastern Zimbabwe paid attention to broad variations in landscapes and soils. Their vocabulary included terms for low-lying land, *gova;* wide, level land between hills, *pani;* sand, **-céké;* and (as we have already seen) **-tòpè* (mud) and **-toolo* (bog). Things would change in the closing centuries of the first millennium, as farmers recognized finer gradations in types of soils and variegations in the landscape. Beginning in the eighth or ninth century, people speaking proto–East Central Shona called sandy soils of low fertility *-shapa;* red clay soils, *jiho;* and soil mixed with detritus, *mhukutu.* By the eleventh or twelfth century, their linguistic descendants, speakers of proto–Central Shona, recognized, in addition to the above, *dofo* (a soft vlei) and *wova* (rich red clay soils).[12]

Proto-Shona speakers and their linguistic descendants identified and named different landscapes and soil types because they understood that land possessed different qualities and that some types would not sustain their agricultural pursuits. For these farmers, *-tsapa,* the sand soils of low fertility, would not have been as desirable as *mhukutu,* the soils enriched by detritus. Likewise, **-toolo* and **-tòpè* landscapes were probably unsuitable for cereal cultivation, and water pooled on their surface may have bred mosquitoes.[13]

In the Nyanga highlands after 1200 CE, farmers built extensive terraces and constructed ridges and watercourses to irrigate their fields.[14] Some scholars have suggested that agricultural intensification was driven by external pressures. For David Beach, the inhabitants of the Nyanga highlands settled on hilltops, cultivated the slopes, and intensified agriculture because they were surrounded by hostile neighbors in Maungwe, Manyika, Baruwe, and Budya. Beach saw the Nyanga terrace complex as evidence of "a culture of losers."[15] More recently, Innocent Pikirayi suggested that Nyanga farmers settled on hilltops in response to the growing power of the Great Zimbabwe state.[16] Similarly, Heike Schmidt attributed settlement patterns in the Honde valley to hostile neighbors, especially the Gaza Nguni, who raided the area beginning in the 1830s.[17] Together, such accounts form what Lowe Börjeson called a *siege hypothesis.*[18] Such a hypothesis ascribes agricultural intensification to threats of violence that prevent farmers from expanding from their locales. But this cannot explain the persistence of this type of farming.[19] In fact, aspects of the Nyanga culture's settlements and agricultural practices—cultivation ridges, pit structures, and enclosures—were adopted on lands settled by the supposedly hostile neighbors of the terrace builders.

Two factors seem to have been particularly crucial to the long occupation of the Nyanga highlands.[20] Light sandy soils derived from granite cover most of the Zimbabwean plateau.[21] These soils are of mediocre fertility. Nyanga terrace builders took advantage of more fertile dolerite-derived clay soils.[22] Archaeologist Robert Soper noted that dolerites accounted for barely an eighth of the bedrock in the otherwise granitic Nyanga hills, but they underlay slightly more than 40 percent of the 18,468 hectares of terracing. Terrace builders clearly understood that dolerite-derived clay soils were more fertile than sandy granitic soils.[23]

The earliest settlements of the Nyanga culture were established on the hilltops when climate conditions in southern Africa were cool and dry.[24] When more humid conditions developed beginning in 1600 CE, settlement in the Nyanga highlands moved downslope to utilize freshly weathered slopes with relatively deeper soils. The settlements' occupants terraced their fields. This investment of labor and time in terracing (instead of leaving for new, virgin lands) belies images of people in precolonial Africa constantly on the move, clearing new lands and moving on after a few years to repeat the process elsewhere.[25] The practice, which some scholars called shifting cultivation or slash and burn, rested, in their judgment, on the underpopulation of precolonial Africa—the idea that land was plentiful and labor scarce. Many historians writing during and after the colonial period followed suit in portraying precolonial times as a golden age of abundant productive land, inadvertently revealing more about the traumas of colonial dispossession than about the thirteenth-century world of the Nyanga highlands.[26]

In other parts of the Zimbabwean plateau where the topography is more forgiving than in the eastern highlands, people's decisions about where to live and farm were informed by their encounters with other aspects of the environment. Rainfall variability and access to groundwater were two such factors. The farming men of northeastern Zimbabwe generally avoided areas that were prone to drought, plague, and disease. Vabocha elders make this point by recounting that the early inhabitants of the Bocha area under headman Mabvengwa abandoned it because of a devastating epidemic.[27]

Bocha lies in the rain shadow of the eastern highlands and is prone to periodic droughts. Across northern and northeastern Zimbabwe, the droughts of 1511, 1517, and the 1530s were particularly devastating.[28] These droughts might have coincided with the emergence of the polities in Bocha, Manyika, and Maungwe, polities that are recorded in mid-sixteenth-century Portuguese documents. If this was indeed the case, residents, suspicious of the ability of their newcomer rulers to ensure the area's fertility, might have connected these calamities to inadequate rainmaking ceremonies. Others might have dreaded the locality and concluded that those who lived there would be hounded by dark, mystical forces.[29]

SOCIAL DISTINCTION, SOCIAL DIFFERENCE, AND LANDED INEQUALITIES

The proto-Shona speakers who settled on the Zimbabwean plateau in the fourth century recognized social differences. Their language contained a set of words that name people who stood out in farming, hunting, and other economic activities. Already in the first millennium, proto-Shona speakers were calling "ordinary" farmers *murimi,* from the verb **-lìm-* (to cultivate). They, however, called the most successful farmers *huludza,* apparently a compound of *-kúdú* (big) and **-dusa* (to winnow). This probably reflected the large crops of grain that these very successful farmers harvested.[30] Similarly, proto-Shona speakers of the first millennium AD called "ordinary" hunters *muvhimi,* a noun derived from **-gúim-* (to hunt), and somewhat more successful hunters *mudzimba.*[31] They called expert hunters *hombalume/hombarume,* a lexical item that, like *huludza,* may have reflected their superior standing in society. Syntactic compounds (built of two full nouns) such as *hombalume/hombarume,* Kathryn de Luna tells us, "are uncommon except with names and titles" and usually constituted "an earned, respected title, a kind of named person."[32] Other skilled individuals, including iron smelters and smiths, also enjoyed superior social standing associated with the esoteric knowledge that they possessed and their control over a scarce and valuable resource.[33] Thus, with skill came fame and with fame, an elevated social standing.[34]

Success in farming and hunting enhanced an individual's status or social standing in society. Gender, in contrast, appears to have governed the rhythms of life within the household. Direct evidence for this is lacking, but the organization of the home space offers clues to how this may have played out beginning early in the first millennium AD. By the time they settled on the Zimbabwean plateau around AD 300, proto-Shona-speaking farmers had abandoned the square houses (**-júbò/*-jú/*-jó*) built by their linguistic ancestors in the Congo basin for the **-jùmbá,* a round house with a thatched roof. Before the ninth century, their linguistic descendants extended the meaning of **-jùmbá* beyond the dwelling structure.[35] In polygamous households, the term referred to a wife's house and to her household, consisting of the woman, her children, and other dependents.[36] Among speakers of proto–Eastern Shona, a speech community that might have emerged as a distinct dialect by the tenth century, **-jùmbá* also referred to the cooking house, the kitchen. Within the cooking house, one found the hearth, **-jooto.* Both the cooking house and the hearth would have been predominantly women's social spaces.[37]

The cooking house and hearth were distinct from the **-bánjá.* Once, in the earlier Bantu world, **-bánjá* generally referred to the courtyard.[38] It also meant a "building site, place of authority."[39] Among proto-Shona speakers and their descendants, the term appears to have held both this generic meaning as well as another, more specific, connotation as "the outside space, where the male head of a household lived."[40] Where homesteads were nucleated into a village, the **-bánjá* was the meeting place of the men of the village. The hierarchical implications of this gendering of space may be discerned from the earlier meaning of **-bánjá* as a "place of authority." The **-bánjá* appears to have been the place where senior men ruminated over the affairs of their households and/or village, while the household's womenfolk carried the burden of preparing food on their hearths.

Beginning early in the first millennium, members of the household were socially differentiated by seniority, understood in terms of both generation and age. Proto-Shona speakers retained **-kúdú,* the proto-Bantu word for elder or senior or big. This seniority was generational in the sense that a nephew could, by age, be older than his uncle and remain his junior because siblings of one's father belonged to his father's generation regardless of their age.

Seniority extended beyond paternal (and maternal) relations. For instance, the women of a polygamous household occupied different statuses. Proto–Central Shona speakers distinguished the first wife from subsequent wives. They called the former **-kócì* and the latter **-dongo.* In earlier times, going back to proto-Bantu times, some four or so thousand years before the proto-Shona speakers settled on the Zimbabwean plateau, **-dongo* was understood to mean "line; row, ten, kinship," or lineage.[41] By calling junior wives **-dongo,* proto-Shona speakers recognized these women as those who came into the polygamous marriage after the first wife. Their statuses derived from the idea of having followed the first wife in the line of marriage. The term **kócì,* which once meant a "strong or mature person [or] extended family head," signalled the first wife's seniority, the responsibilities that came with her position, and the wisdom, maturity, and leadership attributes required to keep the large polygamous households intact and prosperous.[42] This seniority was in relation to the senior woman's standing vis-à-vis her co-wives, the children, and all the other dependents of the household. But even the most powerful senior wife was subordinated to the household's patriarch. It seems proto-Shona-speaking societies were organized on patrilineal lines, and their marriages were virilocal. That is, upon marriage, wives moved to live among their husbands' kinsmen. There, they remained outsiders and could not be heads of extended families.[43]

Exclusions rooted in lineal identities were reinforced through religious practice. Proto-Shona speakers believed that the dead continued to influence the affairs of the living. In prosperity and crisis, they propitiated the spirits of their departed ancestors, **-dìmù.* The belief in ancestral spirits had a very deep history, although those whose spirits were placated varied over time.[44] Jan Vansina thought that **-dìmù* originally "referred to heroes . . . to the spirit of a long deceased leader, whose personality and perhaps even whose name had been forgotten and then rediscovered when he wrought wonders."[45] Later, proto-Mashariki speakers understood **-dìmù* as the spirit of the ancestors of the community.[46] The proto-Shona-speaking people of the Zimbabwean plateau might have maintained both of these conceptualizations, but at some point, **-dìmù* became restricted to the family ancestral spirit. Whether understood in terms of the family or the clan and community, belief in **-dìmù* was married to an ideology of belonging. The ancestral spirit protected members of a community, clan, lineage, or family. The act of honoring departed ancestors reinforced the power of those who already held authority in the household and the wider community. Once, this might have been the family head, the big man, the **-àmi* and the **-kúmù.*[47] Later, when linguistic descendants of proto-Shona speakers restricted **-dìmù* to family spirits, these were male heads of households.

Near the end of the first millennium, social differences among the people of the plateau were magnified—at least as reflected in the archaeological record—as farmers increased the size of their cattle herds. Cattle bones dominate Late Farming Community bone assemblages, and animals were slaughtered in their prime at sites occupied by the elites of the community.[48] Such patterns of slaughter were not consistent with general principles of herd management that would have culled old and sickly beasts.[49] These bone assemblages probably reflected the consumption habits of powerful members of the community, because their sites contain numerous trappings of power but no structures that could have served as cattle kraals.[50]

Cattle also assumed greater importance in the lives of most plateau residents. They made up a large part of **lobol-*, the wealth paid by the groom's family to that of his wife. To underscore their importance, proto–Central Shona speakers used the word **-tàngá* (cattle pen/cattle post) to refer to the wealth exchange. Cattle, or rather their control, could also entrench unequal power relations. At the household level, young women were essential to the accumulation of this wealth. Yet patriarchs essentially controlled it. A brother might use cattle paid as bridewealth to a sister in his own marriage, but only with approval of the family patriarch, rendering junior male members of households supplicants for access to the resources that family heads might use to marry more wives and extend their social and economic power. However, cattle were not the only form of bridewealth payments. Proto–Central Shona speakers incorporated terms such as *-padza* (hoe) and **-júmà* (beads) into the language of bridewealth. Beads and hoes were not prestige goods and were therefore less likely to be controlled by family patriarchs or monopolized by ruling elites.[51]

Yet control of cattle entrenched other forms of inequality. Those who were without cattle sometimes tended the cattle of their more fortunate counterparts in what was essentially a patron-client relationship. Central Shona speakers invented a term, *-ronzer-*, for this practice. Here, wealthy owners entrusted some of their cattle to less fortunate individuals to herd and enjoy certain benefits such as milk and manure without the power to dispose of them. Some of the cattle that ruling elites kept away from their capitals may have been distributed through the *-ronzer-* system. Sometimes the cattle owner might gift a heifer to his herder. Central Shona speakers captured the precarity of this situation in the following phrase: "*Mombe yekuronzerwa kama wakaringa zhira/nzira*" (When one is milking a cow that they obtained through the *-ronzer-* system, they should not become overly comfortable. The owner may show up at any moment and repossess it).

In parts of northeastern Zimbabwe, the disparities in cattle wealth influenced access to good agricultural lands. Communities with far fewer cattle than their neighbors occupied marginal lowlands in Nyanga. Most of them built simple stone enclosures without the pit structures that functioned as cattle pens in the highlands. Such pit structures as there were in the lowlands were considerably smaller than those in the highlands.[52] The people who resided in the marginal lowlands environments may have settled there because they did not have cattle. That is, they were poor and marginalized.

At the same time, gender increasingly shaped the dynamics of power that derived from important industries such as iron working and pottery making. Throughout the first millennium, the power that came with iron production may have been shared by men and women, both young and old. Both iron smelting and smithing took place in the domestic space of the homestead, where restricting access to the smelter and the knowledge and power that sustained it would have been difficult.[53] However, in the second millennium AD, iron smelters and smiths practiced their trade away from areas of human habitations. There, they could exclude women through a series of taboos and restrictions. In an industry that required "a great deal of" technical, ritual, and herbal knowledge and where such knowledge could "be augmented by inherited power," these exclusions enabled men to monopolize the knowledge of iron production and the power that came with it.[54] Meanwhile, potters, who may have been mostly women, likewise enforced a monopoly over knowledge, and the power that came with it, through their own restrictions and taboos. They, for example, prevented menstruating women and young boys from quarrying the potting clay.[55] Such exclusions closed avenues for accumulation to those subjected to the exclusions, while opening opportunities for those who could access the expertise: men in iron making and women in potting.

POLITICAL OFFICE, COLLECTIVE WELL-BEING, AND POWER

For some time, scholars of the Zimbabwean plateau's deep past have suggested that the region's earliest herder-farmer societies were "non-stratified village communities."[56] They suggested that social stratification first appeared among those who had settled the dry fringes of the Kalahari in the last decades of the first millennium.[57] This interpretation rests on archaeological evidence of external trade, including precious metals, beads, ceramics, majestic stone structures, and large cattle herds.[58]

However, some form of social structure was required to put the wheels of external trade in motion; the social and political systems that anchored such structures may have emerged from locally generated wealth.[59] Moreover, not all powerful kingdoms left monuments.[60] But the existence of polities prior to both the Zimbabwean plateau's participation in international commerce and the turn toward monument building is evidenced by the existence of words for political leaders. Portuguese writers who in the mid-seventeenth century described the capital of the Mutapa state as "made of wood" and soon in ruins and reverting to bush after its abandonment also noted the use of **-kúmù* to refer to the chiefs of this area.[61] The word and the political office that it named had been in existence for a very long time.

They can be traced back to proto-Bantu times, some four or so thousand years before proto-Shona speakers settled on the Zimbabwean plateau in the fourth century of the Common Era.[62]

The basis of the **-kúmù*'s authority might have shifted between the time that this institution emerged among proto-Bantu speakers and the sixteenth century, when the Portuguese first encountered it on the Zimbabwean plateau. In the ancient tradition, the **-kúmù* might have been the "big men" of the district, the village, or the household. According to Jan Vansina, the term "shares an etymology with terms meaning 'fame,' 'honor' and also 'to become rich.'"[63] Other scholars suggest that the term might have referred to an "honored person" or an individual with a ritual rather than political role.[64]

Among proto-Shona speakers, a **-kúmù*'s authority may have rested on both ritual and economic power. These communities do not seem to have employed a lexical distinction between communal and ritual leaders. With the emergence of a separate ritual position in the form of the *mhondoro/mphondoro* sometime after the ninth century, however, wealth and the ability to distribute it became essential to **-kúmù* assumption of political office.[65] At least, that is how the Portuguese understood it when they encountered this form of chiefship. Although the Zimbabwean plateau had kings, observed a Jesuit missionary, Father Monclaro, in 1572, it

> is governed by fumos [**-kúmù*] and petty rulers. . . . When one has cows, millet, or naqueny which he can give them and spend, they elect him fumo and his dignity lasts as long as he has something to spend. When they have eaten up his property, they cast him out of the office, and preeminence is the most that they give him. . . . Over these [*fumos*] is the Monomutapa, who is like a king, both in the obedience rendered to him and in the mode of succession.[66]

A little later, in 1648, another Portuguese missionary, Antonio Gomes, noted that the newly installed **-kúmù* offered gifts of cloth to elders, presumably both men and women. In addition, he presented women with jewelry. The gifting, Gomes noted, went on

> until he is left with nothing and when he had nothing else to give they make him a carnival king and throw mud at him and straw bags of fruit from the forest. . . . He tries to get away and they continue after him until in the end he succeeds in finding a safe place. Two or three days later the senators come to his house to comfort him and it would not befit him to be different and that doing the same as his ancestors he will gain and from there they

will recognize him as an elder. They give him a walking cane and something like a hat made of straw and then he is very happy and on account of those insignia, he is respected.[67]

At the time that the Portuguese encountered the *-*kúmù* in the sixteenth and seventeenth century, then, fame, honor, wealth and its sharing, and the ability to protect subjects were important for ascendancy to this position.

*-*Kúmù* was not the only form of chiefship known to proto-Shona speakers and their descendants. They also recognized chiefs whom they called *-*éné,* a title derived from a noun meaning owner or master.[68] On the Zimbabwean plateau, our knowledge of this chiefship derives mostly from Portuguese documents. Both the institution and its name predated the settlement of proto-Shona farming communities south of the Zambezi.[69] They may have emerged as a subsidiary conceptualization of leadership in a society ancestral to Mashariki Bantu that "viewed the *-*àmi* and *-*kúmù* as owners (*-*jéné*) of their kin."[70]

With time, claims to ownership extended beyond kinspeople to territory. It was in this sense that, much later, the rulers of the Mutapa kingdom might have assumed the title of *mwenemutapa,* a compound of two nouns meaning owner (*mwene*) and conqueror (*mutapa*). This deep history of the usage of the term *-*jéné* as a reference to a person of authority among the inhabitants of the northern half of the Zimbabwean plateau is instructive. The subjects of the Mutapa kingdom were titling their rulers by a term that was known to their linguistic ancestors. These were leaders who initially based their claims to authority on ownership, figuratively speaking, of the members of their kin groups and, later, of wealth and territory.[71] Such claims were reinforced by conquest.

Clearly, chiefship and the ideology that sustained it did not remain static, and neither did the broader political landscape. By the early centuries of the first millennium AD, large and powerful kingdoms had emerged, but even these existed alongside autonomous smaller polities.[72] The people who led these polities understood that their authority rested on more than instrumental power—the material resources necessary to "create patron-client relationships or in the power of the military threat to cause social change."[73] It required creative power, which "operates in the words, pauses, and gestures that healers and political orators use to make people well and to sway political opinion."[74]

Creative power conjoined political authority to the land and to the processes of place-making. The precise way that this played out divides scholarly opinion. For decades, archaeologist Thomas Huffman has suggested that since the early centuries of the second millennium CE, Chishona-speaking people recognized a sacred leader. He ruled with the assistance of a sister and lived in a decorated palace.[75] His power arose from a "mystical association with the land and a related link between leaders, their ancestors and God."[76] It was also, Huffman argues, "associated with the majesty of mountains" because "hilltop settlements provided ritual seclusion from physical and supernatural danger."[77] In this view, Shona chiefs and/or kings possessed political and ritual power, and the projection, protection, and distribution of this power were revealed in settlement patterns and symbolism.[78]

Those who question this interpretation challenge Huffman's distinction between the areas settled by the political leadership and those reserved for ritual and initiation activities. They see his reading of Vashona societies as static and based on a misunderstanding of Vashona peoples' succession and ritual practices.[79] For these scholars, the layouts of these capitals reflected the settlements of successive rulers. In this view, each king's dwelling would have become a ritual space where his successors looked up to his spirit.

In critiquing the particularities of Huffman's argument, some scholars have painted an essentially homogeneous image of "Shona" religion. Rejecting Huffman's suggestion that ritual power at Great Zimbabwe was in the hands of kings, whereas in the Mutapa kingdom it was in the hands of spirit mediums, they found "no reason why the Mutapa religion would be different from that of Great Zimbabwe because both were authored by the same people with a similar worldview."[80]

Across the Zimbabwean plateau, chiefs and/or kings encouraged their subjects to look up to the spirits of their ancestors as underwriters of their polity's collective well-being.[81] With further elaborations, this scheme persuaded subjects to revere not just the spirits of departed chiefs and/or kings but also the places the chiefs and/or kings and their lineages had settled while living, including those that were eventually abandoned, the **-tongo.* Equally revered were the leaders' burial places, *mapa.*[82] By establishing their own courts—*mizinda* (singular, *muzinda*) or *dzimbabwe,* a compounding of **-jùmbá* (house) and **-bùè* (stone)—moving their courts and thus leaving **-tongo,* and burying dead chiefs in specific locales, ruling lineages tied chiefly rule and/or kingship to the land. They created ritual sites that would become central to claims to power over the territories and peoples that they ruled. These ideas together with widespread belief in **-zimu*—ancestral spirits at the familial or kinship level—were held in common among the descendants of proto-Shona-speaking peoples.

By the fifteenth century, if not earlier, however, there were significant regional differences in beliefs about collective well-being beyond the boundaries of kinship and polity. The networks of shrines dedicated to Mwali/Mwari, the High God, located in the Matopos hills in southwestern Zimbabwe, appealed to people in most of what is now southern Zimbabwe, northern South Africa, and eastern Botswana. They drew little obeisance from the northern half of the Zimbabwean plateau.[83] In the Zambezi valley, other institutions such as the "cults" of Karuva and Dzivaguru held sway.[84] Across the northern half of the Zimbabwean plateau, including the northeast, there was widespread belief in spirit possession (*mhondoro,* or lion spirits). This bore some resemblance to the chiefly spirits discussed above, but the *mhondoro* were often associated with powerful individuals other than past chiefs. Crucially, the influence of the most powerful *mhondoro,* unlike that of chiefly spirits, transcended the boundaries of several polities. But the *mhondoro* did not have sway in most of the southern half of the Zimbabwean plateau.

The *mhondoro* institution probably emerged among farming people speaking northern dialects of central Shona sometime after the eleventh century. With the rise and expansion of the Mutapa state during the fifteenth century, its influence may have grown among these people as well as speakers of Eastern Shona. Unlike their counterparts, their southern neighbors where the institution held no sway, these communities extended *mhondoro* and its variation *mphondoro* to name the spirit, its medium, and the lion.[85]

The *mhondoro* were spirits of departed notables who made their wishes known through a human medium, also known as a *mhondoro.* Adherents believed that before it entered its human medium, the spirit first entered a lion. Consequently, the animal itself was revered. As a Portuguese official learned in 1687, when the people of the middle Zambezi basin encountered lions, they greeted "them with reverence . . . [and] clap[ped] their hands, which is a courtesy afforded to their elders and talk to him [a lion] as if he could understand what they say."[86]

The people among whom the *mhondoro* institution emerged, like those who turned to Mwari's shrines in the Matopos, had lived long enough with the local environment to recognize that their ritual repertoires, including the belief in **-zimu* (ancestral spirits), occasionally failed them.[87] At the same time, ambitious political actors would have begun to project their own ancestral spirits as more important than those of other families. But some questioned the centralizing impulses of the emerging elites and found succor in *mhondoro.* Ruling elites could claim that their own ancestors were *mhondoro,* while commoners challenged such claims by pointing to *mhondoro* whose power transcended chiefly boundaries. At any rate, as lion spirits, the *mhondoro* defied attempts to territorialize them. Like the lions they were believed to possess before they possessed their human mediums, *mhondoro* spirits roamed the land, literally and figuratively.[88]

By this time, proto–Central Shona speakers clearly possessed an acute sense of territoriality. This found expression through place-making activities such as the burial of kings and the establishment and abandoning of settlements to create **-tongo.* These activities were about ritual space-making, as well as about staking claims to a landed domain—territory. Indeed, when subject peoples looked to the spirits of ruling lineages and contributed to their veneration at places where past chiefs and/or kings had lived or were buried, they affirmed their recognition of the lineage's claims to authority over the territory in which they resided. After all, they understood these spirits as guarantors of collective well-being in this territory.

Just as the humanizing of the landscape through settlements and burials was important in staking claims to the land, so too were the physical features of the landscape central to mapping, at least conceptually, the boundaries of a territory. Mountains and rivers were important in all this. So were burial places of chiefs, *mapa.*[89] Indeed, proto-Shona speakers extended the meaning of *-tunhu,* which originally named a small hill, to mean both territory, particularly that which was administered by a member of a ruling lineage, and the distance between two places. From the middle centuries of the second millennium AD onward, ideas of territory became increasingly central to the legitimation of power by lineages presiding over smaller polities, as they came to terms with the presence of large kingdoms nearby.

By that time, the people of northeastern Zimbabwe had known the land for more than a millennium. As centuries went by, they refined their knowledge of the landscape and of soils, undertaking the conceptual work of naming each category that they identified. By the mid-sixteenth century, they had words for wetlands, sand soils, black loam soils, red soils, and soils enriched by detritus, among others. Some of these soils were more desirable than others, and access to lands with such soils depended on one's social standing within the household and the broader community, for by then, the people of northeastern Zimbabwe had developed intricate social hierarchies. These hierarchies did not merely inform patterns of access to resources; they also governed the rhythms of everyday life. Far from living in nonstratified villages, northeastern Zimbabwe's farmers had, from the beginning lived in hierarchized communities led by the **-kúmù* and **-jéné.* But social stratification as well as the ideologies and material conditions that sustained it did not remain static. By the beginning of the second millennium AD, ruling elites imbricated land in their schemes of governance. They did so by creating ritual centers around their own settlements and burial places and then by persuading their subjects to look up to their ancestors as guarantors of collective well-being. Those subjects who lived under these chiefs recognized their powers as well as their claims to the lands whose fertility they supposedly ensured. This was an attempt to centralize ritual and political power by the chiefs and the lineages that supplied them. But power remained moderated because chiefs were never able to silence all the healers. In fact, by the mid-sixteenth century, northeastern Zimbabwe's powers were moderated by *mhondoro,* whose appeal crossed the boundaries of individual polities.

2 ~ In the Shadow of Kingdoms

POWERFUL KINGDOMS developed between the Limpopo and Zambezi Rivers in the first half of the second millennium CE. The largest (and most famous) of these, Great Zimbabwe, flourished well into the fifteenth century. Existing alongside Great Zimbabwe, at least in its later years, were two other polities: Torwa and the Mutapa. As Great Zimbabwe's sun set, these two emerged as the largest centers of political gravity on the Zimbabwean plateau.[1] Their dominance lasted until the late seventeenth century, when they were eclipsed by the Rozvi state. Across the Zimbabwean plateau, these large states existed alongside many smaller polities.[2]

Standard histories of the Zimbabwean plateau suggest that many of the region's small polities became clients of these powerful kingdoms and that local leaders owed their power to the elites of those states. I argue, to the contrary, that the power of local chiefs in northeastern Zimbabwe was grounded in local relations and local politics. As they came to terms with the existence of powerful, even imperious, kingdoms seeking to incorporate them into their empires, ruling families in this region based their authority on their relationships with their subject people and the land. This remained true even after some ruling families began to claim, late in the seventeenth century, that the Varozvi, the elites of the Rozvi state, appointed them as chiefs and gave them the land over which they presided. This is crucial both for understanding the imbrications of society, land, and power and in appreciating that in these settings power was always mediated and never entirely centralized. Chiefs' powers were challenged and even rivalled by people who presided over rituals. The power of these ritual actors stemmed from the fact that they performed tasks that were believed to be crucial in ensuring the fertility of the land, general collective well-being, and political stability. Meanwhile, access to agricultural land was mediated by various relations of power, including those that were rooted in kinship, and status.

THE LONG SHADOWS OF THE MUTAPA STATE AND THE MAKING OF TERRITORIAL AUTHORITY

The Mutapa state emerged circa 1450. About the same time, several polities emerged in Manyika, Maungwe, Bocha, and adjacent territories. The Portuguese who first learned about these polities in the sixteenth and seventeenth centuries assumed that they were subordinate to the Mutapa state.[3] But this belief reflected what the Mutapa elites wanted Europeans to know: that Mwenemutapa was the most powerful African leader in the hinterland of Mozambique and "want[ed] to lord it over all those lands and paths as far as the fortress."[4]

This understanding shaped Portuguese views of land, minerals, and authority in the region. One missionary observed in 1573 that Mwenemutapa was "a great ruler who possesse[d] many leagues of land and great kings and rulers as his vassals."[5] Almost 125 years later, another claimed that Mwenemutapa received tribute "from the *regulos* and other important *Cafres* to whom he has given some parts of his empire and according to what the land produces."[6] Among the *regulos* was the king of Manyika, a territory that the Portuguese understood to have not previously had kings but only a *donatario* (grant) from the "Emperor Monomotapa."[7] In essence, many Portuguese writers of the seventeenth and eighteenth centuries portrayed the Zimbabwean plateau as the estate of a small group of powerful rulers, led by the Mwenemutapa, whose vassals reinforced their positions as they derived wealth and power from land and mines.

Yet many of the supposed grantees asserted their autonomy from the Mutapa state. As early as 1516, the Portuguese captain of Sofala, Joham Vaz d'Almada, reported that Nyamunda, king of Chiteve, had "risen against the king of Bonapotapa [Mutapa]."[8] A few decades later came another Portuguese report that Mwenemutapa's "vassals . . . [had] risen against him."[9] In the 1670s, the Mwenemutapa reported difficulties caused by rebellions in his vast kingdom. Following these rebellions, Portuguese mercenaries from Sena "went out several times with their armies to quieten" the rebellious regions, but this was not "enough to put down the trouble in the kingdoms of Manica."[10] By the mid-eighteenth century, Manyika and many of the polities formerly claimed by the Mwenemutapa kingdom had become autonomous.[11]

Well-known scholars such as David Beach, Innocent Pikirayi, and Stan Mudenge have pointed to conflicts over succession and Portuguese interference as sources of weakness in the Mutapa empire that enabled successful breakaways by its former parts.[12] But this interpretation reflects the view from the center—from the heart of the large kingdoms of the Zimbabwean plateau. It depreciates the initiative of those who lived with, but not in, these states. To understand the making of authority in Manyika, Bocha, Maungwe, and many other areas of northeastern Zimbabwe (see map 2.1), we need to consider how leaders in those places explained the sources of their power.

In Manyika, Maungwe, and Bocha, power lay with the immigrant ruling families who rooted their authority in localized social processes, captured in the core images of local oral traditions.[13] These suggest that dynastic leaders were heroic hunters who entered areas inhabited by groups without knowledge of fire-making. The newcomers taught the autochthons to make fire and cook their food. They also married their daughters and assumed power when the leading autochthonous families recognized their superior status.[14]

Consider the following implications of these stories. On the Zimbabwean plateau in the sixteenth century, fame, power, and leadership generally derived from wealth produced by farming, cattle herding, or control of long-distance trade. Hunting was quite different. Hunters were accepted into existing kin networks because they possessed valuable expertise. By killing dreaded animals, they helped to tame the environment and to ensure

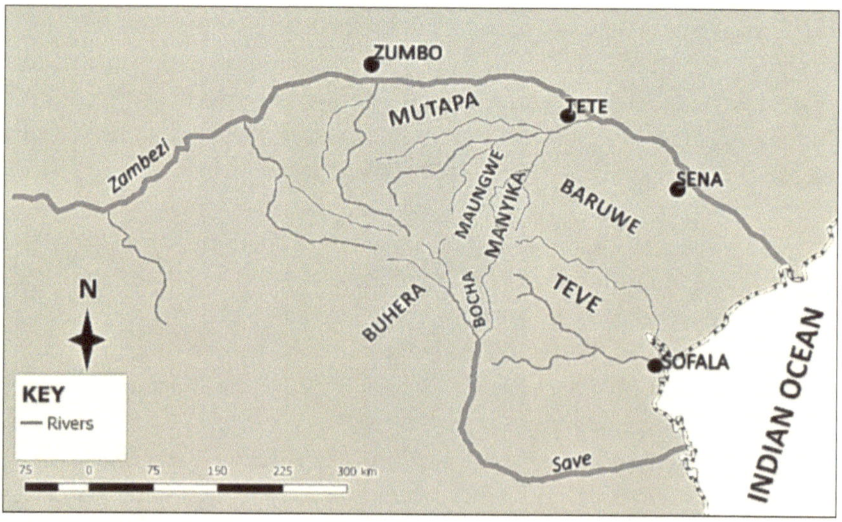

MAP 2.1. Map showing some of the territories on the Zimbabwean plateau and the surrounding lowlands between the sixteenth and the mid-nineteenth centuries. Map drawn by Sekai Kashamba.

collective safety. What is more, bushcraft—incorporating knowledge of hunting and the bush—and the technology that came with it offered individuals "a novel path to singularity, fame, friendship and ancestorhood."[15] It changed local understandings of the landscape and undermined the foundations of autochthonous political and ritual authority in the agricultural economy.[16]

The qualities of a hunter, then, paved the way to positions of power. But to consolidate power, dynastic-founding hunters required both persuasion and coercion. The protective shield offered by the hunters' skills was clearly a cogent inducement. Manyika oral traditions capture the coercive element. Nyamandoto—the successor-son of the dynastic founder, Nyamubvambire, and the woman he married from the autochthonous Muponda—killed his maternal uncles because, although their lineage was slowly losing its power, they were likely challengers of the Nyamubvambire line's claim to land formerly ruled by their fathers.[17] That the violence against the members of the Muponda dynasty was, in this case, credited to the son of the founder of the Manyika dynasty is revealing. The consolidation of power was a gradual process that might take several generations.

As a way of consolidating power, violence was quite blunt. To rationalize and legitimate their authority in more creative ways than the bludgeoning of their subjects into submission, ruling lineages crafted narratives around eating and hospitality that reinforced gendered, generational, and political hierarchies. Mid-seventeenth-century Portuguese writers learned about the practices behind these discourses. "If some outsider entered the settlement, and when a stranger comes there, the chief gets word of it immediately and orders him to be fed according to his standing," Father Antonio Gomes observed in 1648. "If he is an ordinary person," the missionary continued,

> he is taken home by the first person who meets him, and he goes in confidence and tells where he is coming from and where he is going to. If he is a person of standing, there are specially built houses for that purpose and they send him chicken, rice, and maize flour, and for his people, a basket with rice or maize and a cow or sheep . . . and this together with compliments saying that the town is honoured with his visit and excuses for any deficiencies in the way they were received etc.[18]

Just as there were special houses for visiting men of high social standing, so too were there parts of animals (and even animals) reserved for individuals occupying positions of power. Ruling lineages claimed that their founders killed an animal and then offered their autochthonous counterparts the opportunity to choose the piece of meat they wanted—though the choice was fraught, as certain animals and particular cuts of meat were associated with subservience. "My friend, I am greater than you," Chipunza oral traditions recount of the conversation between Sabarawara, their founder, and the autochthonous Madziva. When asked why he was making such a claim, Sabarawara replied, "Because I taught you so many things for the good of your people. I also told you to choose the meat you liked best. You chose the wrong meat. That meat is for women at home, not for men who can hunt and fight."[19]

In the political work of remembering conducted by oral traditions, northeastern Zimbabwean chiefly families portrayed dynastic founders as brave men who defeated autochthonous ruling lineages and tamed hostile environments to the benefit of everyone.[20] In masculinizing dynastic founders, these lineages simultaneously feminized the conquered autochthonous groups. Manyika oral tradition recalls that when Nyamubvambire claimed his chieftainship, he told the autochthonous Muponda and his people that they were now his wives.[21] This feminization of subjects underscored the patriarchal nature of chiefly power.[22] This was neither new nor unusual. "All the Portuguese in this [Mwenemutapa] empire," wrote Francisco de Sousa in 1697, "have the same privileges as those that are attributed to the wives of the emperor and this captain [of the trading post of Massapa] is referred to by him as his first wife."[23]

Ruling lineages also claimed that their founders were harbingers of civilization. They introduced the technology of fire-making to the autochthons. Claims that dynastic founders introduced fire to subject populations carried a political message. The "King of Benametapa [Mwenemutapa]," observed a Portuguese writer in the early sixteenth century,

> sends each year honourable men throughout his kingdom to all the seigniories and places that are in it to give them new fire, to ascertain if they are obedient, that is to say, each man of them having reached a place causes all the fires that are in it to be extinguished in such a way that in all places no fire is left, and when all have been put out, all go to him to take it from his hand as a token of amity and obedience so that the place or town that does not choose to do this is immediately accused of rebellion.[24]

When ruling dynasties claimed to have taught autochthonous communities to make fire, they underscored their political superiority. This preeminence emerged out of the founding chiefs' encounters with people who became their subjects.

Yet by grounding their power in the encounters between their founders and the autochthons, chiefly lineages recognized that they did not occupy empty lands. Their claims to land and power over people rested on the idea that they had outmaneuvered autochthonous communities whose identity was wedded to the land. All of this reminds us that even when large states cast their long shadows over the political landscape of the Zimbabwean plateau, power was locally constituted—at least until the closing decades of the seventeenth century.

CHANGING POLITICAL LANDSCAPES AND THE MAKING OF AUTHORITY OVER LAND AND PEOPLE IN NORTHEASTERN ZIMBABWE, 1680s–1830s

The ways in which power was rationalized across most of the Zimbabwean plateau began to change in the 1680s, with the rise of a man known as Changamire Dombo. Reportedly a one-time herdsman of the Mwenemutapa's cattle, Dombo is mostly remembered as a formidable strategist who defeated the Portuguese, forced them out of the plateau, and founded the Rozvi state.[25] Thereafter, Portuguese sources portrayed the Rozvi ruler and his successors, all of whom held the title of *changamire*, as all-powerful. "All the [people in the] lands of the Mocaranga," and "maybe even all the Rivers," wrote missionary António da Conceição in 1696, so feared the Rozvi Changamire that they were unable "to put [up] the smallest resistance"—so afraid that they "trembled only at the very mention of his name."[26]

The legend of Rozvi power grew during the eighteenth and nineteenth centuries. Several chiefs across the Zimbabwean plateau portrayed the Varozvi as the ultimate power behind their thrones.[27] The Chikwaka ruling family claimed that the Rozvi installed their ancestor, Benhura, as chief. In nearby Rusike, the Rozvi were said to have given Mutonga, the dynasty's founder, and his younger brother Mutota the land and chieftainship.[28] Historian Stan Mudenge identified several other Rozvi interventions in the appointment of chiefs, including the removal of the ruler of the Manyika kingdom in 1695 and his replacement by Changamire Dombo I's own nominee. In Makoni, Chiendambuya was said to have been made king by the Rozvi contrary to tradition that would have crowned his older brother. In Chirumanzu, the first chief was supposedly appointed at the whim of a Rozvi *mambo* who was impressed by the long robe (*hanzu*) that he wore.[29]

Beginning in the mid-twentieth century, many researchers took such claims as bone fide indications of the power of the Rozvi elites.[30] "At the height of Rozvi rule, and in the same region even long after the demise of Rozvi dominance," Mudenge claims, "no ruler could legitimately exercise political authority unless he had been first invested with that authority by the ruling Rozvi Mambo (king) or representative."[31] More recently, Gerald Mazarire has similarly noted that "the Rozvi *mambo*s had the final say on who would be a vassal chief."[32] By these accounts, local people were able to elect their ruler according to local practice, but the Rozvi *mambo* could veto their choice and even bypass the lawful hereditary heir in favor of another whose chief claim "was friendship with the Mambo."[33]

There are several problems with such accounts. First, they ignore the possibility that the Portuguese overstated the capitulation of northeastern Zimbabwe's chieftainships at the hands of the Changamire.[34] Second, they interpret oral traditions from the vantage point of the powerful kingdoms rather than from the view of the dynasties that told them. Although closer association with the Rozvi differed from older ways of claims-making perfected by older dynasties in Manyika, Bocha, and Maungwe, it sought the same end: the legitimation of authority over land and people. As Paul Landau reminds us of communities on the South African highveld, "an aspiring chief could join the *ha rotse* [Rozvi] domain, or claim it, as a feature of realpolitik."[35]

Finally, claims that the Rozvi elite superintended other dynasties reduce more than a century of relations to particular moments in time within specific areas. In northeastern Zimbabwe, there were moments when Rozvi power was on the ascendancy and long periods when it was nonexistent or was simply ignored by the region's ruling elites. As Hoyini Bhila observed, after the 1693–95 wars the "Changamire made himself lord of the kingdom of Manyika, appointed a Chikanga of his own liking, and exercised some sort of effective political authority over Chikanga for at least a decade or so."[36] Thereafter, effective power rested with the Chikangas themselves, and Rozvi influence in the region progressively dissipated.

Indeed, for most of the period of Rozvi preeminence, in Manyika, power remained locally grounded. The Rozvi did not intervene in Manyika politics. Neither did Manyika chiefs periodically seek confirmation from the Rozvi. In fact, between 1695 and the 1830s, the Rozvi were only twice mentioned in Manyika succession politics.[37] The first was in 1695, when Changamire Dombo is said to have replaced the reigning Chikanga with his own appointee.[38] Bhila cautions against reading much into this claim: "The relationship and the terms of tribute between Chikanga and Changamire were . . . unknown, except that Chikanga was ordered to 'govern the Kingdom of Manyika and watch over its *revolucoens*.' [It is possible] that Manyika princes may have been fighting for the throne and that a prince who had fought on Changamire's side during the 1693–5 war was approved in accordance with Manyika traditional practice."[39]

The second incident was a century later, in 1796, when Chikanga Nyarumwe sent emissaries to the Rozvi Changamire asking him to come to or send his representatives to Manyika so that they could confirm his investiture. The impetus here was local. When Nyarumwe first ascended the throne of Manyika, he faced competition from his brothers. It was then that he sent envoys "to beg Changamire to confirm his investure." At much the same time, Nyarumwe responded to Portuguese complaints about disturbances at the *feira* of Chipangura by stressing his inability to deal with them "until Changamire had confirmed him as king of Manyika."[40] Clearly Nyarumwe invoked the Changamire's name to legitimate his own position. There is no evidence that Changamire offered the support he requested.

Claims that the Varozvi appointed all tributary chiefs and apportioned land, in Manyika or other areas, therefore, need to be regarded with circumspection. From the perspective of those who told them, such narratives were more about internal power politics (within or between specific ruling lineages) than they were about Rozvi power. Almost all oral accounts of the Rozvi conferring chieftaincies relate to the seizure of power by usurpers.[41] Traditions relating to the Chikwaka chieftainship, suggesting that the Rozvi granted Benhura power over a territory then ruled by his father-in-law, rationalized one such power grab.[42] Local traditions of succession envisaged that following the passing of the dynasty's founder, his sons would succeed him, brothers succeeding one another with eventual reversion to the eldest son of the eldest brother.[43] With time, the descendants of these brothers became the *dzimba* (houses) in which the chieftainship rotated. Under this system, Benhura was forever excluded from the chieftainship held by his father-in-law. As Central Shona speakers understood, "*Mukuwasha haagare nhaka kwaatezvara*" (A son-in-law does not have a claim to his father-in-law's estate).

Adelphic-collateral succession (brother succeeding brother as above) not only excluded outsiders but also proscribed the rise of a junior member of a lineage ahead of his seniors. Thus, it reinforced exclusions on the basis of both belonging and seniority. As in the case of Chikwaka, the outsider, there were cases where juniors ascended to power ahead of their seniors, and this too could be legitimated by invoking the Varozvi. This is what happened with Chiendambuya.

Gaining a throne often depended on intradynastic maneuvers—the supposed Rozvi interventions notwithstanding. In Chihota, for example, a leader named Zhanji was said to have been appointed by the Rozvi. A cousin named Mutenda whose own brother, Chiputire, had been overlooked, objected and mobilized his men to kill Zhanji. But Mutenda died shortly afterward and Zhanji's brother Chikudza became Chief Chihota.[44] In the end, the people of Chihota got their chief, not because of the Rozvi interventions but because of political intrigues within the ruling lineage.

Likewise, in Manyika in the eighteenth century, local rulers conducted business and dealt with the Portuguese without a hint of allegiance to the Rozvi elites. They traded in ways contrary to Rozvi preferences and blocked trade without consulting Rozvi leaders.[45] In 1794, the frustrated Portuguese asked Changamire to discipline the Manyika king—to no avail.[46] A year later, the Portuguese residents of Sena resolved to relocate the *feira* of Manyika from Chipangura to Ruangwa, still in Manyika but close enough to Baruwe, under the rule of another king, to whose territory it could move with ease if necessary.[47] Nothing came of the Portuguese resolution. The *feira* remained at Chipangura not because the Rozvi intervened with the Manyika but because the Portuguese official who received the resolution had no authority to sanction the relocation.[48]

CONSOLIDATING POWER, EXTENDING TERRITORIAL CLAIMS, AND REINFORCING LANDED INEQUALITIES

In the three centuries after the mid-sixteenth century, even the most powerful chiefs of northeastern Zimbabwe never completely eliminated competitors. In efforts to consolidate their power, some settled members of their lineage in outlying parts of their territory referred to as *dunhu*. Known as *washe* or *muchinda* (headmen in colonial parlance), these individuals and their descendants upheld the authority of the chief. Describing this practice in Chidima (in the lower Zambezi), Albino Pacheco wrote that the territory was "divided into fiefs governed by princes of the most importance (close relatives of Muanamutapa) who rule over it as absolute lords." These princes helped in the conquest of the territory and were "considered perpetual owners of those districts with succession rights as a token of gratitude for service rendered."[49]

Generally, those given fiefdoms would relinquish their claims to the main chieftainship. Manyika oral traditions capture these developments in the early nineteenth century.[50] When Nyamandoto was old, he asked Nyarumwe, his younger brother, to take over the chieftainship, but once Nyarumwe did so, he grew arrogant and failed to properly respect his older brother. Nyamandoto sent men to kill him and made Govera, another brother, chief of Manyika. Fearing that Nyarumwe's sons would revenge their father's death, Nyamandoto persuaded four of them—Saruchera, Zindi, Mandeya, and Sakarombe—to settle to the north of Bingaguru, the capital of the kingdom, to keep a watchful eye on potential enemies.[51] When the brothers learned of Govera's death, they returned to the Manyika capital to see him buried and, presumably, to join the succession battle. However, Manyika elders declared that "those from Mushonga who climbed the Mapwepwe Mountain should not meet the chief."[52] They and their descendants were excluded from the Manyika chieftainship but were then officially recognized as headmen of their *matunhu* (singular, *dunhu*).[53]

There were several advantages to this kind of arrangement. Those who settled the new lands still belonged to the polity and were invested in its survival. They became key to ensuring that their chief's territory survived attacks from neighboring polities and distant neighbors.[54] Furthermore, the exclusion of *muchinda* (ward rulers) from the chieftainship limited the number of houses (*dzimba*) that might aspire to the position of chief without undermining their allegiance to the polity. This was, by and large, good for the cohesion of the chieftainship.

In other cases, social and political conflicts forced people from their community. Anthropologist Igor Kopytoff called this process the reproduction of the African frontier, as outward migrations led to the settlement of contiguous lands by related peoples and the development of societies whose structures mirrored those of the mother communities.[55] This process played out in Maungwe with the establishment of the Makoni and Chipunza dynasties. According to local traditions, the founders of these two dynasties were half brothers. Muswere, the younger of the two, left the territory settled by their father, Sabarawara, to establish his own dynasty (which he called Makoni) because Chipunza, the older half brother, was heir to the Sabarawara dynasty.[56] The frontiers into which the immigrants moved were not empty lands.[57] But by characterizing resident communities as uncivilized, newcomers undermined the legitimacy of autochthonous claims to the land and legitimated their own right to occupy it.

On occasion, newcomers evicted firstcomers from their territory, and proximity to power enabled these displacements. Early in the nineteenth century, Mandeya, a member of the Manyika ruling family, settled at Howeta, in Nyamhuka, where he would soon assume the headmanship, and instructed his wives to go and cultivate groundnuts in the Webengo area—so the tradition says. The autochthonous Dumbwi chief objected to this because the women cultivated the area without informing him. A skirmish ensued. The Dumbwi peoples lost, and the Nyamhuka appropriated their land. We do not know the subsequent fate of the Dumbwi people, but it is possible that they moved to less desirable lands than those from which they were displaced.

Various forms of social inequalities, including wealth and poverty, deepened landed inequalities. One of the ways in which claims to land were established was through its clearance; proto-Shona speakers extended the meaning of *-*sakul* (to weed) to include "to clear" and then derived the noun for "land left fallow," *gura,* from that root.[58] Once a household had cleared land for fields, descendants could claim abandoned tracts by arguing that they had only left them to fallow. However, a household's ability to clear land rested on its ability to mobilize labor.[59] This was facilitated by polygyny. Here, wealthy men held an edge over their poorer colleagues. Manyika men were said to "marry as often as they wish and can afford according to their possessions. Whoever hath more wealth and giveth more to the parents of the women they marry will get more wives."[60] With wives came children and in time their labor. The fewer wives a man had, the less land he was able to utilize. Wealth in things thus reinforced wealth in people, which in turn led to land inequalities.[61]

Wealthy men also accepted daughters offered in marriage by poorer households in lean times. Droughts and locust infestations—which produced these lean times—were not unknown in this region. In 1511, the hinterland of Sofala, including the Zimbabwean plateau, suffered a drought that lasted until 1517.[62] A terrible famine caused by locusts struck the northern parts of the Zimbabwean plateau in 1561 and lasted for two years.[63] Two decades later in the 1580s, severe droughts and locust swarms hit the Zambezi region, resulting "in the displacement of population . . . [,] internal migrations[, and] extremely unsettled conditions."[64] Another plague of locusts hit the Zambezi valley from 1736 to 1745, with devastating consequences. During the worst of the locust plagues, "neither crops nor cultivated or wild trees were left alone, that being one of the reasons why many natives died of hunger, and why others gave themselves up voluntarily as slaves to the Goanese or to some other rich countrymen in exchange for a small portion of grain, enough to last a day."[65] Many daughters left their natal homes as brides under similar arrangements in a marriage practice that descendants of proto–Central Shona speakers called *kuzvarira.* Both *kuzvarira* and pawnship allowed poor families to survive lean years, but the greatest beneficiaries were the rich. They increased their labor pool while poor families remained trapped in a vicious cycle of poverty and precarity. Drained of their labor, they cultivated smaller portions of lands than their more fortunate counterparts and had less to pass on to their descendants.

MARRIAGE ALLIANCES, POWER, AND WOMEN'S AUTHORITY

The material conditions that forced poor households to marry their daughters through *kuzvarira* in many ways differed from those that prompted ruling families to arrange marriages for their daughters. While the former's marriage ensured that their natal families survived famine, the latter entered their marriages as brides in a political game dominated by men. This was because dynastic chiefs sought to build alliances through marriage.[66] But not all of these elite women were pawns of male power players. Many female members of ruling lineages also exercised considerable power. In the Mutapa state, noted Antonio Bocarro in the 1560s,

> the principal one is called Mazarira, who is always one of the king's sisters. She is the mother of the Portuguese, speaks for them, and treats of their concerns with the king, therefore the Portuguese send her presents. . . . The second woman is called Inhahanda and speaks for the Moors. The third is called Nabuiza; she is his [the king's] real wife, for she is the only one who lives in the palace with the king. The fourth is called Nauemba; the fifth Nemangore; the sixth Nizingoapangi; the seventh, Nemangoro; the eighth, Nessanhi; and finally, the ninth is called Necharunda.

Although Bocarro listed these women as Mwenemutapa's wives, he also noted that all but one of them were "his relations or sisters . . . [or] the daughters of the kings and lords who are his vassals."[67]

The powers these women wielded were immense, and their privileges equaled those of leading men. Mazvarira and Nehanda oversaw the *mutapa*'s trading relations with the Portuguese and the Arabs.[68] All had "houses and estates of their own," and some had "many lands and vassals, and . . . kingdoms pertaining to their houses." Their power over their vassals included the authority to punish or put them to death.[69] Two centuries later Nehanda was said to have privileges not unlike those of the king; to have many servants, subjects, or captives; and to bear the title of empress.[70]

Women held similarly powerful positions across the northern half of the Zimbabwean plateau. For example, in 1778, a women appointed by the king of Manyika controlled parts of the territory that included the Portuguese *feira* at Chipangura. As a "princess of that region," the woman had taken residence in the *feira*, from where she observed its trading activities and "received as her due a length of cloth originally small but now [in 1788] large, so constituting a new tribute which every person entering Feira on any business whatsoever . . . [was] obliged to pay."[71] Svosve dynastic traditions also mention at least two women who held power in the history of this polity.[72] One was Vachikombo, a sister of Dandenyoro, chief of the Svosve area and the founder of the dynasty, who settled and controlled the hills west of the Wenimbi River after her brother's rise to the chieftainship. These hills were then named Masikana, literally, "the girls." The second was the daughter of Dandenyoro's successor-son Mukanganise, who moved into the Masikana hills to live with his aunt. On Vachikombo's death, Mukanganise granted his own daughter authority over the land between the Ruzawi and Karimba Rivers.[73] Generally, the king's mother also held enormous influence over her son. Before King Mwenemutapa determined that the Portuguese missionary Gonçalo da Silveira should be killed, he consulted his mother.

RITUALS, COLLECTIVE WELL-BEING, AND THE MEDIATION OF CHIEFLY AUTHORITY

Silveira's fate was sealed when his enemies claimed that, in addition to being a Portuguese spy, "the priest was a Moor, bringing the sun and famine in a dead man's bone and many other spells so as to take possession of the land and kill the king."[74] In short, he was a wizard. Rulers understood wizards to be a threat to their rule. In their wizardry, they harmed the land, destabilizing the polity. "If a king lays hold of a sorcerer," said Álvaro Fernandez of the ruler of Manyika in 1573, "he kills him because he does not suffer any other sorcerers besides himself, considering himself and being considered as a great sorcerer."[75] But rulers could not kill every wizard or witch. To temper the threat posed by medicine men and women, northeastern Zimbabwe's ruling lineages almost invariably claimed political as well as ritual power. Indeed, one of the great achievements of second-millennium state-makers was to create capitals that, with time, also became ritual centers and to create ritual sites around sacred groves and caves (*ninga*) where they interred their leaders.[76] At these spaces, ruling lineages propitiated the spirits of their ancestors, requesting good and adequate rains as well as protection against pestilences and disease.[77] In Manyika at the end of the eighteenth century, these rituals were performed with great ceremony. Sacrifices offered by the king to the gods were "pompously performed by his great magicians or priests called Massumba [*sic*] [the big lions], whom they also call *muzimo* [*mudzimu*] believing that the soul of his father, the previous king, has transmigrated into him, and not only this one but all the others into whom the souls of their ancestors have transmigrated take the name they had in real life."[78] In the assessment of contemporary observers, the Manyika peoples believed in "the transmigration of the souls of men into the bodies of others and consider those godly, and also into animals such as lion, crocodile and others."[79] These, in short, were the *mhondoro* at work.

For all their efforts, rulers and their lineages were never able to centralize healing and political power. The people of the Zimbabwean plateau sought to limit the power of their leaders to those necessary to ensure their collective well-being. Reasoning that, if unfettered, power would allow leaders to "stand up to them and dominate them," rank-and-file residents of the Zimbabwean plateau thought it "a good idea to weaken him [the king] before he develops such ideas and, if he does not accept this, they consider him a traitor and seek other ways of thinning out his wealth."[80] Among these ways was denouncing the king as a wizard on the appearance of high rates of illness and death among his people.[81] Droughts and excessive rains were further grounds for impugning leaders as selfish wizards. "If there is much sunshine," one missionary noted, subject peoples told their leader "to free the rain, if it rains a lot, they tell him to let the sun out, that he gathers so much wealth because he has the sun trapped in his house and does not let it shine over other people's crops."[82]

What is more, by the sixteenth century, the people of the Zimbabwean plateau had succeeded in separating the spiritual and temporal powers from the control of one man. Indeed, not even the powerful rulers of the Mutapa state controlled both ritual and political power.[83] Moreover, to borrow Steven Feierman's words, "it was, impossible," for chiefly families "to eliminate every sort of healer who claimed the ability to bring rich crops."[84] On the Zimbabwean plateau, men of medicine were many and varied.[85] To cap it all, some of the most important *mhondoro*—the spirits and the mediums that channeled them—did not belong to the ruling patrilineages. Instead, their powers and appeal transcended the boundaries of chieftainships.[86]

By way of illustration, in times of drought or some other calamity, the Vanhowe made offerings at a ritual site called Dziva Ranyamhita (Nyamhita's pool).[87] Nyamhita (also known as Nehanda or Nyamhita Nehanda) was an important figure of historical imagination among Zezuru and Korekore speakers.[88] Although Nyamhita Nehanda's spirit and its medium Charwe were connected in the twentieth century with anticolonial resistance and postcolonial nation-making, this important ritual figure was historically associated with rain and fertility.[89] Several oral traditions relating to the peopling of the Zimbabwean plateau by ancestors of Central Shona–speaking peoples and the founding of the Mutapa state suggest that Nyamhita committed ritual incest with her brother, an act that was central to the ritual of *kupinga pasi* (to tame the land) and to ruling lineages' attempts to centralize creative and instrumental power.[90]

When ruling dynasties claimed that their founders committed incest, they suggested that they were providers of wives to their own lineages. For this reason, their ability to ensure the fertility of the land, bring rains, and end misfortunes such as pestilences—in short, to ensure social health—belonged to their lineages, not the spirits of outsiders. This was based on the understanding that those who provided wives were the guarantors of fertility.[91] However, when the Vanhowe propitiated the spirit of Nyamhita, they acknowledged that they did not have control over the forces of fertility in their own territory. This is because Nyamhita did not belong to their lineage. According to Vanhowe traditions, she was the wife of the early Nhowe rulers and, therefore, an outsider.[92]

But even when rulers and their families could guarantee the fertility of their own territory, as the Mutapa elites claimed, they were unable to monopolize power. Within the Zambezi valley, ritual actors associated with the Mutapa ruling lineage faced competition from the Dzivaguru-Karuva "cult" controlled by the Tavara people conquered by the kingdom's founders in the fifteenth century.[93] The Tavara were not the only conquered people to retain ritual power even as they lost their political autonomy. Autochthonous subject peoples in Manyika also claimed spiritual control over the land and its products, and their conquerors, the Nyamubvambire dynasty, relied upon these subjects to communicate with their ancestral spirits to ensure the prosperity of the land.[94]

The continuing existence of powerful ritual actors outside the ruling lineages pitted power against power.[95] Ritual sites and actors (such as the famous shrines at Matopos, the Musikavanhu territorial cult, and the Marumbi Karivara cult) were sources of authority alongside chiefs and their lineages.[96] Their importance, in the eyes of many members of subject populations, was indicated by an elder who told a researcher that "those who rule should be the people who perform the rituals that bring rain (*anenge ane rushanga*), the tools that were bestowed by the dead, the real owners of the chieftainship (*tsvimbo dzekupihwa navafi varidzi vanotonga hushe*)."[97]

Other ritual actors whose authority rivaled that of chiefs included an official known among the Wamanyika as the Sahumani. This individual performed two related rituals: one venerating the survival spirits understood to extend the longevity of the chief; the other a ceremony known as *kugara ngwena* (to sit on a crocodile). This ceremony was conducted at two points in the chief's life: at coronation and in honor of a chief whose rule had been long and productive.[98] The first of these ritual moments was described at the end of the eighteenth century. "For his [the chief's] coronation, apart from many other extravagant ceremonies, they catch a live crocodile of which there are some very big ones in the rivers Ruanga and Hose [Odzi?], tie it by the neck and make a bed on top of it on which the king has intercourse with a princess, one of his daughters and afterwards sits on the crocodile."[99]

The Sahumani lived in Manyika territory, but he was almost autonomous. He did not perform the ceremonial clapping of hands (*kuwombera*) to show his respects to the king.[100] The Sahumani did not pay tribute to the chief, a clear marker of his independence.[101] He was also permitted to appropriate the king's cattle if they strayed onto his land.[102] In his autonomy, the Sahumani mirrored the Gosa, a man who, while living within the Mutapa territory, did not attend ceremonies called by the Mwenemutapa. Owing to his greatness, da Conceição said of this man in 1696, Gosa was "not due the curtseys and prostrations the others have to do."[103] Gosa's greatness, unlike that of the Sahumani, stemmed from the fact that his lineage provided the guardians of the powerful Dzivaguru and Karuva cults known as Nechiskwa.[104]

The status of the Sahumani and the Gosa clan in relation to the power of chiefs and/or kings underscored the fact that chiefly power could be circumscribed. Those who checked rulers' impulses to centralize authority over land and people came from within and outside ruling lineages. They performed rituals that ensured collective well-being, a ruler's long and productive reign, and ultimately the stability of a polity. Although these individuals and the institutions they represented were not directly involved in land allocation, their powers rested on both a wider moral order and their role in securing collective well-being. The latter had become especially important as descendants of proto-Shona speakers came to terms with the fact that land with all the ingredients to sustain cereal cultivation and animal husbandry was limited. This limited land was not accessed by everyone in equal measure. Leaders like Mandeya and other members of the ruling lineages could displace autochthonous communities as remembered in Manyika oral traditions. In those instances, proximity to power enabled access to good, productive land.

3 ⁓ Changing Geographies and Old Registers of Power

IN THE 1830s, the Rozvi kingdom—the dominant polity in the Zimbabwean plateau after the late seventeenth century—collapsed, but many polities and other institutions of power remained. This chapter traces these changes and continuities and what they meant for social and political relations in the region up to 1890, when most of the Zimbabwean plateau became the British colony of Southern Rhodesia. It argues that, as before, the ways in which people related to one another and to their neighbors shaped how they lived and farmed, but new political realities amplified old ways of rationalizing authority, even as old threats to political power within dynasties persisted, forcing rulers to secure their positions against members of their own lineages. Among some chieftainships, this led to the appointment of female rulers to preside over a very patriarchal institution in which kinship and seniority remained important determinants of position and power. However, most women remained structurally subordinated to men and were only able to access land and other resources through them.

THE CHANGING GEOGRAPHY OF SETTLEMENTS AND FIELDS

When English artist and explorer Thomas Baines reached the Manyame River in the late 1860s, he saw "formerly extensive" fields and settlements, by then abandoned.[1] A little later, Frederick Selous, traversing the land near where Harare now stands, also encountered recently abandoned settlements and fields.[2] Similarly, "large patches of cultivated land now abandoned" were visible farther east, between Umtali and Salisbury, as late as 1893.[3] To European travelers this indicated that once densely settled areas had experienced a demographic collapse.[4]

In fact the people who had once cultivated the abandoned fields had moved to new, secure locations, some near their old sites and some more distant. Having passed several deserted fields in Chief Chivero's territory, south of the Manyame River, the traveler Walter Montagu Kerr soon "came upon numerous . . . patches of cultivated ground" and "a lovely green valley where . . . cattle could be seen grazing." This valley "was walled-in by low mountain ridges, and overlooked by the rocky fastness of a Mashona chief."[5] North of the Manyame River from Chief Chivero's territory, Kerr found bare, flat, sparsely settled country, but far to the east the horizon was broken by a chain of craggy mountains—"stark upheavals of spire-like rocks whose . . . recesses concealed Neanda [Nehanda], a large Mashona town, of which Setauro [Chitauro] was the chief."[6]

Historically, it was quite common for chiefs and their close associates to live on hilltops. These locations were associated with power.[7] By the late nineteenth century, however, many Mashona homesteads were perched on top of rock formations.[8] One of Chief Svosve's subjects had his homestead "uphill . . . where one had to wait for 2 hours before one was allowed inside."[9] Selous described "several Mashuna villages" "perched amongst the rocks of little stony hills" that studded the landscape.[10] Near the confluence of the Ruzawi and Karimba Rivers, the houses were built "upon the ledges" and on the highest parts of "an outcrop of enormous masses of bare rock [and] gigantic smooth, rounded boulders."[11] Indeed, when German geologist Karl Mauch reached two "small villages in the plain" in 1872, he remarked that this was "something rare because [villages] are generally built on rock kopjes."[12] Many of these places were nucleated settlements. Several travelers remarked that even "outlying kraals"—distant from the centers of African political power—consisted "as a rule . . . of a dozen or more huts" surrounded by a large number of granaries.[13]

The concentration of people in hilltop villages and hamlets was on the one hand a way of dealing with pestiferous insects such as tsetse flies and mosquitoes and on the other, a response to security concerns.[14] Many stockaded settlements on the northern half of the Zimbabwean plateau were built in response to the presence of Portuguese *prazo*holders and their Chikunda armies.[15] In the mid-nineteenth century, raids by these parties reached communities in the upper Mupufure watershed and the headwaters of the

Save River.[16] Later, Portuguese warlords such as Kanyemba and Manuel Antonio de Souza, popularly known as Gouveia, raided large swaths of land in northern and northeastern Zimbabwe.[17] Some of northeastern Zimbabwe's smaller communities were raided by more powerful Shona-speaking neighbors. In the Nyanga highlands, Chihombo's village, tucked up on "rocky mountain slopes," was pillaged by Chief Mutoko's forces in 1872.[18] Nguni speakers raided plateau lands from the 1830s onward and drove locals into safer landscapes of hills and mountains.[19] Gaza Nguni warriors also attacked the settlements in the eastern highlands in the 1860s. But both the Ndebele and Gaza raids were intermittent. The Gaza Nguni's practice of moving their capitals—and their people—meant that their influence on the central watershed and northern parts of the eastern highlands waxed and waned. When the British occupied the Zimbabwean plateau in 1890, the balance of power was shifting in favor of some Shona-speaking communities with access to Portuguese and Afrikaner guns.[20]

Defensive retreat into the hills often came with costs. "To live among the rocks," G. W. Knight-Bruce commented condescendingly in 1891, "the Mashona will sacrifice even a good water supply."[21] This sacrifice bore especially heavily on women who made frequent trips up and down the hills to fetch needed water and firewood. Other burdens were borne by those (such as the people of Chief Nyandoro, who retreated in the 1880s from the open lands between the upper Manyame and Munyati Rivers to Samuriwo's refuge at Matsvitsvi) who left their own lands to live among neighbors as outsiders. Easy familiarity, a sense of belonging, deeply rooted ecological knowledge, and in many instances any claim to ancestral land all stood forfeit to such strategies—and they brought no guarantee of safety or stability. Both Nyandoro's and Samuriwo's peoples eventually took "refuge in Nhowe" a few years after Nyandoro led his subjects to Matsvitsvi as raids continued.[22] The Nyandoro peoples were never able to regain their lands in Tsunga, which were parceled out to white farmers by the colonial government.

Access to good defensive sites was informed by existing hierarchies of power. Where good locations were scarce, poorer people sometimes had to scatter homesteads, for want of easily defensible space in one location.[23] Where lands with defensible hills were limited, those who occupied the lower rungs of the social ladder settled on the defenseless plains. Between the Tugwi and Runde Rivers in south-central Zimbabwe, the lower-class members of the community "descendent from inherited mothers" were located on the plains where they were vulnerable to Ndebele raids, while higher-class Mhari occupied mountainous strongholds.[24]

It was not just the defensible sites that tended to be few and far between. By the end of the eighteenth century, productive land was in short supply in some areas of northeastern Zimbabwe. This may have prompted Chief Marange Chirukamaswe to occupy two areas in northern Bocha and induced the Mutsago dynasty to settle the marginal lowlands of southern Bocha.[25] A half century later, land pressures might have been felt in parts of the central watershed, particularly the lands between the headwaters of the Nyaguwe and Manyame Rivers. In the 1870s, little game was to be found in the lands between Chief Chikwaka's territory and Mount Wedza because there were "a good many natives in the district."[26] Many of these people had fled Ndebele raids between the Manyame and upper Munyati Rivers.

But even when large areas were left unsettled, they were not without owners. As noted in the preceding chapter, **-kur-*, the act of clearing land, conveyed a lasting claim to it. Likewise, chiefs regularly claimed territory to some boundary, even though large parts of their domain remained uninhabited.[27] By contrast with European landowners, who essentially derived rents from their land, chiefs in northeastern Zimbabwe asserted their authority over both the land and the people who lived on, or traversed through, it by demanding tribute. When Thomas Baines hunted near Manyame in 1869, he learned that local chiefs in the area enforced "the law observed by Portuguese hunters" that "half of any slain animal that touched the ground belonged to the chief, and till he had taken his, the hunter must not touch it."[28] The incorrigible traveler Walter Montagu Kerr was twice admonished for killing game without giving any to the chief "to whom the whole country belonged," as well as entering a chief's territory "without asking him permission, or sending him a present to let him know he was coming."[29]

NEW POLITICAL REALITIES, COMPETITION FOR LAND, AND OLD MODES OF LEGITIMATING CHIEFLY POWER

Chiefs could apply levies to hunters hunting in their territories because they retained control of their lands. But in the mid- and late nineteenth century, many ruling elites and their subjects lost their lands. This was not unusual. Most dynastic traditions concede that chiefly lineages displaced other people whose lands they settled. In the eighteenth century, several dynasties in south-central Zimbabwe lost land and power to immigrant dynasties from the northeast.[30] What was different in the mid-nineteenth century was that the long-powerful Rozvi ruling houses fled their own lands. Mutinhima went into exile in the Mai ya Vahera Hills with the Ndebele hot on his heels. The Tumbare, Mavhudzi, Nerwande, and Chihunduru houses fled to the northwest of their former territory. Other Rozvi houses took refuge in the upper Save River basin to become Chiduku, Tandi, and Rozani groups. In the south, the Gumunyu and Jiri houses found a place among the Duma in Bikita.[31]

Those who moved into the upper Save River basin occupied lands protected by the defensive ramparts of the Mavangwe, Bepe, Dombwe, Nyamupara, Maninga, and Musvawu ranges. This land lay on the borderlands of several territories, but the Rozvi understood that it was not unclaimed. To legitimate their presence there, they sharpened the argument that they had always assigned land and installed chiefs, then further refined this idea as they adapted to colonial rule and sought to revive the Rozvi *mambo*ship in the twentieth century.[32] Rozvi chieftains continue to espouse this claim because it is useful in contemporary conflicts over boundaries.[33] Aware that they have been in the area barely a century and a half, they imply a longer presence to elevate their status in relation to that of their neighbors.[34] Chief Mbava, a Rozvi leader who lived in the upper Save River basin from the late nineteenth century to the 1920s, encapsulated this thinking when he claimed, "King Chiduku of the Warozvi ruled over the country of the Mawungwe, the Manyika, the Mabocha, the Wanyashanu, the Makombe and the Mazezuru. After this time the Warozvi were the overlords of the whole country, and chose all the new chiefs."[35] But this was not the case in northeastern Zimbabwe. Such assertions took their place in a long line of claims made to land and authority. To be sure, Changamire Dombo had operated in Maungwe and Manyika between 1684 and 1696, but there is little evidence that ruling houses in northeastern Zimbabwe consistently sought Rozvi investiture thereafter.[36] In any event, the ruling houses in Maungwe, Manyika, Bocha, and Mbire were long established before the rise of the Rozvi state in the 1680s.[37] Far from receiving land from Rozvi elites, some of these lineages accommodated the diasporic Rozvi ruling houses of the nineteenth century in their territories. "These days, Mazise and Gwangwava live in this country of Jiri. Mbava and Ruzani and Bhasvi and Benhura are in Mbire. Chiduku and Mavudzi are in Makoni's country," confirmed a member of one of the Rozvi ruling houses.[38]

Many more political actors appropriated old registers in claiming land and making authority. As late as the 1890s, some members of northeastern Zimbabwe's ruling families were seeking to reproduce the frontier in ways others had done in the past, by leaving well-established communities to escape social conflict and establish their own polities elsewhere.[39] Thus, in 1896, some six years after the British annexation of Manyika, Chimbadzwa, Chief Mutasa's son, left his father's territory together with his supporters to establish his own dynasty near the territory of his uncle, Makombe, the king of Baruwe.[40] Chimbadzwa's migration to Baruwe mirrored the near-contemporaneous move by the famous Mapondera, from the upper Mazowe valley to the Zambezi escarpment.[41]

SECURING POWER, MAKING FEMALE RULERS

Although many political elites utilized old ways of claiming land and authority to their own advantage in the nineteenth century, all understood that their positions were open to contestation—especially from kin and neighbors.[42] As chiefs sought to undercut these threats, the long-standing strategy of settling competitors from their lineage in outlying parts of their territory and then offering them the title of *muchinda* (discussed in the previous chapter) continued.[43] Those who took the position of *muchinda* not only settled and exercised power in new lands but also remained integral members of the polity and were invested in its survival. Despite "the fissile nature of their internal politics," observed historian David Maxwell, "it was in the interests of all the agnates of the ruling dynasty that it should continue. . . . Without a *mambo*—chief—of their clan or worse still with a new *mambo* of another clan, members of the dynasty would lose the slight edge they had over local *vatorwa*—outsiders."[44]

These measures lessened rather than extinguished political intrigue.[45] Some chiefs, therefore, took other steps to secure their power. These included marriage alliances, and, again, in time tested fashion, the appointment of female members of their lineages—aunties (fathers' sisters), sisters and daughters—to oversee portions of a chieftainship and stave off rebellion. Upon the death of a Manyika *muchinda*, an early colonial official reported what he understood of the process by which a successor was chosen:

> Bones were thrown to determine the cause of death. The diviner reported that the deceased's area was responsible. The chief then consulted the great spirit of the tribe (*Nyamandoto*) through a medium. The spirit replied that the country of the dead *muchinda* needed a *muzari* [*sic*] and not a *muchinda*. *'Let a Washe,'* said the spirit, "light her fire there and rule the people." "If you put a *muchinda* in charge again, he will rise in rebellion."[46]

And so a headwoman was appointed to preside over the area in question and avert the fragmentation of the polity.

These princesses held the title of *washe* (plural, *madzihashe*). When the British occupied Mashonaland in 1890, several *madzihashe* presided over parts of Manyika, Jindwi, and Bocha.[47] One of these, Makanaka, was an aunt of *mambo* Tendai Mutasa Chifambausiku. She "was a powerful chieftainess, owning sway over many kraals in the valley watered by the Revue river, and stretching away from Umtali towards Mase-Kesse."[48] Washe Makanaka presided over a territory that encompassed the old Portuguese *feira* of Chipangura. Whether there had been continuity in the succession of *madzihashe* in this territory we cannot tell, but Makanaka governed the same part of Manyika that was administered by a female ruler a century earlier. Washe Chikanga, the daughter of Chief Tendai Mutasa, lived in a kraal five miles west of New Umtali.[49] To the southwest of Manyika, in Bocha, Washe Mupomwa—the daughter of the reigning chief, Marange—presided over the affairs of a part of her father's territory that was only ten miles from the chief's court.[50] A little farther south, again in Bocha, "Darokasoa's village" was under the authority of a "chieftainess" who was the daughter of Mutsago.[51]

Far from being women used as pawns in male chiefs' power games (as the narrative of their appointment to stanch rebellion suggests), *madzihashe* possessed real power. The *washe* who governed the *feira* of Chipangura in 1788 monitored the Portuguese and African traders there (an immense responsibility that confirmed the confidence that Manyika rulers had in her) and collected and kept levies, which allowed her to accumulate wealth and, with it, power. Female rulers also presided over sensitive matters such as witchcraft, theft, and murder—at least in the nineteenth century. These matters were mostly reserved for chiefs because they were fundamental to both the material and symbolic aspects of authority. Adjudicating murder cases allowed rulers to accumulate wealth from fines. It also allowed them to combine political and ritual power. Chiefs not only monopolized the power to try witchcraft cases but also, as owners of the land, monopolized authority to perform rituals meant to cleanse the land that was assumed to have been polluted when murder was committed. The retention by northeastern Zimbabwe's female rulers of the authority to preside over these cases is testament to the immense powers that they possessed.

Madzihashe further revealed their status and power by conducting their business in ways similar to those of male chiefs. When "Mambo Candie . . . , a [male] member of the family of the reigning Muanamutapa," met Pacheco in Chidima in mid-January 1862, he lived "like all chiefs surrounded by wives, and children and by a great number of hangers-on, whom he calls *vanhae* (*vanyayi*) [messengers]. These men," Pacheco later explained, "on seeing a gesture or hearing an expression, however crude it might be, broke into deafening burst of clapping accompanied by the monosyllable *di, di*."[52] Likewise, when Rose Blennerhassett and Lucy Sleeman, two British nurses working at the newly established Anglican mission near Umtali, visited Washe Chikanga in 1891, they found her with an entourage of fifty or sixty men.[53] The *washe,* Blennerhassett and Sleeman observed, commanded the highest respect. Whenever she spoke, all the people in the room clapped. "Once she went to the door and spat outside; they all clapped solemnly." Meanwhile, no other woman dared approach the "council hut."[54] This room, then, represented patriarchal rule at work. However, at its head was a female member of the ruling family.

Washe Chikanga continued her performance of power the following day when, returning Blennerhassett's and Sleeman's favor, she visited the two nurses at their camp. She arrived in the company of sixty or seventy people—old and young men, and boys of all ages. Inside, "the 'Queen' seated herself on a box, while her husbands—[they were clearly her aides]—sat on the ground beside her."[55] Both the command of retainers and the etiquette of seating signaled the hierarchy of power. Here, too, the *washe*'s status was similar to that of her male counterparts.[56] Indeed, when Chief Chuzu met Walter Montagu Kerr near his court in 1871, he was "accompanied by a number of . . . girls" who "answered his beck and call with due humility."[57]

A *washe*'s power, like that of her male counterparts, was reinforced through gifting. When Blennerhassett and Sleeman visited the *madzihashe* Makanaka and Chikanga, they gave each of the two leaders gifts of cloths and beads.[58] Protocol required that gifts or other pleasantries meant for the leaders were handed to an aide who then passed them to the ruler. As Montagu Kerr learned, it was "not regal etiquette . . . for a chief to receive a present into his own hands."[59] The logic of this, though, was more than just royal etiquette; it was also security. Rulers feared that they might fall victim to poisoning or witchcraft if they received gifts directly. Their suspicions deepened when the gift-giver was an outsider, something that escaped Blennerhassett and Sleeman when they offered Washe Chikanga coffee and she asked her aide to taste before she declined it.

In all this and more, northeastern Zimbabwe's female rulers disrupted the baggage of gender norms that Europeans brought with them to the Zimbabwean plateau. Consider, for example, how Blennerhassett and Sleeman responded when Washe Chikanga declined their coffee and then told them that "she understood, and liked, whisky better."[60] "We told her that 'fire water' was the drink of men, not women, but could not make her see the force of the argument. If the white men liked it and drank it, why should not white women do so? What was good for men, was good for women too, at least for the chieftainesses!" The two female missionaries confessed, "This Woman's Rights argument . . . amused us greatly."[61]

Neither Washe Chikanga nor other *madzihashe* subjected themselves to the social institutions that sometimes normalized female subjection.[62]

These institutions included marriage and the payment of *roora*.[63] "The marriage customs of these headwomen were irregular," an early colonial official noted with some disapproval. "Lobola [*roora*] was never paid for any of the sisters or daughters of Mutasa," and

> when a married *muzari* [female in the chiefly lineage] became a *washe* [headwoman] she took her *nehanda* [a man whom she "married" who was usually a chief's friend] with her. But she was rarely faithful to him, and it was always recognized that she could consort with any man to whom she took fancy. As a matter of fact, all the *wazari* used to be notorious for their loose morals and were extremely bad examples to all the Manyika women.[64]

As powerful women, *madzihashe* and other female members of the ruling lineages did not fit the stereotypical women envisioned by either the African or the British patriarchy. They were as powerful as their male counterparts.

LIMITS TO CHIEFLY POWER

Rulers, male or female, and the lineages that supplied them exercised power within set parameters. If they underperformed they could be sanctioned.[65] Vabocha oral traditions recall the loss of territory by Chief Marange. The chief gave a part of his land to Mabvengwa as a reward for seeing the severed head of Marangeni, his wife, murdered while looking for food in nearby Jindwi.[66] The chief was penalized for failing to ensure good rains and exposing both his family and his subjects to hunger and danger.

Chiefs could also be sanctioned for overstepping the boundaries of their authority. Vabocha tell another tradition in which their chiefs lost land because they were implicated in the death of a stranger (*mubvakure*) named Newunze.

> What happened was that the Mukwadas appeased a ngozi [avenging spirit] by pledging a girl to the wronged family. They also carved a piece of territory from their jurisdiction which would be controlled by any man who was to marry this girl. The girl was not supposed to move out of the Mukwada family on getting married but the suitor was the one who had to have children with her without paying lobola. . . . The children born in this family were not supposed to join the [biological father's] clan even if they used his surname because they were regarded as children born to compensate the deceased. Up to now, they occupy the Newunze area as it

was called and the Mukwadas and Maranges have no jurisdiction in that locality despite being within their overall territory.[67]

The act described here recalls a widespread practice of appeasing *ngozi,* the avenging spirits of strangers killed by clan members. The practice "derives from the belief that if a person kills another human being, he or she has to acknowledge their wrong doing and pay restitution to prevent the victim's spirit from coming back and haunting the killer and the members of his or her extended family."[68] In these instances, restitution was paid to the victim's family.

When the victim's family was unknown, families that believed they were being afflicted by the *ngozi* of a stranger built a small hut known as *chimba chemupfuko* (plural, *zvimba zvemipfuko*) (literally, little hut[s] for avenging spirits) which they placed under the care of a young girl. The young girl was understood to be "the ritual wife of the spirit for which the hut was built."[69] She was allocated a piece of land by her father, which she managed herself.[70] When the practice involved chiefly lineages, as the Mukwada case shows, a portion of the territory rather than a space for a hut would be set aside to appease the stranger's spirit. The lands that the chiefs surrendered as restitution to the deceased stranger became autonomous. All this underscored the point that if chiefly lineages crossed the boundaries of law and morality, they, too, could be sanctioned. In local custom, chiefs were expected to protect and not to take away lives.

In the meantime, across the Zimbabwean plateau in the mid- and late nineteenth century, old institutions of the *mhondoro*—both the medium and the spirit that it hosted—continued to serve, as they had done in the past, as centers of power that rivalled or even eclipsed that of chiefs. "Nebeza or Nhatangue," Pacheco noted of the Matope spirit and its medium, "is consulted by everyone and the natives hold his prophecies to be sacred. . . . Nebeza is[,] then, the spiritual head of both Chedima [Chidima] and Dande."[71]

Nebeza was associated with the founding of the Mutapa state and therefore a powerful political figure, at least in the legends of the Mutapa dynasty. In its glory days this state covered both Chidima and Dande, but by the time Pacheco visited these areas in 1862, the old kingdom was in its sunset. The Mwenemutapa dynasty retained control over a much-reduced territory, Chidima, between the Zambezi and its tributaries, the Musengezi and Ruenya Rivers. Dande, the other old constituent of the Mutapa state, to the west of Chidima between the Zambezi's confluence with Musengezi and the Sanyati, was ruled by several independent dynasties.

In Dande, several mediums operated in what G. Kingsley Garbett called "spirit provinces."[72] These were areas "of varying size, each of which . . . [was]

associated with, and named after one of the original Karanga invaders, a descendent of theirs, or occasionally an autochthon" that the spirits were believed to protect. These lands were bounded by physical features: hills, streams, rivers, and so on.[73] Nebeza's spirit and its medium were, by contrast, recognized as powerful across the boundaries of provinces and individual chieftainships. This recognition was actualized by the fact that Nebeza received "valuable gifts from all the *mambos* and *príncipes* from both territories, those from the Muanamutapa being the most valuable."[74]

Nebeza was part of an elite group of *mhondoro* who commanded power and respect across wide areas and whose authority rivaled that of chiefs. Others in this group included Pasipamire, the late-nineteenth-century medium of Chaminuka (d. 1883), who operated from his base at Dungwiza (Chitungwiza), in the central watershed. Pasipamire's power was recognized by several groups of Chishona speakers and by the Amandebele, who "considered [him] a very powerful Umlimo, or god."[75] According to Frederick Selous, writing in 1881, Pasipamire was gifted cattle and young girls by Lobengula, the Ndebele king.[76] Another equally powerful *mhondoro* lived in Chief Nemakonde's territory in 1891.[77] His mother, reported the Methodist missionary Isaac Shimmin, "was also a prophetess . . . acknowledged by the mighty Moselikatse [Mzilikazi], the first Matabele king."[78]

The power of these nineteenth-century *mhondoro* was recognized by rulers beyond Central Shona territory, but their authority was especially felt in many Shona polities—or so Europeans were made to believe. There, no serious decisions were made without the *mhondoro*'s assent. Shimmin's experiences are illustrative. The missionary approached Chief Nemakonde with a request for land to establish a Methodist mission station, but he was told that the chief and his principal men "could not act in the matter until the consent of their great prophetess had been obtained."[79] Similarly, Selous's visit with Chief Mutoko in January 1891 was delayed for several days while the chief communicated with a "mondoro or 'lion god,' a sort of High Priest who appears to have more power in the country than Mutoko himself."[80]

Mhondoro derived status by (supposedly) ensuring collective well-being and political cohesion. One medium encountered in Chidima in the Zambezi valley in 1862 claimed to have been "present with God at the creation of the world." He was said to receive the petitions and gifts of the people and to give sunshine and rain when he pleased; he foretold the future and warned of calamities that might happen in a given period.[81] Contemporaries regarded Pasipamire as "the foremost rain-maker" on the plateau, and his services were much sought after.[82] Legend had it that following Pasipamire's death at the hands of a Ndebele *impi* (army), "no rain fell and the country was sorely afflicted with drought: the crops failed, the cattle died; people wandered about gaunty and hungry; there was general distress. The heavens remained like rock, not a drop of rain—for was not the great rain-making medium slain?"[83] In Makonde, too, the leading *mhondoro* was said to "make rain, govern the harvests, avert sickness, or bring punishment." She held, as the missionary Shimmin learned, "the power of life and death, and to disobey her voice means destruction for the present and future."[84]

SOCIAL RELATIONS, ACCESS TO LAND, AND INEQUALITY

The female mediums channeling spirits with the "power of life and death," like *madzihashe,* occupied privileged positions. Most women in northeastern Zimbabwe were treated as men's subordinates.[85] This systemic subordination, the work of patriarchy, shaped control of, and access, to resources. In the 1870s and 1880s, critical resources such as land and cattle were controlled by men; males also monopolized control over society's reproductive capacity through their control over women as wives.[86] These gendered inequalities were reinforced by ideas of belonging. Upon marriage, women became outsiders in their husbands' communities because marriages were virilocal.[87] Women were not only denied control of land, they also lacked the support of kin to sustain claims to this resource. In the early colonial period, colonial officials were informed by African interlocutors that access to land depended on membership within a community—a patrilineage or the so-called tribe. This denied women rights to land because grandmothers, mothers, wives, and daughters-in-law did not belong to the lineages into which they married.

Power in the households of the nineteenth-century plateau resided firmly with the husband. This was underscored by the identification of some of each household's fields with the family patriarch. By naming these fields and the crops harvested from them *zunde rababa, chishanu chababa,* or *mushumo* after a sacred day (Chishanu) on which work of any kind was prohibited, the implication was clear: the powerful patriarch's lands were to receive the same respect as the community's ritually sanctioned day of rest.[88]

Gender and belonging were not alone in shaping differential control of land within households. As in the earlier centuries, disparities in wealth, ideas of seniority, and an emphasis on generational respect entrenched differences in landholdings and unequal power relations. Fathers, for example, maintained their power over their sons because they retained control over resources essential to the social reproduction of the household. They also presided over a host of ritual practices that helped to reinforce their power over junior men. When a married son wished to establish his own homestead, he had to inform his father, who in turn approached the chief or the chief's local representative with the request for land.[89] The household patriarch ceremonially dug the first hole before the young man could construct his new homestead, a practice known elsewhere on the Zimbabwean plateau as *kutema rupango* (to cut the first pole).[90] These practices meant that younger male members of the household required the blessing of the family patriarch to achieve a modicum of independence, just as they depended on the approval of their senior male counterparts to marry and acquire land. This strongly reinforced the authority of fathers over their sons.

Although seniority, generation, gender, and wealth entrenched disparities in power and landholding, they did not totally preclude those subordinated by these structures of power from accessing land. The ways in which the terrace builders in the Nyanga highlands exploited different environments well into the nineteenth century illuminate this point. As this complex of terraced fields, pits, and ridges was understood by Robert Soper, its leading archaeologist, terraced fields and cultivated ridges seemed to be devoted to different crops. In Soper's assessment, "outlying terraced fields were devoted to the main grain staples"; large outlying cultivation ridges were given over, in their wetter areas, to root crops.[91] Because cultivation of both ridges and terraces required heavy labor, Soper considered it unlikely that they were used simultaneously by a single community.

An alternative account sees terraced fields and ridges cultivated by people from the same community with men and women utilizing the different areas.[92] Elderly women, relaying wisdom passed from generations of mothers, aunts, and grandmothers, told me that, historically, women alone grew *tsenza* and *madhumbe*. The latter was grown on ridges in wetlands while *njera* and *tsenza* were grown on higher ground. The women who cultivated *madhumbe* were in all probability responsible for creating the ridges on which they grew this crop. This spatial distribution of fields in different microenvironments hedged against crop failure, but it also afforded women autonomous control of fields beyond those controlled by the family patriarch.

This gendered access to land had its own hierarchies, and these mirrored the orders of seniority among the women's husbands. Just as junior men required the cooperation of older men to access land, daughters-in-law accessed independent plots for the cultivation of *madhumbe* and *tsenza* through their relations with their mothers-in-law. On the eve of colonial rule, seniority differentiated power relations among women.

Generational differences underlined how land was accessed within a household or a patrilineage. Social conflicts, which often emerged from internal contradictions within African households and the fractious nature of politics, led some people to seek land beyond their patrilineages. "My great-grandfather," said a Bocha elder, Charova, "left Chief Mutema's area with his siblings to escape squabbles that rocked their father's polygynous household. They were hunters and used their hunting skills to gain acceptance among the Vajindwi, who gave them wives and pieces of land to settle near the Wengezi River." The family then moved to Bocha when the Southern Rhodesia administration conveyed their land to a white farmer.[93]

Charova's ancestors settled as strangers, using their hunting skills to gain acceptance. Other peoples forced out of the lands of their patrilineages by conflicts used maternal relations to find new land. Consider, for example, the context in which Makuvise Chigonero's family ended up living in the Chihota area in the late nineteenth century. Chigonero's parents initially gave Furamera, their *muzukuru* (nephew/sister's son), land when he left his patriclan because of conflicts over succession to the Chihota chieftainship. Furamera eventually won the support of his own people, returning to Chihota to assume the chiefship. He then reciprocated his uncles' gestures by inviting them to settle in his territory. Similarly, Rwambiwa Chari's parents moved from Goromonzi to Chihota in the late nineteenth century to live with their maternal uncles.[94]

The role of maternal relations in creating access to land was important in subverting the colonial idea that access to land depended on membership in a patrilineage or the "tribe" as conceived by colonial officials and anthropologists in the early colonial period. The patrilineage or the tribe of these men and women was a unit of agnates with descent that could be traced to a common ancestor through a patriline. Yet not everyone accessed land in this way. Even when they did, such access was not in equal measure, for it was mediated by seniority and gender. Ideas of belonging further served to include and exclude others from communities and to undermine the claims of those who were deemed to be outsiders. African male elders who stood to benefit from this framing of how land was accessed in their communities stressed it to colonial officials, who were in turn steeped in their own myths of "tribal" Africa with the hope that this would strengthen their own positions.

4 ~ Imagining Traditions, Making Authority

THE BRITISH occupation of the Zimbabwean plateau in late 1890 altered the world of the region's indigenous peoples. Willfully ignorant of the fact that the Zimbabwean plateau's societies had developed institutions to limit the power of their leaders, the colonial state, over the next several decades, sought to remake authority and patterns of landholding to meet its own interests and turn leaders into little autocrats. Together with other Europeans, including missionaries and amateur ethnographers, colonial officials infused their preconceived notions with information they gathered from local informants, mostly male chiefs and elders, to construct a narrative of Africans living in a patchwork of tribes under the authoritarian power of male chiefs. These men and women, so the discourse went, practiced communal land tenure. That is, they accessed land based on membership within a community, the "tribe," or at times the patrilineage.[1]

This chapter is about these discourses and the practices of power and landholding in the reserves of northeastern Zimbabwe from 1890 to the late 1920s. During this period the colonial state held strongly to its idealized views of African social and power relations and systems of land tenure. Although such views were intended to strengthen the authority of male chiefs and elders over women and junior men, these hopes were not always matched by developments on the ground.[2] The colonial state pursued a series of contradictory policies. Its interventions in the legal sphere, for example, could undermine chiefs, the very authorities it sought to prop up. Moreover, Africans' participation in the colonial economy led to new dynamics of accumulation, which in turn threatened senior men's control of resources, including land, and by extension their authority over junior men and women. Further, unequal access to wage labor and markets, among other factors, deepened social differentiation with concomitant effects on patterns of landholding. Thus, despite the colonial state's attempts to rely on a version of custom that strengthened the patriarchal power of chiefs and male elders, in the colonial era as in the precolonial past, power was contested and land was not accessed in equal measure. Of course, the forces underlining these contestations and inequities were not the same as those that had obtained in the precolonial period. The task in this chapter, then, is to highlight these new forces and their influence on how Africans related to one another and to the land.

COLONIAL IMAGINARIES OF AFRICAN POWER DYNAMICS, LANDHOLDING, AND THEIR LOGICS

British colonizers arrived on the Zimbabwean plateau with preconceived ideas about both the modes of power and the systems of landholding among the region's indigenous inhabitants.[3] They assumed that the chiefs of Chishona-speaking peoples fell into a hierarchy and immediately sought to "ascertain who . . . the principal chiefs in the country" near Fort Salisbury, their new seat of power, were.[4] The new colonial administrators were prepared to find a "supreme chief" but not anyone else capable of checking the powers of such leaders. But as discussed in chapter 3, many chiefs waited to consult their *mhondoro* before making important decisions.

The fate of the *mhondoro* in the formal politics of authority over land soon became tied to African resistance to colonial rule. In the aftermath of the 1896–97 Chimurenga uprisings, the colonial state accused *mhondoro* and other religious leaders of inciting Africans to rise against company rule.[5] It branded them as dangerous to the peace of the colony, placing under surveillance those that it had not executed or incarcerated for leading the rebellions.[6]

European officials' attitudes toward African religious leaders in these early years of colonial rule stood in sharp contrast to how they related to chiefs. To be sure, the British South Africa Company (BSAC) regime killed or imprisoned those chiefs whom it viewed as instigators of the Chimurenga risings of 1896–97.[7] It replaced such leaders with pliant individuals. Thereafter, the state viewed chiefs and headmen as the sole and "customary" authorities whose powers it ought to, at a minimum, uphold. Often, it sought to prop up their powers.

Studies in the history of customary law have increased our understanding of how the colonial state and its African interlocutors created this regime of authoritarian "tribal" chiefs. Anxious to avoid social disruption, these studies show, colonial governments codified "customary" law, strengthening, in the process, the authority of African chiefs by centralizing, in these leaders' hands, power that had formerly been diffused.[8] Chiefs, for example, began to preside over family matters that previously lay within the domain of patri- and matrilineages.[9] The assumption of judicial power by chiefs was especially important in fortifying their authority. "This compulsory expectation that chiefs and headmen attend courts and take part in the delivery of judgments," commented Martin Chanock, "altered their role across much of central Africa. The judicial processes provided an important avenue for those who were seeking political authority, little enough of which was available to Africans under British rule."[10] Mahmood Mamdani concurred. "Without Native Courts that enabled Native Administrations to turn their writ into law," he said, "the Native Authority would have been emasculated as an active agent."[11] The centralization of power was assumed to have been completed when the colonial state assigned African access to land to the customary sphere dominated by chiefs.[12]

The colonial state and its interlocutors believed that, in this customary sphere, land tenure was "communal." That is, access to land depended not on individual initiative or rights but on membership within a corporate community, its imagined "tribe."[13] "Land," elaborated one administration official in 1903, "is held under the tribal system & is as a rule divided under sub-chiefs who are sons of the ruling house. . . . The sites of the gardens are shown to his people by the headman of the kraal. After picking the sites for his own and his immediate relations' gardens the headman allows the remainder of his people to pick their lands in succession according to their status in the kraal."[14] In this system, those who occupied the lowest rung of the social ladder would almost inevitably occupy the marginal lands left unclaimed by the members of the ruling families. Moreover, while heads of households could pick fields for their families, nobody owned land, not even the chief, who was sometimes called the owner of the land (*muridzi wenyika*).[15] "The chief himself, while in practice is recognised as the landlord," wrote Charles Bullock, a Native Department official with significant anthropological interests, "was believed to be the earthly vicar only of the real owner."[16]

The claim that African land tenure was "communal" was tied to similar imaginations of the African family. As colonial ethnographers (mis) understood African societies in the early twentieth century, "a system of control based exclusively on kinship was antecedent to the tribal system and . . . the latter—in those instances which are no longer kinship units—were patterned on the former."[17] In this system, so the argument went, individuals did not matter much in the African family, just as they could not own land. Even "the minor [nuclear] family [was] found to have only an insignificant place in the arrangements for carrying out the conscious and the unconscious purposes of tribal life. The individual's and the minor family's identities," W. H. Stead elaborated, "are considerably eclipsed by the identity of the extended family and, within the extended family, the sib, i.e., the agnatic group within which relationship is traceable reasonably close stands out distinctly from the rest." The sib, Stead explained,

> is the stressed unit in tribal life. Its members have common descent, reciprocal duties and behaviour patterns, obligations to support and protect each other, and a strong sense of solidarity binds them together. An injury or insult to one is an injury or insult to all. They are a single entity who share rights or privileges and have joint responsibility to other similar entities in the body politic. Property is owned by the sib and held in trust by its senior member.[18]

Bullock, a contemporary of Stead's, added that "the *paterfamilias* is the representative of the family, but he is also the link between his predecessor and his successor. He is *of* the group, not a separate individual with individual rights of property, etc. He cannot then alienate the control of the *familia*, with all the rights and duties involved. He is the representative and custodian for his lifetime only."[19] The father of the family, then, served the same function that the chief, said to be the earthly vicar of the land, did at the level of the "tribe." And the clan, consisting of members of the same patrilineage (constructed through patrilineal descent), constituted the community.[20] One's position within the patrilineage constituted the clan hierarchy or what the administrative official described as one's "status within the kraal."[21] The status was granted according to ideas of patrilineal descent, seniority, and gender.[22] "As a general rule," noted W. S. Bazely at the time, "the eldest son of the deceased inherits his father's bow, and with it his name, his wives, his property and the guardianship of the younger children."[23]

The idea that the patrilineal community took precedence over individual rights and interests, and that land was communally owned, gained traction because, from early in the colonial period, it served a variety of interests. In the colonial context of Southern Rhodesia, officials favored the language of communal land tenure and the privileging of the community over the individual because they thought that it strengthened the powers of chiefs and elders. These were the people that the colonial administration used in its scheme of rural rule.[24] Members of the Morris Carter Land Commission (1925) captured this sentiment. Claiming rather disingenuously that "the people generally know no other form of tenure," the commissioners told the colonial administrators who had appointed them that "many of the chiefs are obviously afraid of losing their already diminishing influence and power if individual natives of their tribes are given the opportunity of, and encouraged in, acquiring land of their own."[25] They recommended that the state should retain the system of "communal" land tenure in the reserves.[26] Colonial officials and their acolytes insisted on the idea that African land tenure was communal for a second, equally sinister, motive. Members of the 1925 Carter Commission used this argument to justify racial segregation in land allocation.[27]

Meanwhile, African elders emphasized the communal nature of African landholding to underscore the inalienability of the resource and to critique the avariciousness of a colonial state that dispossessed whole communities and assigned that land to a single settler. Moreover, when elders claimed that access to land depended on membership within a patrilineage, they articulated their own idealized vision of how kinship relations ought to structure access to land and how the system accorded them authority over junior men and women of their households.

Interestingly, as many young men left their rural homes to look for jobs in the emerging mines, settler farms, and towns, they also invoked the idea of communal land tenure hoping to retain claims to land in their communities even when they were away. This was not peculiar to labor migrants from early colonial Zimbabwe. Young labor migrants from the northern regions of Nyasaland weaved a similar narrative of authority and landholding because they felt that, in their absence, chiefs would protect their local interests in land and cattle. Chiefs would also enforce controls over the young migrant men's women and children while they were away, earning money in Southern Rhodesia and South Africa.[28] Labor migration, then, was a common experience that made youths in south-central Africa support ideas rooted in custom to safeguard their interests. The position of Southern Rhodesia's Africans was worsened by land shortages created by racialized colonial land alienation.

LAW, PRACTICE, AND THE POLITICS OF AUTHORITY

There is no doubt that some male chiefs and elders used the narrative of society power and landholding that they, together with early colonial officials, propagated to strengthen their own power. But this did not mean that they succeeded in holding absolute power. Changes brought in by colonial rule opened gray areas where authority could be contested. The colonial state's interventions in the legal arena through the 1898 Order-in-Council, in particular, withdrew judicial power from chiefs. "Strictly speaking," explained Clarkson Henry Tredgold, the colony's attorney general, in 1904, "native chiefs have no more right to try cases than any ordinary individual."[29] What muddied waters in the exercise of chiefly power was that this legal position did not, in practice, prevent chiefs from adjudicating cases brought to them by their subjects. Attorney General Tredgold recognized this, insisting that "should however any two natives take their case to be tried by the chief and consent to its being done, the Chief acts as an arbiter."[30]

Limits to chiefly power were further reinforced by the redefinition of offenses against chiefs as offenses against the state or criminal offenses.[31] These included witchcraft accusations and murder.[32] Similarly, native commissioners rescinded fines—called *maropa* (from *ropa* [blood])—imposed by chiefs for cases of murder committed by their subjects. These interventions shook the material as well as the ideological bases of chiefly claims to power and to a landed domain. The chiefs' prerogatives to try murder and witchcraft accusation cases enabled them to accumulate wealth that was crucial in retaining patrons. However, the material side of the fines was not what mattered most, because new and older sources of revenue, including the monthly allowance that chiefs received from the colonial state, compensated for the loss of *maropa*. Instead, it was the loss of the symbolic power embedded in these practices that signaled the erosion of chiefly power. Chiefs retained *maropa* arguing that they used it to perform rituals meant to cool the land that the accused "heated" by spilling blood in their territory. Chiefs monopolized the authority to "cool" the land because they claimed its "ownership." "Cooling" the land also gave chiefs legitimacy over their competitors.[33] This legitimacy is what the colonial state denied these leaders when it banned practices meant to "cool the land."

The colonial archive records several interventions of this nature. In 1904, the Manyika chief Chakanyuka Chiobvu Mutasa fined one Kachete four cattle, forty-two goats, and £3 for the death of one Nyamatore. The native commissioner for the district of Inyanga overturned this fine because the colonial state no longer recognized the practice.[34] In that same year, the native commissioner for Inyanga reported that Chikomba, another chief from the same district, had seized a woman and handed her over to Chief Mutasa, the area's paramount chief, as payment of *maropa*. The native commissioner told him that the custom was no longer recognized by the government.[35] Years later, in 1917, the superintendent of natives at Umtali accused Chief Makoni of failing "to report a case of homicide in his district although he was informed of the fact by the head of the kraal at which it occurred." Chief Makoni, the native commissioner charged, "had fined the Kraal and taken cattle as 'maropa' in settlement of the act." Worse, he had also appointed and installed a headman under Chipunza's people without informing the native commissioner or receiving the consent of the administrator.[36] The superintendent of natives ordered the chief to return the cattle he took as *maropa*. Chief Makoni protested that he was acting as his fathers had done, but this did not prevent the colonial state from punishing him by slashing his subsidy.[37]

The way colonial rule reshaped the politics of land and authority in rural northeastern Zimbabwe did not merely involve intervening in the ritual and political struggles for power among Africans. The state itself became entangled in these conflicts by dictating where and how Africans should live and farm. Until wartime shortages encouraged industrialization in the 1940s and necessitated the permanent accommodation of African labor in the urban areas, the colonial state envisioned the colony's African population as migrant laborers whose home was in the reserves.[38] The reserves also served another function. They were meant to divide Africans into governable ethnic minorities, each residing within neatly bounded territorial localities.[39] This policy of ethnic spatial fixing—to borrow a phrase from Donald S. Moore—allowed the colonial state to rule through local chiefs and to divert grievances toward these now bureaucratized leaders.[40] But ethnic spatial fixing had unintended consequences. Instead of creating native reserves exclusively occupied by particular "tribes," the colonial state produced rural areas in which communities belonging to more than one chieftainship occupied each reserve. This raised problems for the smooth exercise of power by chiefs and colonial administrators. The native commissioner for the district of Inyanga found himself with "one of the most difficult districts to manage," noted the superintendent of natives for Umtali in 1908. He added, "Umtassa, the paramount chief, lives in Umtali District and this fact has more or less thrown him out of touch with his sub-chiefs, each of whom is now more or less independent. Instead of having only one or two chiefs to deal with Mr. Moodie has about seventeen."[41] Thus, argued Superintendent of Natives Thomas B. Hulley, Chief Mutasa was slowly losing authority over his former territories and the subchiefs who presided over them. At the same time, the native commissioner found himself with more chiefs to deal with, expanding his administrative burdens. The superintendent of natives lost the irony that the colonial state had manufactured the positions of paramount chiefs that chiefs like Mutasa, Makoni, and many others had come to occupy. The same colonial state had also manufactured "tribes" where none had previously existed, creating the problems of governance that it was encountering.

Chiefs' authority also increasingly came under threat from the influence of new religious practices, particularly Christianity. Christian institutions, especially the mission station, offered an exit route to those subjects who sought to challenge the power of chiefs and African male elders. The Catholic mission center at Triashill, for example, accommodated women who ran away from their homes seeking refuge from their husbands and fathers. When the husbands came for them, they refused to go.[42] "On one occasion," reminisced a priest at the center, "the husband brought the paramount chief to collect the girl and when she refused the P. Chief grabbed her, but she evaded him and ran away. The chief went lumbering after her but could not catch her and the school children burst out laughing to see him trying to catch her and after that there was no more trouble in that way."[43]

This increasing loss of control over female subjects was not lost on chiefs. In 1925, Chief Chiobvu Mutasa complained that emerging mining centers, native commissioners, and missionaries were a tripod of evil that undermined their efforts to control women from their communities. "Our wives," he moaned, "leave us and go to Penhalonga. All the advice of the Native Commissioner is to get divorce. Our wives go to Missions. We are prevented from taking them."[44] This loss of control over women's sexuality had wider significance. "Because female fertility was also associated with the fecundity of the land," Elizabeth Schmidt informs us, "control over this vital resource also determined whether a people would eat or starve."[45]

African Christians' opposition to African religious practices also undermined the epistemological basis of chiefly claims to land. These claims rested on chiefs' ability to ensure the fertility of the land. Yet some who converted to Christianity refused to participate in these rituals.[46] The Christians claimed that they ensured the fertility of the land through prayer and fasting. Chiefs, who understood the implications of these claims for their power, excluded Christians from rituals meant to ensure the fertility of the land.[47] Some of the chiefs petitioned the colonial state to ban some of the activities of the Christian converts in their areas. In 1918, Chief Muradzikwa and six of his headmen complained that "the situation caused by the revival movement of the American [Methodist] Episcopal Church among his people has become unbearable . . . young people run to the mountain crying out 'that they have the Spirit of God in them.' They yell out their past offences in a sort of confession of sins. Immorality is rife among both old and young. There will be starvation as the preparing of lands is in a neglected state."[48] The language of morality masked elders' anxieties about the progressive loss of control over their young men and women and the threat that the African converts to Christianity posed to their claims to power over land. The chief complained that "the native in charge of the station at Shetora has been going about among the kraals and in some parts has broken pots and upset beer."[49] Interestingly, pots and beer, among others, were the things that chiefs and elders used to supplicate the ancestors to ensure the fertility of the land, and it was likely for this reason that the chief expressed fears about starvation.

ADMINISTRATIVE INTERVENTION, INTRA-AFRICAN CONFLICTS, AND CHALLENGES TO CHIEFS' POWERS

Besides undermining the ideologies and practices that had previously legitimated chiefly power, the colonial state complicated chiefs' standing and authority in other ways. One of those ways was the colonial state's tendency to appoint chiefs based on their potential as administrative officers and not their legitimacy as heirs to the throne. Such interventions occasionally led those who felt that the chief lacked legitimacy to defy his authority or even seek his elimination. In 1901, supporters of the late chief Chingaira Makoni, executed by the BSAC during the 1896–97 uprisings, raided his successor, Ndafunya Makoni, seeking to kill him—or so colonial officials believed.[50] These men, the acting native commissioner reported, "have always been very bitter against the present chief as they consider that he is not the lawful Paramount and helped the white men to kill the old chief."[51]

There were other cases of opposition to chiefs appointed by the colonial state. In 1913, colonial officials identified a man named Revesai as "a continual thorn in the side of the present [Chief] Umtassa." "He," reported the native commissioner for Umtali District, "was one of the Manyika tribe who refused to 'wombera' the present Umtassa but deliberately acknowledged Shiobvu as Chief in defiance of the Government and of native law of succession to the chieftainship of this district."[52] *Kuwombera*, or *kuvuchira*, literally meant the ceremonial clapping of hands either in exchanges of pleasantries or in recognition of differential power relations between two individuals. In the politics of chiefly authority, this took a particular salience. "At his installation," anthropologist Jon F. Holleman noted, "a new chief receives gifts of tribute and recognition (*civuciro*) [sp. *chivuchiro*, from *kuvuchira*] from his ward-heads, village headmen, and important members of his family under his control, and even neighbouring chieftains who wish to avoid the impression of being hostile to him will send gifts in kind or money."[53] Holleman explained that "these gifts, which vary from a half crown to a head of cattle, have a dual purpose of being expressions of rejoicing (*kupemberera*) and of recognition of his political superiority (*Kuvuchira*) by his subjects. In the latter sense they are in practice obligatory, as failure to give them immediately raises the presumption of insubordination."[54] Holleman made this observation after conducting ethnographic fieldwork in Uhera, not far from Manyika. What the Hera called *kuvuchira*, the Manyika called *kuwombera*. When Revesai refused to "*wombera*" the incumbent Chief Mutasa in 1913, he openly showed his insubordination to the chief.

Elsewhere, Africans refused to recognize the authority of the local chief because their legitimate chief resided in a neighboring reserve or even another colony.[55] When the Anglo-Portuguese boundary was settled in 1892, about one thousand Wavumba who occupied the highlands southeast of the present city of Mutare fell into British territory. The rest, including the chief, Chirara, found themselves in Portuguese East Africa. The native commissioner for Umtali soon found it "difficult to work them through Zimunyu whom they have never recognized as chief."[56]

COLONIAL IMAGINARIES, AFRICAN SOCIAL PROCESSES, AND ACCESS TO RESOURCES

As with the imagined power of "customary" leaders, the language of African access to land developed by colonial officials and their informants in the early years of British rule captured the ideal more than the lived experiences of many Africans. Emphasizing membership in patrilineages as the basis of landholding among Africans, this discourse constructed an African who was essentially a cultural and not a socioeconomic being. It maintained that an African could only access land based on his or her belonging within the cultural sphere of the patrilineage and the "tribe." But Africans were social and economic beings, and their decisions about where to live and farm were influenced as much by ideas of belonging as by their own social relations, by the imperatives of survival in a colonial economy, and by state interventions in their lives. Significantly, access to resources and markets (and lack thereof) influenced the social geography of landholding among northeastern Zimbabwe's indigenous peoples. They contributed to social differentiation and inequality, deepening disparities in landholding not only between white settlers and Africans but also among Africans.

To be sure, many Africans in northeastern Zimbabwe, as elsewhere on the Zimbabwean plateau, deployed kinship to access land. But agnatic kin or even men were not always the main actors in important social processes such as the distribution of a deceased patriarch's estate, including, in Bullock's phrase, a right to tenure.[57] "It is quite in accordance with Manyika custom for a dying man to make arrangements for the care of his infant children and property," a colonial official noted in the early 1920s. "He calls his sons-in-law (actual and prospective), his sisters and the elders. He may declare that he is unwilling to allow his nearest male relative or even any of the males in his clan to be guardian and he may then hand over the care of his wives, his children and his property to a son-in-law or his sister or to one of the elders or to one of his friends," the official elaborated.[58] This flexibility to choose somebody other than the lineage's surviving eldest male was meant to accommodate instances in which family feuds made it impossible for somebody to entrust the lives of his children to members of his patrilineage.

Such flexibility sat uncomfortably with the normative claim that patrilineal inheritance reinforced the patriarchal power of male elders. As the same official learned, among the Manyika, "the heir . . . [was] actually nominated by his *Samukadzi,* (eldest sister or nearest female relative of the same clan and generation). . . . She," he wrote, "pours beer dregs (*masese*) on the ancestral bow and hands it to him. The heir is not allowed to refuse to *adiate* (accept the inheritance)."[59] It did not occur to this official, and many others thereafter, that such a practice granted the *samukadzi,* a woman, wide discretionary powers to nominate somebody else of her choice rather than the most senior son of the deceased patriarch.

Within the colonial context of Southern Rhodesia, these practices were especially crucial. As settler land alienation reduced the amount of land available for Africans, younger generations increasingly depended on plots passed down from grandfathers and fathers. Land was thus added to the list of property that had to be shared among the children of the deceased household patriarch. And its distribution could depend on the choices made by the *samukadzi.* Moreover, the idea that male seniority guaranteed privileged access to land inherited from a deceased patriarchy failed to realize that, ideally, by the time of the father's death, it was the youngest son who would have remained at the family homestead, inheriting both its dwellings and the fields.[60]

More importantly, here, as in other parts of Africa, "both kinship and territorial relations constitute[d] semantic resources which [we]re put to rhetorical use" by different individuals in their struggles for land and authority rather than firm and unchanging structures.[61] Precisely because kinship served as part of a broader ideology of claiming land, it did not always guarantee access to the resource. In many ways, the reality of social conflict—and, in the case of women, marriage—saw many individuals leaving their kin groups to live with non-kin. In these cases, individuals understood the importance of forming new networks of kinship. For some men, the key to the forging of these new relations of kinship was marriage.[62] This allowed families and communities to accept and settle outsiders who became their sons-in-law. However, as studies in the histories of women and gender show, for the most part, this practice created opportunities for men more than women. Among the Shona, upon marriage women moved to live with the families of their husbands, where they could face discrimination and exclusion as outsiders.[63]

SOCIOECONOMIC CHANGE, AGRICULTURAL INNOVATION, AND LANDED INEQUALITIES

Ultimately, social processes such as the distribution of a man's estate combined with other forces to shape patterns of access to resources including productive agricultural land. African participation in the colonial economy was one such force; in the early days of colonial rule and even later, this was quite uneven. From the onset of colonial rule, some enterprising and fortuitously located Shona men and women began to experiment with new crops to exploit the market opportunities created by the emergence of colonial urban and mining centers. Their success drew occasional praise from the otherwise prejudiced colonial officials. "I have in various reports from Lomagundi and Melsetter mentioned that in my opinion the Mashona works his lands better than any other native tribe I know," Thomas B. Hulley, the native commissioner for the district of Umtali, wrote in 1897.[64] "And the willingness they show to learn anything about agriculture, they will plant anything they think they can get a sale for," Hulley continued.[65] In fact, Africans in Umtali District were "eager to get any seed of any grain or vegetable which would find ready sale with the Europeans." They were particularly interested in "potatoes, cabbage, cauliflower, onions, cucumbers, beans etc growing for which the native had no previous knowledge."[66]

However, it was mostly those Africans located near markets or those who had access to means of transport who were able to turn to enterprises like those that impressed Native Commissioner Hulley. In this respect, the experiences of Africans located in the districts of Goromonzi, Marandellas, Makoni, and parts of Umtali generally differed from those who resided in Inyanga and the outlying areas of Umtali District. In 1921, for example, the African inhabitants of Goromonzi District "harvested excellent crops . . . and disposed of approximately thirteen thousand bags of grain to traders and others."[67] In that same year, Inyanga District's African farmers reportedly sold about five hundred bags of grain to Europeans.[68]

Several factors account for these differences. Goromonzi and parts of Marandellas were close to Salisbury and were combed by European traders who purchased grain for sale in the colony's capital.[69] Mining centers such as Arcturus provided further markets to Goromonzi farmers. Similarly, the Chiduku Reserve in Makoni District was located near the railway line that connected Salisbury with the border city of Umtali and, ultimately, Beira on the Indian Ocean coast.[70] In contrast, in Inyanga District, crops were mostly grown for home consumption, "the trading done being small owing to the distance from any market."[71] Apart from the emerging administrative center of Inyanga, there was no other center of a sizable population in the district. The nearest mining community at Penhalonga was almost a hundred kilometers from Inyanga's center. Umtali was even farther away. The lack of local markets was compounded by the unforgiving rugged topography of the eastern highlands, which made it difficult to establish transport networks necessary for the transportation of bulk grains. "The natives possess no vehicles of any sort," noted the native commissioner for the district of Inyanga in 1913. He added that "the nature of the country is all against that."[72]

While those Africans in Inyanga faced serious challenges in trying to reach the market, the difficulties of negotiating the mountainous terrain in the eastern highlands were felt even by those who were in the Umtali District. But there, the proximity to a market center stimulated innovation. To take advantage of the emerging market in Umtali, the more enterprising farmers turned to other crops that seemed more profitable. By 1921, those Africans farther afield from the town of Umtali had discovered that, under the existing conditions, growing potatoes for market paid better than mealies (maize) and finger millet, with the result that, for the market, these farmers cultivated these tubers more extensively than formerly.[73] Those fortunately living within the vicinity of the town and at Old Umtali had by that time captured "a fair amount of the green grocery trade." The vegetables they produced took "a lot of beating for variety, size, and quality."[74]

Combined with "pockets of precolonial accumulation which had survived the violence of the 1890s, the productive investment of wage labour" in agriculture as well as innovations with cropping techniques and access to markets deepened social differentiation among Africans.[75] A new class consisting of "cultivators covering the spectrum of independent household producers stretching from middle peasants whose family labour and land sufficed to reproduce themselves through to rich peasants on the brink of transforming themselves into capitalist producers" had emerged by the 1920s.[76] "Although occasionally indistinguishable from their poorer neighbours in terms of standards of consumption," Ian Phimister points out, these rich farmers "increasingly came to occupy a quite different place in the social relations of production." They normally possessed "large or above-average size herds of cattle and fields, monopolized communal grazing and at certain times of the year . . . employed labourers to till their fields and harvest their crops."[77]

This new group of farmers further invested in agricultural implements, especially plows, allowing it to expand production and open more lands for cultivation than its poorer counterparts. Table 4.1 gives us a sense of the distribution of the plow in five districts in colonial northeastern Zimbabwe between 1909 and 1922. Clearly, during this period, the ratio of plows to the population of each district suggests that those who owned the implements constituted a very small minority. Even in places such as Marandellas, which saw a significant rise in the number of plows from 1916 onward, the ratio of the tool to the district's population in that year was still one plow per thirty-six people. Going by the formula used by native commissioners to calculate the number of people in their districts, for every household that had a plow, nine did not have one.[78] The gap was even wider in Inyanga, where there were, reportedly, only nine plows in 1916 among the 18,572 residents of the district.[79]

TABLE 4.1. PLOWS OWNED BY AFRICANS AND ESTIMATED POPULATION OF AFRICANS IN GOROMONZI, MARANDELLAS, MAKONI, UMTALI, AND INYANGA DISTRICTS, 1909–1922

Year	Goromonzi		Marandellas		Makoni		Umtali		Inyanga	
	Plows	Population	Plows	Population	Plows	Population	Plows	Population	Plows	Population
1909	0	15,880	0	15,341	1	20,463	1	no data	0	17,000
1910	2	16,533	0	18,084	2-3	20,704	2	25,000	0	17,700
1911	4	17,470	1	18,084	X	20,704	3	18,450	X	17,800
1912	5	17,933	1	18,762	X	20,704	3	19,100	0	17,800
1913	12	18,928	4	19,301	5	22,011	8	20,050	1	17,000
1914	13	19,915	18	19,848	5	22,239	X	22,256	1	17,000
1915	X	no data	26	20,440	X	22,550	X	no data	X	18,388
1916	34	21,962	104	21,894	30	23,328	X	23,759	9	18,572
1917	41	22,298	280	22,144	X	24,024	X	23,970	9	16,674
1918	43	22,409	380	23,015	X	24,770	X	23,390	X	17,539
1919	52	22,192	440	24,450	X	26,270	X	23,387	X	22,463
1920	57	22,649	600	26,228	X	27,870	75	23,765	X	22,984
1921	63	24,999	X	27,258	X	28,392	X	24,153	X	24,081
1922	71	19,740	X	27,364	X	28,392	X	24,759	X	23,548

Source: Constructed from the figures provided in native commissioners' annual reports for each of the five districts from 1909 to 1922.

Note: An *X* in place of a number for plows indicates that the officials did not state figures but used comments such as "no noticeable improvement," "has not extended beyond five kraals," or simply "increasing."

The slow uptake of the plow reflected its cost. In Goromonzi, the district closest to the colonial capital of Salisbury, the supply of plows was "very irregular and the prices . . . high" as late as 1919.[80] In nearby Marandellas District, the demand for plows that year was greater than during the previous year. This was largely on account of the excellent harvest reaped in the 1918–1919 agricultural season and "the fact that large quantities of grain were sold by the natives at remunerative prices"; yet many Africans in Marandellas "were prevented from buying ploughs on account of the greatly increased cost."[81] Worse still, owing to the exorbitant prices charged by merchants, worn-out plows were not being replaced.[82] The cost of the plow and the investment in repairs and in draft-animal power (cattle and donkeys) meant that not everybody adopted the implement, at least in the early twentieth century. Early plow owners were relatively wealthy individuals. Among the four people who owned farming implements in Marandellas District in 1913 was a chief who, in addition to plows and harrows, owned a scotch cart. The other owners of implements were traders.[83] Apart from expanding production, plow owners accumulated additional profits by hiring out the implement, for a fee, to those who were without it.[84] Thus, plow ownership simultaneously depended on possession of wealth and deepened social differentiation.

Further, use of the plow affected the social geography of African land use and landholding. Africans who adopted the implement expanded the acreage that they put under cultivation.[85] They also opened lands in previously ignored environments. Most farmers on the central watershed located their fields in wooded areas and on hillsides because they believed that where trees did not grow, crops would not do well.[86] However, they did not stump the wooded lots on which they cultivated their crops, because they used the hoe. Instead, they just chopped the tree branches. Land cleared in this way could not be easily plowed because the stumps obstructed the oxen and the plow itself constantly got stuck on roots. The plow induced African farmers to make use of open lands that required less clearing and stumping. "The old fallacy of theirs [the Mashona] that where trees will not grow crops will not thrive," the native commissioner for Goromonzi District noted, with some measure of condescension, in 1913, "is dying out, and there are a few cases of lands being made in the open country."[87] By 1917, forty-one plow owners were "taking to the open land and vleis for cultivation purposes and [were] not dependent on thickly wooded parts for their lands as in former times."[88]

Precisely because very few households could afford to invest in the plow and livestock, it was those better-resourced farmers who were able to expand their landholdings by opening fields in a variety of microenvironments. As of 1914, most Africans in Goromonzi District cultivated wooded parts of the reserve; the thirteen plow owners who were "working open lands" were the exceptions, although they also retained their fields on the wooded lots while they were expanding into the open lands.[89] Once these claims were made, they became permanent. The initial act of clearing and cultivating the land formed the basis of one's claim to the land. Many of those who had used the plow to open new lands could afford to let them lie fallow and still invoke the concept of *gura* (fallow land) to claim lands they formerly cultivated but had abandoned.

The adoption of new agricultural implements had other consequences. It created opportunities for cooperation both inside and outside kinship groups. Plow owners strengthened relationships with their neighbors by plowing for them. Expansion in areas under cultivation increased demand for labor for weeding and harvesting, much of which was mobilized through beer parties (*humwe/hoka/nhimbe*). Such gatherings offered the hosts opportunities to flaunt their wealth and gain a good reputation that would help mobilize huge gatherings in subsequent seasons.

Cooperation extended to the transportation of crops to the market. One elder, David Kamusoko, explained how this worked: "Say at one area they may have two scotch carts, so they would make a contract, where they put their sacks in the cart and they each produced cattle to be spanned so that they could pull the cart."[90] Exclusions were common. Another elder, Makutu Taonezvi, pointed out that the organization of transport to carry grain to the market involved *chizivano* (nepotism), adding that scotch cart owners would charge high or low amounts depending on their relationship to the person seeking their services.[91]

The expansion of new implements together with African participation in the migrant labor economy affected gendered relations of production. At the time that the native commissioner for Makoni reported the arrival of the first plow in his district in 1909, he also claimed that "many native women are becoming averse to heavy work in the lands," adding, with some optimism, that "this will become an important factor in inducing the men to follow European methods of cultivation."[92] The assertion that women were opposing heavy labor was rooted in a stereotype and was clearly an exaggeration. The point, though, was that some women in the rural areas appreciated the value of farming implements and believed that the adoption of these tools lessened their workload.

This recognition of the labor-saving capacity of the plow by Vashona women eluded subsequent discussions of the impact of agricultural mechanization on household labor. These discussions emphasized the increasing burden that befell women. This stemmed from the fact that Africans adopted the plow, expanding the areas under cultivation and, therefore, requiring more hands and time in planting, hoeing, harvesting, and threshing crops at precisely the time that many men were drawn into the colonial migrant labor market.[93] This observation is in many ways apt, but it also ignores the importance of off-farm income in the social dynamics of agricultural production. From the early days of African participation in the migrant labor economies, those with access to off-farm income began to hire labor. "The natives of this district employ quite a number of natives from other Districts (principally Mrewa and Mtoko) during the ploughing season, the usual wage being 10/- [shillings] per [month]," reported Goromonzi District's native commissioner in 1909.[94] In that same year, his counterpart in Makoni noted that "some of the Native Messengers who are constantly employed do employ other natives on a monthly wage to do their cultivation."[95] In interviews, elderly women emphasized this point by coding it in the moral language of real "husbandhood." A "real man," one elderly woman told me, would remember to send money so that his wife could mobilize labor for the cultivation of the fields; he would remember to send money to his wife so that she would pay the tax for the household's livestock and land.[96] Those who did this expanded both their fields and their yields. They also bequeathed to future generations larger pieces of land than was the case with their counterparts who did not have resources.

By the time society expected "real" husbands working in cities and mines to send money to their wives to pay workers tilling land and herding livestock in the reserves, colonial rule had shaken Africans' lives as they had lived them before. It had, among other things, intensified competition among chiefs, African male elders, and other power players. Together with the emerging urban and mining centers, new institutions such as mission stations created potential exit routes for those seeking to escape the authority of their male elders.[97] At the same time, the new colonial economy ushered in additional forms of accumulation, heightening social differentiation. Wages earned from migrant labor, for example, gave young men opportunities to subvert the power previously held by elders. This power stemmed from elders' monopolies over resources that were crucial in social processes such as marriage and the development of new households. Aware of the potential for generational conflict and the undermining of the authority of African chiefs and male elders, colonial officials, amateur ethnographers, and the Africans who served as their informants constructed versions of custom that sought to strengthen the so-called customary leaders—a hierarchy of chiefs and headmen—and the male heads of households. Yet by the 1920s, colonial officials were conceding that chiefs were not as powerful as they imagined them to be or, at a minimum, were losing their grip over their subjects.

5 ~ Changes in the Law

UNTIL THE end of the second decade of the twentieth century, native commissioners frequently reported that chiefs were doing their jobs satisfactorily. But beginning in 1919, their assessments of chiefs took a remarkably different tone. "Nothing to report except the unanimous conclusion of all Native Commissioners that the power of the native chiefs is fast disappearing," wrote the superintendent of natives for the Umtali Circuit that year.[1] Thereafter, such comments marked most annual appraisals of chiefs by native commissioners.[2] The negative assessments of chiefs' powers were accompanied by similarly disparaging remarks about African agricultural practices. "With the exception of only a few cases, the natives have not made any attempt to improve the productive power of the soil," the native commissioner for the district of Salisbury wrote in his 1920 annual report.[3] "The younger generation of men from the reserves who go and work for European farmers," another Native Department official noted, "no doubt retain in their minds a recollection of the methods of their employers, but on return to the reserves, quickly revert to the methods of their fathers."[4] A third official stressed that they regularly impressed upon the Africans the benefits of manuring their lands, "but the majority appear [*sic*] to be quite satisfied with simply scratching the surface, sowing the seed, and trusting to luck."[5]

In the ensuing years, the colonial state sought to change African agricultural practices and reinforce the power of chiefs, headmen, and kraalheads with the twin objectives of limiting Africans to the small reserves without expanding these areas and using "customary authorities" in tax collection.[6] This chapter investigates the implications of these policy interventions on the social relations of land and power among Africans in northeastern Zimbabwe until the 1960s. As in the previous three decades, the outcomes of colonial policies remained contradictory. Attempts to shore up the power of customary authorities through two legislative interventions, the Native Affairs Act (1927) and the Native Law and Courts Act (1937), were, for example, contradicted by the subsequent policies of native development, which in principle left land matters in the hands of a technical bureaucracy. And until the passage of the latter law, the colonial state did not recognize chiefs' legal powers, undermining a source of authority that strengthened the power of "customary" authorities elsewhere in colonial Africa.[7] At the same time, colonial agrarian interventions entrenched gendered and generational disparities in land allocation. Yet the participation of young men in the colonial economy undermined the powers of male elders.

THE RETURN OF CHIEFS' POWERS?

Having convinced themselves that chiefs and headmen were slowly losing power over their subjects, officials in the Department of Native Affairs sought ways of averting this. The move was self-serving. Increasingly deskbound, native commissioners hoped to strengthen "customary" authorities to help in "extracting tax and labour, duties that [the commissioners] could no longer undertake in person."[8] Their starting point was a search for the source of the perceived weakening in the power of chiefs. They found this in new institutions such as schools and mission stations. "Teachers and pupils," wrote one native commissioner, "consider that once a school is established, they are independent and do not come under the control of headmen and chiefs. . . . This has also been the case with several heads of kraals who consented to schools as a direct defiance of their headmen. This attitude of the young generation often leads to implications between them and the older people who are ignored."[9]

To address this issue, colonial authorities argued that, in the reserves, the rising African elites of teachers and agricultural demonstrators should be placed under the authority of chiefs.[10] Native commissioners also called for the formal recognition of the hierarchy of "customary" authorities and of chiefs' judicial powers over civil cases pitting Africans against one another.[11] Such lobbying led to the passage of the Native Affairs Act in 1927. This law codified the hierarchy of native authority—consisting of kraalheads, headmen, and chiefs under the supervision of native commissioners—giving it a stamp of authority and legal recognition.

But the powers that the Native Affairs Act conferred to Southern Rhodesia's Africans were quite limited. "Native chiefs," explained Chief Native Commissioner H. M. G. Jackson in 1930, "have no jurisdiction conferred on them by the Native Affairs Act or any other law to try civil and criminal offences. The growing trend of opinion toward what is called indirect rule cannot be acted upon by us in anticipation of its possible adoption in this colony. No Native Chief must be allowed to assume judicial power unless and until the law gives and regulate such power."[12] Moreover, the Native Affairs Act (1926) strengthened the power of native commissioners more than those of African chiefs.[13] "Now the natives regard the Native Commissioner as the ipso facto Paramount Chief of the district," argued Fritz W. T. Posselt, Marandellas's native commissioner, in 1930.[14]

Besides the recognition by Africans, native commissioners themselves simply grabbed chiefly powers to adjudicate cases that historically legitimated chiefs' claims to the land. These included cases of *makunakuna* (incest), which lay outside the tentacles of criminal law but breached the morality of kinship (*ukama*) that Africans believed hindered the fertility of the land.[15] "Whenever a case was reported to me," Posselt confessed in 1930, "I have had the elders and Headmen present and inquired whether in fact the incest according to Native Law had been committed. The facts having been ascertained, penalties of from two or more head of cattle have been inflicted." Posselt gave a portion of the penalties imposed on the culprits to "the sectional Headman or to the Chief." He then ordered the remaining cattle to be killed on ceremonial occasions, effectively reenacting how chiefs had historically performed ceremonies to "cool the land" heated by this transgression of the morality of kinship. As Posselt put it, he had always "ordered the necessary purificatory ceremonies to be observed, one or more cattle being killed for such rites. This procedure has not only complied with Native Law but has also given general satisfaction." Posselt noted that "in one or two cases I have ascertained that the Chief or Headman have tried to act independently, but I have immediately checked the proceedings and ordered the case to be brought before me."[16] Such interventions, like the categorization of murder and witchcraft accusations as criminal offenses, shook the epistemological foundations of chiefly claims to land and power. In Shona cosmology, *makunakuna* polluted the land, angering spirits and preventing rains from falling. Acts of *makunakuna*, like murder and witchcraft, "harmed" the land.[17] Chiefs claimed that they used fines imposed on those who committed *makunakuna* to undertake ceremonies meant to "clean" the land.[18] And now, native commissioners usurped those powers.

Native commissioners like Posselt not only appropriated from chiefs the authority to settle cases of *makunakuna* but also held final say over the establishment of new villages.[19] This was a legacy of Proclamation No. 55 of 1910. Under this proclamation, Department of Native Affairs officials were empowered to "control inter-district movements, assign land of various purposes, fix the number of huts comprising a kraal and collect taxation."[20] The proclamation's terms were incorporated into the Native Affairs Act that replaced it.[21]

But in the 1930s, a few factors complicated these officials' abilities to exercise this power. First, as they increasingly became deskbound, saddled with administrative paperwork, from the 1920s onward, native commissioners needed the cooperation of local headmen and kraalheads, who, under the Native Affairs Act, had "the added responsibility of preventing the removal of kraals without the N. C's. prior authority."[22] However, this support was not always forthcoming. In 1930, Native Commissioner Posselt complained that "Headman Nengubo had been very lax in the discharge of his duties of supervision in this respect." At the time, Kasege had built his homestead and cleared new fields in Manyaira village, under headman Nenguvo, in Marandellas District, without the native commissioner's approval.[23]

Second, Africans dissatisfied by the decisions of their headmen, chiefs, and local native commissioners could appeal to the chief native commissioner, who, in turn, considered it his duty "to be accessible to all natives presenting their grievances."[24] Posselt summed up the implications of this paternalistic policy: "At present they [Africans], have all to gain and nothing to lose by making fictitious allegations. If this is permitted, I can foresee the time—not far distant—when every order by a district official will be subject to an appeal or a complaint."[25] Posselt made this comment when his own power was being tested by a few of his African subjects. One of these Africans was a man named Mtandwa, who, in the late 1920s, complained that Chief Chihota "had declared his proposed union to be incestuous" and proceeded to forbid it.[26] Native Commissioner Posselt affirmed the chief's decision, but the aggrieved Mtandwa appealed to the Natives Appeals Court. The Natives Appeals Court, in turn, overturned the chief's verdict.[27] The other African to challenge Posselt was the aforementioned Kasege, who, objecting to how the native commissioner had handled his case, escalated the matter to the chief native commissioner. In this case, the chief native commissioner sided with Native Commissioner Posselt, requesting Kasege's removal from Marandellas District. But the point had been made. Dissatisfied Africans could use the NAD chain to appeal the decisions of junior officials.

Moreover, the chief native commissioner did not always side with his men at the district level. One case illustrates this point. In 1930, four men—Bayika, Chera, Mamutsa, and Mauskwa—sidestepped their native commissioner, complaining to the chief native commissioner that their chief, Svosve, had leveled spurious charges of *makunakuna* against them and proceeded to impose unreasonably high fines.[28] Chief Svosve, it turned out, had "always showed a marked inclination to rake up incest cases when he was still a Headman under the name Gambiza." Posselt, his native commissioner, had "rebuked him on several occasions for such undue zeal."[29] But in this case the native commissioner had attempted to shield the chief, inadvertently putting himself on a collision course with his own superiors. When the case first came to light, the assistant native commissioner for Wedza who investigated the complaints concluded that "the fine was excessive." In consultation with elders in the Svosve Reserve, the assistant native commissioner recommended that "2 head fine and one to 'Cheka Ukama' [literally to cut the kinship ties] would meet the case." Chief Svosve was "to return 7 head, 5 to Jambgwa and 2 to Mauskwa."[30]

The assistant native commissioner was Posselt's subordinate. Posselt overruled him. "It would be a fatal mistake, to my mind, to order complete restitution," Posselt argued, reasoning rather disingenuously that "the Natives would not appreciate our motives and would regard it as an obvious act of abrogation of their tribal law, which will lead to no little confusion and dissatisfaction."[31] But there was more to Posselt's thinking. Ever mindful of the usefulness of chiefs in their colonial constabulary role, he feared that the assistant native commissioner's recommendation that Chief Svosve should return most of the complainants' cattle would undermine the chief's power in the eyes of his subjects. Posselt thus recommended a course of action that, in his view, would punish Chief Svosve without undermining the chief's authority in his subjects' eyes. "I suggest we go further than merely restoring the balance of the stock to the parties concerned," Posselt told his superiors. "I propose that the remainder of the cattle should be surrendered by Svosve to me, in my capacity as Paramount Chief, and I will dispose of them at my discretion. This will at the same time be an effective measure of upholding Native Law and a salutary check on Svosve against further attempt to enrich himself, in spite of any plea he may urge of having acted merely as the custodian of state stock."[32] Needless to say, this would have been a lose-lose situation to both Chief Svosve and the complainants.

Of course, the greatest beneficiary of this course of action would have been Posselt. In addition to checking Chief Svosve's avariciousness, he would cement his status as the district's "paramount chief" by arrogating to himself those rituals of cleansing the land that chiefs had reserved to themselves or to their most trusted lieutenants. The chief native commissioner, the colony's attorney general, and the prime minister, who also served as the minister of native affairs, stopped Posselt in his tracks. "It does not seem to me that the steps you think should be taken to check and punish Svosve for inflicting fines of 28 head of cattle in the cases appearing in this correspondence are satisfactory," Chief Native Commissioner Jackson told Posselt. "It is noted that you had already reprimanded this chief of his undue zeal in incest cases, although to my mind 'cupidity' better describes his moral attitude," Jackson pointed out before chipping away at Native Commissioner Posselt's argument that the complainants' family members had indeed committed incest by pointing out that in such cases, there already existed a remedy in Shona practice. This remedy was a payment of a small fee or a cow for *cheka ukama* (to cut the ties of kinship).[33] Jackson reserved his sharpest criticism for Posselt's remedy to the cases: "Where I do not agree with you is your suggestion . . . that the fines inflicted by Svosve should stand as against the complaining Natives, and that the balance of the cattle—rightly described by the Assistant Native Commissioner as 'preposterous fines'—should be handed over to you to be dealt with in your discretion," he stressed.[34] Queried Jackson, "I should like to know in what manner you would propose dealing with this property. To my mind, restitution to the aggrieved parties should at least follow: If a wrong has been done, *fiat Justitia, ruat coelum,*" he said.[35] In these Latin words, Jackson simultaneously pointed to the injustice of Posselt's measures and reminded the native commissioner that what he possessed was instrumental and not creative power. Posselt was not the "owner" of the land and had no standing that allowed him to purify the land that had been polluted by *makunakuna.*

The chief native commissioner's position was endorsed by H. U. Moffart, the prime minister and minister of native affairs.[36] Likewise, the attorney general Robert H. Hudson insisted that chiefs, including Chief Svosve, had no powers to try criminal and civil cases. "A duty is imposed on him [the chief] of reporting breaches of the law to his Native Commissioner but he has no authority to try cases," Hudson elaborated. Recalling the words of Clarkson Henry Tredgold, his predecessor as attorney general, two decades earlier, Hudson pointed out that "it is possible that where natives who are parties to a civil dispute agree to submit their dispute to a headman or chief then his decision in this matter might be upheld as being the award of an arbiter."[37] Building on this opinion, Chief Native Commissioner Jackson instructed Native Commissioner Posselt to ensure the restitution of the cattle. "I must insist that you regard the foregoing instructions as explicit and final," Jackson warned.[38] In these words, the chief native commissioner brought the case to finality, curbing the native commissioner's and the chief's excesses. Early in January 1931, the chief native commissioner issued a circular "warning N.C.s that chiefs were not entitled to try criminal cases, and in any civil action, parties should be given the option to reject his services as an arbiter."[39]

These few cases were undoubtedly exceptional—a point attested to by the fact that they ended up in the colonial archive—and should not be stretched to suggest that the Native Affairs Department hierarchy protected African interests. It did not. But the cases underscore the fact that, as with the colonial state more broadly, this hierarchy consisted of people with different dispositions.[40] Those dispositions at times allowed brave Africans such as Bayika, Chera, Mamutsa, and Mauskwa to draw small victories from the authoritarian hands of both their native commissioners and their chiefs. Licking their wounded egos, such native commissioners fumed, deriding members of other branches of colonial administration—the attorney general, for example—for failing to realize that on the ground, things worked differently from what the colonial laws often intended. Despite the attorney general's position, Posselt, indeed, insisted that "the so-called arbitration by Chiefs is a fiction. [Chiefs] do, or at least in most cases, hear and determine Civil matters in conformity with ancient custom. The term 'arbitration' is therefore merely a means of disguising a fact [i.e., chiefs were judging cases and not simply arbitrating] and giving a legal authority to what might otherwise be considered an illegal proceeding."[41] What Posselt had not learned even after his superiors had overruled him was that chiefs' judgments, like his own, could be challenged or even annulled because, at law, they did not hold judicial authority. In short, then, the differences in the dispositions of the Native Affairs Department hierarchy often produced devastating results to Africans—imagine Native Commissioner Posselt's decision in this matter carrying the day—but also left crevices through which subjected Africans could contest the most egregious abuses of power by both their chiefs and native commissioners.

The cases also allude to the fact that although colonial rule was violent, exploitative, and disruptive, Africans' lives were influenced not only by how they related to colonial institutions or even to the colonial economy but also by how they related to one another.[42] Chief Svosve's conduct was, undoubtedly, buoyed by his newfound powers as a colonially appointed chief. It was also steeped in local conflicts. His appointment had not been "popular in all quarters." He was "resorting to reprisals to that section of the community that opposed his appointment."[43]

Likewise, the matter that took Kasege to the chief native commissioner's doorstep can be understood in terms of local rivalries and competition over land among Africans with varied access to colonial sources of power. At a minimum, this is what Kasege wanted Chief Native Commissioner Jackson to believe. Kasege told the chief native commissioner that he used to live at Chiremba village near Epworth Mission on the outskirts of Salisbury but had obtained permission to relocate to Marandellas District, where his brother, who was a teacher at Nengubo (now Waddilove) Mission, also lived. He then accused Lemuel, the son of a native messenger called Simon, of causing his problems. Lemuel, Kasege claimed, had caused his brother to be transferred from Nengubo Mission, where Lemuel replaced him. Kasege also claimed that Lemuel had taken his land and that the local headman, despite promising to give him another piece, had not done so. Finally, Lemuel and his father had caused the arrest of Kasege's relative. They were angry when Kasege paid his relative's fine, and Simon promised to use his position as a native messenger to cause the native commissioner to remove him from the area. "The Native Commissioner did not order me to leave," Kasege claimed. "Simon told me to move and said it was the Native Commissioner."[44] "Simon," Kasege continued, told Kasege's wife (outside the native commissioner's office, where she was dragged on behalf of her husband, who was away at work) that "'as you cannot get on with my son Lemuel, you must move away from where he lives.' My wife returned home, and Lemuel again told her that we must move, as we did not get along with him."[45] The native commissioner for Marandellas alluded to this conflict by stating that he had attempted to settle a dispute between the wives of Kasege and Lemuel.[46]

This case then implicated conflicts among Africans in the colonial state's efforts to make Africans legible.[47] Native Commissioner Posselt ordered Kasege to relocate his homestead in line with the government's policy of ethnic spatial fixing.[48] Through this policy, Africans were to build their homesteads in linear settlements in areas under their own customary authorities. Kasege had defied this by building his homestead in a village different from the one to which he belonged and by doing so without first seeking the native commissioner's authorization.

All this drama played out at a time when voices calling for the strengthening of chiefs' authority were growing increasingly loud in the Native Affairs Department.[49] Indeed, studies in the history of native policy have seen the 1930s as the period when the colonial state restored "customary" authority in Zimbabwe.[50] Historian Murray Steele notes that

> the earlier *laissez-faire* attitude to so called tribalization was now abandoned in favour of a policy directed towards the shoring up of

> customary institutions and values, the principal feature of which was the maintenance of the chief's prestige. As a means to this end, the Government decided to extend formal recognition to the judicial powers chiefs had been unofficially exercising in respect to civil cases within the purview of Native customary law, and a modified form of the 1931 proposal was enacted as the Native Law and Courts Act of 1937.[51]

This shoring up of chiefs' powers did not go very far. The Native Law and Courts Act (1937) was hedged with safeguards that, in the end, limited chiefly authority.[52] Section 10 (C) of the bill read, "Any party to a civil case who is dissatisfied with the judgment of a native court in such case may, in such a manner and within a period as may be prescribed, apply to the court of the native commissioner of the district for the rehearing and retrial of such case by such last mentioned court, and thereupon the judgment of the native court in such case shall be of no effect."[53] More importantly, the bill did not give provisions for execution of judgments and for punishing contempt of court or the giving of false evidence.[54] What is more, "disapproval of Indirect Rule practices continued, despite the policy changes of the later thirties."[55] Much of this disapproval came from members of the Law Department who believed that neither chiefs nor native commissioners were competent to dispense justice—even when this was defective colonial justice!

It was not merely segments of the colonial state who threatened the powers of chiefs; African participation in the colonial economy further eroded chiefly authority. Forced to pay rent on alienated land, some Africans increasingly objected to chiefly demands that previously rested on their claims to a landed domain. For example, in 1933, Chief Mutasa complained that he had requested people under headman Mandeya to repair his homestead, which was burned down the previous year, according to Manyika custom but they "refused to comply with the custom."[56] In refusing, they stated that they had no time to do such work; they lived on mission (Triashill), alienated, and Crown lands and had to find government taxes.[57]

The Nyamhuka people's decision to decline Chief Mutasa's request drove home the point that colonial land alienation had severed older forms of obligations that legitimated chiefly authority over land. To understand this point, it is crucial to unpack the ideological basis of Chief Mutasa's request. As discussed in chapter 2, Mandeya was one of the four exiled sons of Nyarumwe, the Manyika king said to have been killed by his brother, Nyamandoto.[58] Nyarumwe's successor acknowledged the relative autonomy of these four brothers by allowing them to establish their own territories as

Mutasa's *machinda* (headman). In return for recognition of their independence, the four brothers agreed not to contest the Mutasa chieftainship.[59] But, vested in the survival of their kingdom, they recognized the reigning Mutasa chiefs.

For the headman Mandeya, the recognition of this authority was recalled by the practice that each time Mutasa's homestead was rebuilt, his subjects were to build the very first hut. In this way, the *machinda* and their subjects not only renewed their allegiance to the chief of the land but also recognized the chief's claims to "own the land." This affirmation of chiefly power over land was severed when the Nyamhuka people refused to rebuild Mutasa's homestead because they now lived not on the chief's land but that of the missionaries, the colonial state, and private landowners.

TECHNOCRATIC AUTHORITARIANISM, THE POWER OF CUSTOMARY AUTHORITIES, AND LAND INEQUALITIES, 1930s–1950s

In the 1920s the colonial state began to actively intervene in African agrarian practice in the name of native development.[60] The impetus to this appears to have been, among other factors, the hardships that accompanied the post–First World War economic recession and the famine of 1922, but the objectives ranged from conservation to governmentality.[61] Rooted in the racist view that African agriculture and land use were detrimental to the environment and inefficient, native development, as conceived by the colonial state between the late 1920s and the early 1960s, included the employment of African agricultural demonstrators to promote manuring and crop rotation, the separation of fields and pastures (centralization), destocking, and the implementation of soil conservation measures. As conceived in the 1920s, the earliest of these measures were meant to be implemented through demonstration and persuasion. But, by the 1940s and 1950s, measures had become coercive and authoritarian, climaxing with the passage and implementation of the Native Land Husbandry Act (1951).[62]

The implementation of these policies would influence rural Africans' relations with the state at the local and national levels, as well as Africans' relations with one another. All these measures were about the exercise of power from on high. They were also meant to ensure African legibility to the state.[63] The policies of centralization and the Land Husbandry Act, in particular, required Africans to follow a linear settlement pattern. The linear settlements were introduced by the demonstrators, who "did not want the scattered huts because they were a problem to the police. So," recounted Gwatidzo Panyanyiwa, "they decided on having huts built in lines, so that policemen would just follow lines."[64]

By the 1940s, these rural policies were also meant to accommodate the changes in the Rhodesian economy. Wartime conditions had facilitated the takeoff of a manufacturing industry whose labor requirements could not be sustained by the old patterns of migrant labor, which catered to the primary industries of agriculture and mining.[65] The more intrusive policies such as the Native Land Husbandry Act of the 1950s were thus meant to accommodate these changes by creating a permanent peasant population and a class of landless Africans who would provide a stable labor force to the expanding postwar manufacturing economy. Contributing to the bill in 1951, Minister of Native Affairs P. B. Fletcher stated that "the natives must realize that, if they want to become great people and to make a contribution to the development of Africa, they must face the fact that, as the years go by, a smaller percentage of their people will be able to engage in agriculture. Greater and greater numbers must seek a future in industrial development because there is no future for all natives living on the land taking one another's washing."[66] A policy paper that explained the act claimed that the African male kept "one foot in the reserves while dabbling in some paid occupation and tends to be grossly inefficient in both."[67] The act sought to stop this tendency by assigning permanent landholdings to those in the reserves and turning those in the urban areas into landless permanent laborers.

These policies affected the social dynamics of access to land, but many of their lofty goals were not always met. As of 1949, attempts to enumerate Africans in Umtali District to make them visible to the colonial state ran into several problems. Several people were omitted from the census collection because "in some cases the correct classification of the kraals [according to their chiefs] was in doubt; in other cases, kraals were in process of moving, and in further cases kraals were either scattered or their inmates dispersed over [an] extensive area as individual plot holders."[68] At the same time, the implementation of colonial development and agrarian policies was uneven. The Native Land Husbandry Act, that epitome of state intrusion into African social and economic life enacted in 1951, was never implemented in parts of the eastern highlands.[69] In the Mangwende Reserve in the central watershed, the colonial state implemented the same policies with so much zeal, it caused an uprising.

Moreover, where the policies were implemented—which, in colonial northeastern Zimbabwe included the districts of Marandellas, Goromonzi, Makoni, and Mrewa—they influenced relations between the colonial state and its African subjects and also facilitated the emergence of a technical bureaucracy consisting of native agricultural demonstrators, community assistants, and land development officers, whose authority over land use and allocation rivalled that of chiefs, headmen, and kraalheads. Trained at Domboshava and Tsholotsho government training centers, African agricultural demonstrators worked under the supervision of Emory D. Alvord, an American man with a missionary background appointed to the post of agriculturalist for the instruction of natives by the Southern Rhodesian government in 1926. Alvord and his subordinates' mandate was to encourage Africans to adopt crop rotation and the use of manure. Soon, however, the African agricultural demonstrators became involved in land allocation because they worked with the land development officers, demarcating fields from pastures. The appointment of these men coincided with increasing concerns over environmental degradation in the reserves on the part of colonial officials.[70] These same concerns also prompted the colonial state to attack customary land use and tenure and to place land allocation in the hands of the technical officers.[71]

At face value, both the attack on customary land use and tenure and the introduction of a technical bureaucracy to oversee land matters in the reserves were assaults on the power of kraalheads, headmen, and chiefs and entrenchments of technocratic authoritarianism.[72] But, in fact, no such swinging of power over land from chiefs to technical officers occurred. If anything, land allocation required chiefs' approval, and when the African agricultural demonstrators who implemented these policies first arrived in the reserves, they presented themselves to the chiefs, a legacy of the policy of the 1920s, when Native Affairs Department officials were concerned that the presence of these men, like that of teachers and kraal schools, undermined the power of "customary" authorities.[73]

Even those policies like the ambitious and intrusive Native Land Husbandry Act of the 1950s, which were implemented not by the African demonstrators but by the white land development officers, did not sideline chiefs, headmen, and kraalheads.[74] Elders who witnessed the implementation of these policies remembered these technical officers working alongside chiefs. Asked by a researcher if she had seen demonstrators growing up in northeastern Zimbabwe, one elderly woman, *mbuya* Chikonzo, explained that she had not seen the demonstrators who taught people about new agricultural methods when she was still living in Mutasa.[75] This was not surprising; the Native Land Husbandry Act was hardly implemented in the rugged terrain of the eastern highlands.[76] *Mbuya* Chikonzo added, "The ones that I know were the whites (*mabhunu*) who came to demarcate fields. They came and they started to demarcate fields and that is when we left our properties. I only saw the demonstrators when I was already in Bocha." She elaborated, "The land development officers came and worked with the kraalheads," who

> directed them to the arable lands where we grew maize. That is where they began demarcating fields, giving each household small plots of land. We were no longer doing as before when we were growing up. Then we cultivated any piece of land that satisfied the demands of each household. Now they demarcated even smaller pieces saying that we should do this so that everybody gets a piece. The kraalheads were now incorporated in this whole business of demarcating fields. They were now in agreement with the demonstrators and began to say this is the new law that we should follow.[77]

Villagers like *mbuya* Chikonzo distinguished land demarcation from land allocation, maintaining that land development officers demarcated the fields but the "customary" leaders allocated the land to their subjects. Thus, when in a follow-up interview, I asked the elderly lady whether the arrival of the demonstrators and land development officers meant that kraalheads had lost their authority to technical officers, her answer was no.

> People would still go to the kraalhead because the allocation of the household plots was accomplished only because the demonstrators worked with the kraalheads. The demonstrators (which in fact incorporated land development officers) came and worked through the kraalheads. So, the kraalheads adopted this policy. If an individual married, he would go to the kraalhead. The kraalhead would allocate fields from the uncultivated potions of his land. He would demarcate similar acreages to those that were given to others when the demonstrators came.[78]

The distinction between land demarcation and land allocation was not just semantic—at least from the perspective of those in the reserves. It signaled that while technical officers spatially mapped fields and pastures, customary leaders retained the power to allocate land to those who lived under their authority. Thus, kraalheads did not just facilitate the work of a technocratic bureaucracy; they also continued to play a central role in the allocation of rural land. Native development and agrarian policies, then, might have pulled in opposite directions, but they allowed technical officers and "customary" authorities to exercise power over land simultaneously. The result was that power over land remained a subject of competition among various elite groups.

However, these policies did affect the social relations of landholding. In particular, the Native Land Husbandry Act (1951) restructured African landholdings in ways that deepened generational and gendered inequalities. The young men who were most frequently labor migrants stood to lose most from the implementation of this act. When officials reallocated land in the reserves, many young men would fail to meet the act's condition of showing that they had cultivated the land in the previous year because they would have been away at work in cities or mines. Moreover, under the Native Land Husbandry Act, the state allocated individual farming rights to male heads of households, denying women and junior men the chance to legally own farming land.[79]

Also, under this act and even before, the state compelled Africans to perform a series of soil conservation and pasture improvement measures. Thus, in February 1952, the colonial state instructed headmen in Makoni District to hold meetings "to collect labor for roads and soil conservation."[80] "Thereafter," wrote historian Terence Ranger, "the monthly reports of the Land Development Officer for northern Makoni document massive intervention—drain strips, gulley dams, contour ridges, rotational grazing, all these and more were enforced. More and more demands," Ranger added, "were made—there was to be no intercropping; no cultivation of wet gardens near streams."[81] The ban on cultivation of areas near streams further undermined women's independent access to land. As noted in chapter 3, women had historically accessed and controlled land in these areas for the cultivation of *madhumbe* and *tsenza.* Women's access to these plots disrupted the colonial vision of African landholding based on patriarchy. "In *tsenza* plots," wrote anthropologist Donald S. Moore, "women farmed freely (*kurima madiro*) on state-owned land spatially beyond their government allocated fields, legally registered in their husbands' names."[82] The colonial state's expansion of its conservationist measures, outlawing cultivation near stream banks on the pretext that it caused siltation, threatened women's access to these plots.[83]

The Native Land Husbandry Act further entrenched disparity in landholdings rooted in other forms of social difference. "At Sadza village the headman turned out to have twelve acres, and an angry commoner complained that he had been given only three," Terence Ranger learned when he accompanied the nationalist George Nyandoro to Seke Reserve in 1958.[84] Under this act, the standard household acreage in wetter areas like the Seke Reserve was six acres. It was progressively more in drier areas. The source of this disparity between the headman and his commoner neighbor at Sadza village might have been rooted in the fact that customary authorities were, as discussed above, involved in land allocation and would have reserved for themselves plots that were larger than those of their subjects.

As with its attempts to shore up the power of chiefs in the 1930s, the state's interventions in African agriculture did not always structure African societies in the way that policymakers envisioned. Thus, the imposition of new legal paradigms did not end older forms of negotiation over land rooted in "custom." Rather, the two persisted side by side, creating a gap between legal paradigms and "customary" practices.[85] This gap allowed individuals to negotiate their access to land, including buying land from village heads, headmen, and chiefs under the guise of paying a token of appreciation.[86] The commoditization of land in this way persisted into the postcolonial period and has allowed some women, immigrants, and junior men to access land outside the plots allocated to family patriarchs by the state.[87] This reality escaped mid-twentieth-century anthropologists who held on to the caricature that, except for very minor possessions such as personal clothing or tools, property, including land, ownership was communal.[88]

At any rate, implementing some of the colonial state's agrarian measures to the dot proved almost impossible. Part of the problem with these measures lay in the fact that they were meant to sustain racial segregation in land allocation. Consequently, the colonial state was unwilling to transfer land that had been assigned for white settlements to the African reserves even when it was clear that there was a serious problem of land shortage in the latter areas and large portions of land on settler farms were underutilized. These problems were compounded by the fact that the soils and general conditions in the reserves were poor. In 1937, "less than 50% of the land in the Native reserves was arable," Alvord explained. "Of this arable area," he continued, "we find that on several of the large reserves, 40 to 80 per cent of the classified arable land cannot be occupied due to lack of water supplies or rainfall. All areas in the reserves that are best suited for occupation are already fully occupied." Many of these areas were already eroded and yields per acre very low.[89] In these circumstances, people settled beyond the areas the colonial state spatially demarcated for homesteads and fields.

The case of the Svosve Reserve in the Marandellas District illustrates this point. In 1946, the reserve "was in a very critical condition due," in the eyes of colonial officials, "to uncontrolled over tillage, overstocking and the fact that the reserve had never been centralized." "During the past year," a report of an ad hoc committee on the land situation in reserves noted, "this matter has been taken in hand, the reserve declared an intensive conservation area and the Governor-in-Council has declared that the population and stock be decreased to a reasonable carrying capacity."[90] But this did not yield immediate results. A few months later, the director of native agriculture reported that "Svosve reserve is 46% overstocked and on a 6 head of livestock per family basis, it is 166% overpopulated."[91] The extent of arable lands as demarcated for occupation by the land inspector in September

1945, he continued, "constitutes approximately 10% of the entire area less waste. The total area suitable for tillage is estimated at 2400 acres. This at 6 acres of lands per family, would take only 400 families while total number of families in 1945 was 905. If the 2400 acres of tillable lands are divided among 905 families, it would mean an average of 2.6 acres per family."[92] Needless to say, many of the families in the Svosve Reserve had abandoned these demarcated areas. They were growing crops on the banks of streams, vleis, and watercourses.[93]

Indeed, in 1956, the native commissioner for the district of Marandellas complained that "following allocation, this year's ploughing took place and it is regrettable the extent to which boundaries of lands, road strips and drain strips were ignored and how many people cultivated land not allocated to them."[94] Likewise, "there were many reports of exultant acts of deliberate disregard, for the elementary lessons on soil preservation which the extension services had tried to teach for more than a quarter century in their preaching and demonstration work" in the Mangwende Reserve in 1961.[95] Added Jon F. Holleman, an anthropologist who was part of a commission that investigated the African uprisings in this reserve at the time, "There were outbursts of 'freedom ploughing' and of the indiscriminate and wanton destruction of trees, activities which went far beyond the limits of even the most haphazard of traditional farming practices. Against these, sometimes politically inspired, activities," he continued, "most chiefs were virtually powerless and could do little more than try to pour some oil on troubled waters."[96] Holleman overstated the powerlessness of chiefs, many of whom encouraged the practice by assigning their subjects land outside the areas identified by colonial technocrats.[97]

Settling beyond the areas that the state demarcated for homesteads and fields was one way in which Africans responded to colonial interventions in their agrarian lives. Villagers linked this opposition to nationalist mobilization, particularly to the language of *kurima madiro* (freedom farming) that the anticolonial movement evoked to oppose the hated Land Husbandry Act and to mobilize rural farmers to its cause.[98] Through "freedom farming," men and women subverted the colonial state's efforts at spatial reordering of their livelihoods, revealing, in the process, the limits of technocratic authoritarianism.

There was more to this resistance. In the Chihota Reserve in 1947, a land development officer recounted with some condescension the apathy that some in the reserves showed to these policy impositions from on high. "The Demonstrator found it difficult to contend and overcome overwhelming conservatism of the masses of people, the popular idea being that the

Government would eject the people from the Reserve and populate it with Europeans as soon as it was developed agriculturally," he noted.[99] A former demonstrator similarly remembered the hostility that he encountered when he was first deployed to the Chihota Reserve in 1943. "We had a difficult time, I tell you," he said, adding,

> we had nowhere to stay. We could be offered a deserted house left by someone. [We] were in a real tough situation. . . . We could stay out till a few who had compassion admitted us into their homes. . . . We were faced with great difficulty. There was great fear of the government during those days, for people had recently been harassed. . . . They were beaten. . . . The white policemen came and forced people to carry some luggage. . . . So people thought that the demonstrators had also come to deceive them.[100]

Elders similarly remembered subtle oppositions in the form of song compositions that critiqued colonial policies of *chibaro* (forced labor), road construction, cattle culling, contour ridging, and the resettlement of Africans in linear settlements.[101] Composed in the 1950s, elders recounted, the song's lyrics stated that "Mangwende resists cattle culling; all our heads have been destroyed; they started with *chibaro,* followed by road constructions, now it's cattle culling and all that stuff." "It was a political protest song," they elaborated, adding that "if one was heard by the colonial officials singing it, one would be disappeared."[102]

Africans composed this song in the wake of rural protests against colonial agrarian measures in the Mangwende Reserve in late 1959 and early 1960 mentioned earlier. As in many other African reserves, tensions over colonial agrarian interventions had simmered throughout the 1940s and 1950s. However, the uprising in the Mangwende area was so overt that the colonial state dethroned the incumbent chief, exiling him to the Seke Reserve. It was this chief who was celebrated in songs as leading the resistance. In fact, concluded a commission that investigated the risings, "the majority of the agitators" came "from Salisbury [and] were . . . young male migrant labourers from the Mangwende area whom the Land Husbandry Act had rendered ineligible for farming rights in their home area."[103] These young migrant laborers, the commission added, "appeared to be the most vociferous and excitable elements who exhorted their tribesmen to resist land allocation and who threatened to resort to physical violence if people cooperated with the [colonial] administration."[104] The commissioners suggested that migrant workers' actions were facilitated by the fact that their home area was close to Salisbury, the colonial capital. This, they argued, allowed for "the considerable volume of weekend commuters . . . [who] were in close and regular touch with the center of African political thought and ferment, and therefore more exposed to the political exploitation of possible causes of grievances than many others."[105] The commissioners' finding revealed the contradictions of a migrant labor system that was meant to contain Africans but had come to facilitate the movement of anticolonial ideas between town and country. This was not unusual. Migrant workers led the way in rural resistance in South Africa, where similar policies had been implemented under the deceptively titled policy of betterment.[106]

Resistance was not limited to the young men who stood to lose most from the land tenure reforms envisioned by the colonial state, nor was it always a result of nationalist ferment. As the Mangwende case illustrates, "customary leaders"—chiefs, headmen, and kraalheads—also resisted colonial agrarian interventions, even as the colonial state had reduced many of them into mere constabularies. This, in part, was because such measures threatened "customary" leaders' powers.

These leaders also resisted because they understood that, together with their subjects, they were victims of colonial agrarian experiments. One case illustrates this point.[107] In 1950, colonial officials in the district of Umtali identified an area in the northern part of the Maranke Reserve to initiate a pilot project in soil conservation through the use of heavy machinery. The project faced heavy opposition from the local Africans. Two years later, headman Chipfatsura, whose jurisdiction covered the targeted lands, complained about the environmental impact of this pilot project. "I am reporting the damages done by the Department of the Land Development Office here on Sub-chief Chipfatsura, the son of Chief Maranke," he wrote, adding,

> I am humble, acknowledge your noble counsel, about this Department is really spoiled the country and our lands, we are having greater starvation or the terrible hunger this year through the agriculture department. They are mostly very badly. Indeed, they are not giving us proper lands, only throw the good lands away, they gave two grazings areas to the cattle, therefore, especially here on Chipfatsura's area the catterpillars spoiled the lots. Nothing good, only suffering. This Department is not happy to see the black people eating food, and also the line which the houses are in are fully by water coming from the contour ridges and from the dams and the houses are full by the springs, we have nowhere to sleeping all these times. Absolutely nothing all the dams and the rivers and the roads and the streams and the dongas, been made by the catterpillars are fully by the sands coming from the contour ridges.[108]

Chipfatsura's command of the English language was poor, but his message was so clear that it forced the colonial state to act. The state sent an expert to investigate the headman's claims. "Chipfatsura's area," the subsequent report noted, "lies within the portion of the Maranke reserve covered by the Special Project where, for the past two years, large scale soil conservation work with heavy equipment has been carried out. It is," the report confirmed, "unfortunately true that considerable damage was done to those conservation works by exceptionally heavy rains in 1950 and 1951."[109] Studies of similar outcomes of colonial conservationist measures in nearby Lesotho help us understand how this happened. Implemented with inappropriate technologies and without regard to local conditions, including aspects of soil texture and gradient, these measures produced structures that were weak and could not sustain the runoff caused by the often torrential rains that fall during the rainy season in southern Africa. Unsurprisingly, these contour ridges and other structures meant to combat soil erosion failed, leaving behind erosion channels called "imperial gullies."[110]

Chipfatsura's story also reminds us that, in contrast to much earlier thinking about colonial intrusions and African responses, it would be a mistake to view African attitudes toward colonial agrarian measures only through a narrow political lens of nationalist politics, for, as in this case, not all of that was inspired by nationalist agitation.[111] Chipfatsura, noted the Umtali native commissioner, "is a disgruntled obstructionist who is consistently uncooperative and hostile towards all efforts to teach good husbandry in his area."[112] The official believed that Chipfatsura disliked colonial land allocation or any form of control and this was the real reason for his complaint. The Umtali native commissioner was not alone. The land development officer who investigated Chipfatsura's case reported that the majority of Chipfatsura's people felt that the size of land allocated was too small, and that they would therefore starve.[113] The possibility of starvation, more than political mobilization, accounted for their opposition to colonial soil conservation measures.

But not everybody resisted these policies, revealing the complex array of political and personal interests that informed African lives under colonial rule. Many other villagers adopted the changes introduced by the demonstrators without abandoning their old practices. In response, the colonial state withdrew Master Farmer and Master of Tillage certificates that it had awarded these villagers (see figures 5.1 and 5.2).[114] Those who embraced these measures saw their benefits in local struggles for land and authority, just as some might have resisted these measures based on how they related to their neighbors.[115] For Acting Chief Chihota in the mid-1940s, the conservationist

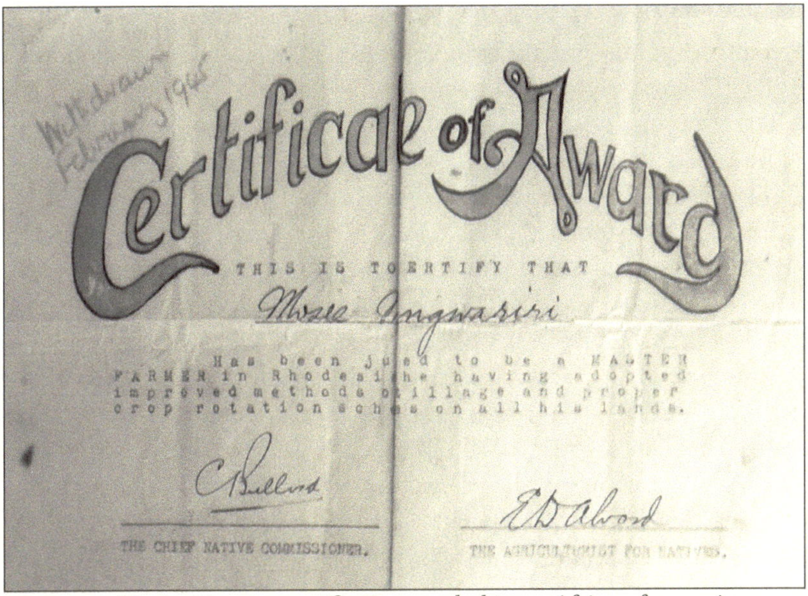
Withdrawn February 1945

Certificate of Award

THIS IS TO CERTIFY THAT

Mosee Ingwariri

Has been judged to be a MASTER FARMER in Rhodesia he having adopted improved methods of tillage and proper crop rotation schemes on all his lands.

C Bullock

THE CHIEF NATIVE COMMISSIONER.

E D Alvord

THE AGRICULTURIST FOR NATIVES.

FIGURE 5.1. Master Farmer certificate awarded to an African farmer in Marandellas District.

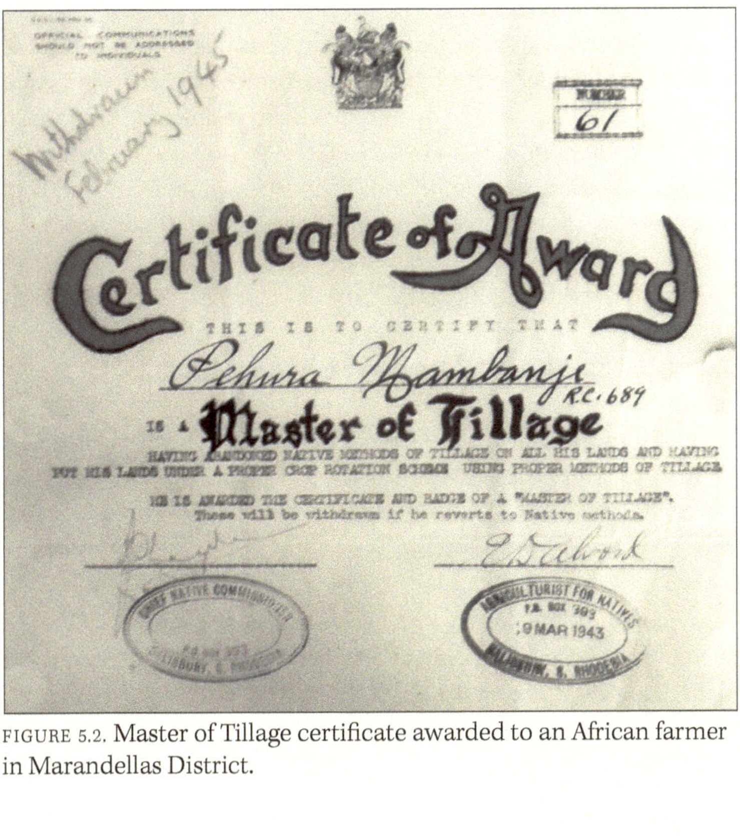
OFFICIAL COMMUNICATIONS SHOULD NOT BE ADDRESSED TO INDIVIDUALS

NUMBER 61

Withdrawn February 1945

Certificate of Award

THIS IS TO CERTIFY THAT

Pehura Mambanje R.C. 689

IS A Master of Tillage

HAVING ABANDONED NATIVE METHODS OF TILLAGE ON ALL HIS LANDS AND HAVING PUT HIS LANDS UNDER A PROPER CROP ROTATION SCHEME USING PROPER METHODS OF TILLAGE

HE IS AWARDED THE CERTIFICATE AND BADGE OF A "MASTER OF TILLAGE". These will be withdrawn if he reverts to Native methods.

E D Alvord

CHIEF NATIVE COMMISSIONER P.O. BOX 393 SALISBURY, S. RHODESIA

AGRICULTURIST FOR NATIVES P.O. BOX 393 9 MAR 1943 SALISBURY, S. RHODESIA

FIGURE 5.2. Master of Tillage certificate awarded to an African farmer in Marandellas District.

measures offered him the opportunity to clearly demarcate the boundaries of his territory. The acting chief requested that "he be allowed to define by pegging the lands around his kraal that his kraal inmates cultivate" and offered to contour ridge the area.[116] Moreover, colonial cartography became useful in local struggles for land. Trymore Jena alluded to this when explaining how, in the Wedza Reserve, conflicts over land that involved "immigrants" and "firstcomer" patrilineages were resolved. These conflicts, he pointed out, ended when the firstcomer communities threatened to take the cases to the district officers. Both parties, Jena explained, knew that the maps kept in the district office contained exact boundaries.[117]

However, by the late 1950s, it had become clear to the colonial state that the cost of resistance to its projects of rural rule far outweighed the perceived benefits of implementation. Faced with increased rural resistance and nationalist agitation, the colonial state abandoned the high modernism of the Native Land Husbandry Act and replaced it with the policy of community development. This policy shift began in 1959 when the Rhodesian state sought technical assistance from the United States government through its International Cooperation Administration (precursor to the United States Agency for International Development [USAID], established in 1961). The US International Cooperation Administration recommended that Rhodesian officials should hire James Green, an American expert in community development, as a consultant. Green worked in this capacity for the Rhodesian state between 1960 and 1964, but midway through his term, in 1962, the Rhodesian state announced the suspension of the Native Land Husbandry Act (1951). Officials disingenuously claimed that community development was "an active, planned and organized effort to place *responsibility* for decision making in local affairs on the freely chosen representatives of responsible people at the community and local government level."[118] In practice, despite the facade of decentralization, the colonial state remained paternalistic and authoritarian.[119]

By the 1960s, however, the colonial state was circling back to its earlier attempts to strengthen the power of "customary" authorities, this time as a tactic to deflate African nationalism. And the colonial and postcolonial state would continue to swing between this promotion of "customary authorities" and their replacement by other actors.[120] Of course, as in the past, these competing actors would, in practice, exist side by side while the policies they implemented tended to entrench gendered and generational landed inequalities.

6 ~ Accessing Land and Contesting Authority outside the Reserves of Northeastern Zimbabwe

SHOWN THROUGHOUT the preceding pages are the environmental, social, and political relations that undergirded contestations over land and authority among Africans in precolonial Zimbabwe and how these were impacted by colonial rule. But colonialism did more than affect relations among Africans. It led to a large-scale dispossession of African lands, which the colonial state parceled out to European settlers. By 1908, some eighteen years after the British occupation of the Zimbabwean plateau, 90 percent of the Africans in the district of Inyanga lived on alienated land.[1] A little later, in 1912, half of the African population in the district of Umtali and a quarter of the Africans in Makoni District resided on land claimed by European companies and settlers as farms.[2] They became tenants and "squatters" on lands they had possessed for generations. Many of the dispossessed people remained on alienated lands until the colonial state forcibly removed and resettled them in African reserves in the 1940s and 1950s. In this chapter, I turn to the struggles surrounding these people's access to land.

The struggles involved multiple players and ideologies. Some Africans remained on alienated land for more than a half century because this was advantageous to colonial capital. Others did so because of their tenaciousness. In fighting to remain on land alienated for white settlement by the colonial state, these men and women deployed arguments rooted in custom and tradition, while those who were opposed to their continued occupation of this land often deployed arguments rooted in ideas of environmentalism. By paying attention to all of this, the chapter returns to the argument with which the book opens, that is, when we conceive the questions of land in Zimbabwe and other former settler colonies, we should not think merely in terms of the actions of colonial and postcolonial states. Neither should we simply conceive this question in terms of conflicts pitting Africans on the one hand and the colonial state and white settlers on the other. The question of African tenants' rights (and obligations) not only produced conflicts between Africans and settlers or Africans and the colonial state but also often led to quarrels among colonial officials and between colonial officials and European settlers. All of this mediated the patterns of access to land along racial lines, as well as fomenting social conflicts at the level of the African household and community. If, in the precolonial period, social conflict gave people like Charova's ancestors the impetus to leave their families and search for land among non-kin, then colonial land dispossession, I suggest, fermented conflicts among neighbors.

COLONIAL LAND ALIENATION AND THE MAKING OF "SQUATTERS"

After the imposition of British colonial rule on the Zimbabwean plateau, increasing numbers of the colony's Africans ended up living in the poorer lands that the colonial state set aside for their exclusive occupation as reserves (later, tribal trust lands and communal lands). This was mostly because of state compulsion, although, as Terence Ranger argued, some wanted to pursue a "peasant option."[3] The peasant option, Ranger explained, entailed producing for the market and, in the process, undercutting the colonial state's efforts to turn Africans into laborers for settler farming and mining capital. This, he tells us, was particularly the case in Makoni District, where African peasant farmers voluntarily left settler farms for the Chiduku Reserve because the area was ideally suited to African production for the market. The Chiduku Reserve followed the line of the new Beira-Umtali-Salisbury railway and was connected to markets by a network of farm roads. These conditions, according to Ranger, lured Africans from white farms to the reserve to produce for the market.[4]

However, not all of the region's—and indeed the colony's—Africans were able to find land in the reserves. Neither did all of them find it desirable to move into these areas. In the districts of Umtali and Inyanga, as well as large parts of Makoni District, conditions conducive to African exploitation of colonial markets and the pursuance of a "peasant option" in the reserves hardly existed. There, extensive land alienation by companies and individual white settlers left little land available for the establishment of native reserves. It was "particularly unfortunate," lamented the native commissioner of Umtali in 1900, "that nearly all the ground had been taken up here before my appointment and those parts which have been unappropriated are either too small for reserves or not suitable."[5] In Inyanga, "nearly the whole district . . . had been alienated by 1902, and the N/C [native commissioner], unable to select any large unalienated blocks, simply took what was left. The land, was quite unsuitable for reserves, being precipitous, inaccessible, badly watered and generally very poor."[6] This "very rough country," to use the words of one native commissioner, had "little or no timber."[7] The situation was no better in nearby Makoni Reserve. In 1912, Makoni District's native commissioner described the reserve as a broken country that only afforded sufficient room for the families already living there. Those, including Chief Makoni himself, who lived on alienated land "could not find room there for their cultivation and grazing of stock."[8]

In Inyanga and Umtali, after years of hesitation caused by concerns over the establishment of African reserves on land that bordered Portuguese East Africa, the colonial state established reserves in the Honde and Nyamukwarara valleys. These low-lying areas were hot and malarial.[9] The Maranke Reserve was prone to periodic droughts because it was located on the rain shadow of the eastern highlands. Similarly, northern Inyanga, which the colonial state also targeted for the resettlement of Africans, marked the transition into the fringes of the highlands. The area is characterized by unpredictable rainfall patterns and periodic droughts. In 1916, the Vahwesa who inhabited most of this area survived "on wild fruits and such grain they could trade" owing to "a total failure of crops."[10] "Except on the [banks of the] Gairezi [River] where all people live," noted the district's native commissioner at the time, "[the area] is waterless, mountainous and covered with thick bush. [The Vahwesa]," he continued, "are poor and possess few cattle and small stock."[11]

Confronted with the possibilities of moving to these wretched places, most of the Africans in northeastern Zimbabwe, as with many in Matabeleland, opted to remain on the lands of their forefathers as tenants and "squatters."[12] In the early years of the twentieth century, such arrangements were possible because many of the farms in the region were owned by companies who held them for speculative rather than productive purposes. Thomas B. Hulley, the native commissioner for Umtali District, summed up the situation in 1910: "It is interesting to note that four Landowning Companies owning properties totaling 123,151 morgens in the district, at present unoccupied, impose no burden whatsoever on the natives living on their land," he noted. "It is evident therefore that in the Umtali district what is known as 'nigger-farming' is practically non-existent," Hulley continued, adding that "in consequence of the fact that no rental is charged by the large Companies, the number of natives living on these properties and outside the reserve is very great."[13]

Similar underutilization of land obtained on farms owned by individual white settlers. In the early twentieth century, many of these farms were grossly undercapitalized and hardly productive. "With the exception of a vegetable garden—about 30 yards long by 20 yards long—in front of the store, no agricultural work" was being performed on Farm Hannover in Inyanga in 1905.[14] Under these circumstances, colonial officials and their settler constituency believed that "it would be to the advantage of the natives and the country generally if for the present, the land could be held for the natives, as more can be got from it by what is commonly called 'native farming' in the way of tax, rent and indirect revenue than by the sale of the land itself."[15] These conditions, therefore, made it possible for Africans living on alienated lands to remain there.

SETTLER INTERESTS, BOUNDARIES OF AUTHORITY, AFRICAN INITIATIVES, AND THE POLITICS OF TENANTRY

Besides living as sharecroppers—which colonial officials called "native farming," Africans remained on alienated land as labor tenants. Facing stiff competition for labor from mining capital, settler farmers who benefited from this arrangement defended the continued presence of Africans on their farms. They opposed colonial attempts to resettle Africans in consolidated villages, claiming that this would adversely affect their ability to mobilize labor.[16] Concerned over labor shortages, particularly those caused by the concentration of Africans on certain farms, these same farmers pushed for the enactment of the Private Locations Ordinance (PLO) of 1908. The ordinance discouraged the leasing of unoccupied land to Africans by imposing a fee of one shilling per tenant for an "occupied" farm and five shillings for absentee landlords. Under the ordinance, African tenants, whose number was not to exceed forty adult males per 1,500-morgen (about 3,000 acres) farm, had to sign an agreement with each landlord in the presence of their respective native commissioners. Thus, the PLO sought to distribute Africans among the numerous white-owned farms and then to tie them to these lands as cheap laborers.[17]

Such developments undoubtedly tied some of the Africans to settler farms as labor tenants until the 1930s, when the ordinance was superseded by the Land Apportionment Act (1930). These developments also reveal the cooperation that existed between white settlers and the colonial state, which promulgated and implemented this and similar laws. This cooperation, and its corrosive implications for African livelihoods, was not lost on Africans, who responded by, among other things, giving colonial officials names that captured their characters. Africans in Umtali called Hulley *Dambuza* (or *Dambudzo,* one who gives troubles); the assistant native commissioner, W. A. Levine, *Chikanda Mseve* (one who throws an arrow); and the clerk-in-charge at Penhalonga, B. Johnston, *Chiparadzanyika* (one who destroys the country).[18] Those in Inyanga called Native Commissioner D. H. Moodie *Mashumba* (the lion).[19] Meanwhile, Ernest Morris, the longtime native commissioner of Marandellas District, was known by his African subjects as *Muchekanzeve* (one who cuts ears).[20]

The cooperation between colonial officials and white settler landowners was sometimes tempered by other considerations. The imperatives of maintaining law and order, for example, dictated that colonial officials could not completely ignore the plight of their African subjects. In the years that followed the African risings of 1896–97, both the imperial government and the chartered company's directors were anxious to ensure that Africans would not revolt again.[21] Consequently, officials from the Native Affairs Department (NAD) sometimes intervened on behalf of Africans against European settlers in the hope that this would keep the Africans contented.

The interventions by NAD officials also reflected contradictions within the colonial state. Conflicts over land became enmeshed with contestations over the boundaries of authority. Many NAD officials strongly felt that African administration was their domain and would not countenance any encroachment into their territory by other members of the colonial establishment. Consider, for example, the case of Trooper Williams of the British South Africa Police (BSAP), who was stationed in Makoni District. In 1908, Williams received a complaint from G. R. Winsch of Farm Diana that Africans under headmen Nyarota, Madziwa, and Mawowo were cultivating on his farm. Williams coerced those under headman Nyarota to share half of their crops with Winsch and evicted the families under headmen Madziwa and Mawowo from the farm.[22]

Williams received a sharp rebuke from Hulley, the superintendent of natives for the Umtali Circuit. Hulley demanded "to know what inducement he [Williams] held out for these natives to agree to pay Mr. Winsch half of their crops . . . ; by what authority he turned off Madziwa and Mawowo."[23]

Hulley also queried whether the policeman knew the conditions under which the land was granted to Winsch and if indeed Williams had ascertained the authenticity of the beacons demarcating the boundaries of the farm before he evicted the concerned Africans.[24] Hulley further expressed his displeasure at the trooper's conduct. "The Department [of Native Affairs] has been at endless trouble about cases of this nature. The Attorney General has held that natives must have sufficient notice to allow them to clear their crops, and there are other conditions also," he wrote. "With reference to Trooper Williams' high-handed action in turning certain natives from the farm," he continued,

> I would draw your attention to the Order in Council 1898, Section 85. I think that if this man acts in this manner, it is dangerous to allow him the free run of the district, and I think that he should be clearly made to understand his position. In this case, taking the facts from his own statement, he has made these natives agree to give up half of their crops when there was no obligation on their part to do so. He has turned natives off a farm contrary to His Majesty's Order in Council and has generally taken upon himself the duties of Native Commissioner.[25]

Hulley thus railed against Trooper Williams because he strayed beyond the boundaries of his authority into the native commissioner's domain. Nevertheless, the native commissioner's motive in attacking Trooper Williams did not matter much for the Africans involved in this case. Crucially for them, the conflicts between the two colonial officials granted them some relief.

When Superintendent of Natives Hulley rebuked Trooper Williams, this was not the first time he or other Native Department officials intervened against settler molestation of African tenants. In August 1904, Hulley learned that a settler farmer called A. H. Chaser was about to collect rent on Africans living on his farm near Penhalonga. Hulley told Chaser that he was not entitled to charge rent until he had given the resident Africans a year's notice.[26] In 1909, the assistant native commissioner of Umtali told a Mr. Holand that "the natives residing on Farm Hoboken are under no obligation to work for Mr. Nauhaus."[27] In 1916, C. V. Burton, who farmed at Jerain, demanded from his tenants payment in cattle for an undisclosed case. The tenants took Burton's letter of demand to the native commissioner of Inyanga. "Mr Burton," stated the native commissioner, "should be told that he has no right to do this kind of thing," adding, "I have told my natives that they are on no account to take any notice of these scraps of paper."[28] In October 1917, the manager of Premier Estate requested permission to remove one Kulibwanya from the farm. The native commissioner declined to grant the wish.[29]

The interventions by native commissioners demonstrate the dynamics that enabled some Africans to continue living on alienated land. While native commissioners were not advocates of African rights, paternalistic attitudes explain why they might have supported African tenants. Native commissioners thought of themselves as protectors of Africans against settler avariciousness. When Hulley informed A. H. Chaser that he had no right to charge rent to Africans residing on his farm without giving them a year's notice, he concluded by pointing out that, as the native commissioner, Hulley had to see that Africans were protected.[30] Similarly, when in July 1917, Native Commissioner Hulley learned that the Rezende mines were cutting wood on land earmarked for African settlement, he invoked colonial paternalism. "Though it is far from its intention to hamper the mining industry," Hulley wrote, "the principles involved in the regulations regarding the entry upon native reserves, i.e. the protection of native interests by this department should be preserved."[31]

Colonial paternalism aside, native commissioners understood the importance of pragmatism in dealing with settler-tenant conflicts. To understand the roots of this pragmatism, it is crucial to think about how a few colonizers justified their rule over the numerically superior colonized peoples. Colonial rule thrived by differentiating the "civilized" ruler from the "uncivilized" ruled. One way in which colonial administrators constructed their images of civilization was by pretending that they respected their own laws (they also claimed to respect the African laws that were "not repugnant to natural [read European] justice").[32]

Native Department officials strove to maintain the facade that they maintained their own laws. They vehemently opposed those whose actions tore this veil, for this made their jobs difficult. Consider the following case. In 1900, a farmer called Mathew W. White complained that Africans had made their gardens on his farm without his permission. He demanded payment once the crops were harvested. He charged the Africans in question one shilling a week for any hut they had built on the land and two shillings sixpence for each head per month as grazing fees; threatened to destroy any cattle or goats found trespassing; and finally stated that "any native found upon these farms who shall not be employed here, or seeking work undertaking produce to market, will be removed."[33] The native commissioner of Umtali told White that his proposal for reprisals was "most illegal."[34]

Similarly, in 1904, the Umtali native commissioner rejected the request of a settler farmer called C. Weissenborn to seize African crops grown on his land without permission. "It is not within my power to confiscate the crops which have been put on your land," Native Commissioner Hulley wrote.[35] A few weeks later, the native commissioner advised Weissenborn to be less confrontational and to arrange for a reasonable settlement with the so-called squatters, adding that this "would save a deal of trouble and expense."[36] These officials knew that the legal route was slow and expensive. As the Inyanga native commissioner put it in 1907, the cost of suing for rent and filing for conviction was so expensive that the companies concerned with nonpayment of rent on their properties were discouraged from pursuing that option.[37]

As native commissioners wedged into conflicts between settler landowners and African tenants, they deployed a variety of arguments. Because most of the conflicts concerned settler demands for rent and labor, the colonial officials made it clear that they were not opposed to the principle that Africans should meet these conditions to gain access to alienated land. However, they expressed reservations about the timing of demands for rent. A settler farm owner, argued Umtali District's native commissioner in 1904, could not "come at any time and demand rent on his own terms."[38] On a different occasion, Native Commissioner Hulley discouraged another settler farm owner from evicting Africans despite the endorsement of the chief native commissioner because of timing. "Considering . . . how far advanced the rain season is, I think it would be a little unfair to turn out the natives at this very moment," he said.[39] Hulley went further, imploring the colonial state to insert a clause in the permit of occupation "giving natives the right to attend and reap all growing crops."[40] "As natives prepare their lands long before sowing," he argued, "prepared lands [must] be considered in the same manner as growing crops."[41] A few years later, Hulley refused to sanction the forced removal of Africans occupying the Imbeza valley because their crops had been planted.[42] "If it had been intended to eject them this year," he argued, "action should have been taken earlier."[43]

However, Africans' continued presence on alienated land cannot be explained as simply a result of the calculations of colonial agrarian capital or the administrative egos of Native Department officials.[44] African tenants often took the initiative to ensure their continued stay on their former lands. Seizing on gaps in the legislation to contest settler power, these men and women exposed farmers' ignorance of the relevant landlord laws. This forced Native Department officials to intervene on their behalf. As Native Commissioner Hulley explained, many settlers were unaware that when disputes involving rent-paying Africans living on exempted farms arose, the matter was one between a landlord and his tenant and the aid of the Native

Affairs Department could not be invoked to turn Africans off the farms.[45] Indeed, on numerous occasions, Native Department officials declined to evict Africans for this reason.[46]

Even in cases where Africans agreed to provide labor in lieu of rent and were bound by the terms of the Private Locations Ordinance, the agreements were sometimes imprecise. In 1914, Superintendent of Natives Hulley declined to intervene on behalf of a farmer called V. A. Gross, telling him that "your agreement is that natives on your farms shall work for two months each in every year without pay. Nothing is laid down in regard to what particular two months any individual native shall work. . . . Obviously therefore there has up to present been no breach of the contract by the natives."[47]

African labor tenants often resisted settler efforts to specify the exact times that they would work on the farms to fulfill their end of the contract. "The one week-a-month system was extreme and objectionable," one settler complained. "The native, who in many instances occupied the present kraal site and garden plots before the advent of the Whiteman, refused to understand that he is receiving any considerations in return for his services," he added.[48] The farmer also highlighted the limited options that settlers had in such situations. Eviction, the landlord's only practical remedy for noncompliance by the tenant, he noted, was not desirable as it increased the farmer's difficulties in acquiring labor.[49]

Other forms of African resistance to settler power also influenced the pace of implementation of colonial land and segregationist policies. In 1904, a large number of Africans under Chiefs Tangwena, Saunyama, and Mandeya moved to the Portuguese territory in consequence of the warning given to them by landowners that they would have to pay rent or move.[50] In January 1905, Chief Tangwena and his people "flatly refused to pay rent."[51] They argued that rather than pay rent, they would abandon their crops before rent fell due in March.[52] In 1909, the BSAC gave notice that Africans must agree to pay rent or leave the company's land. Many Africans in Inyanga and Umtali responded by moving across the border into Portuguese East Africa.[53] The cross-border migrations prompted the government to postpone the action "in order to avoid trouble."[54]

For many of these people, this movement did not necessarily mean leaving their old farms. Many of them remained in the vicinity of their old homes. In 1904, Chief Chikomba and his subjects moved to a point just beyond the boundary, due east of his old homesteads.[55] Similarly, in 1906, the majority of Africans who left Holdenby block to protest the imposition of rent settled on those lands in Portuguese East Africa that adjoined the border. Some of these people's new homes were less than a hundred yards from the border.[56] They continued to cultivate their lands in Southern Rhodesia, for most of these farms had passed into the hands of absentee landlords.

For Native Department officials, this practice was particularly difficult to prevent. It required the cooperation of Portuguese officials, which was not always forthcoming. In 1918, the superintendent of natives for the Umtali Circuit, Thomas Benjamin Hulley, conceded that little could be done to stop Africans in border communities from relocating their homesteads to Portuguese East Africa and continue cultivating lands in Southern Rhodesia. "With reference to natives living in Portuguese Territory and cultivating on the farms," Hulley wrote, "I cannot get the Natives in this territory. A complaint to the police might have some effect, but it would require a border guard to deal with the case."[57]

The option to move into Portuguese East Africa was especially appealing for those communities near the border. As the native commissioner for Inyanga District noted in 1916, these border communities contrasted conditions in Portuguese East Africa with those obtaining in Southern Rhodesia.[58] Neither colonial system was necessarily benign. Both taxed their African subjects while coercing them to engage either in poorly paid wage labor or in the production of primary commodities for export, but the absence of massive land alienation on the Portuguese side of the region meant that there, the burden of rent was absent.[59] In addition, the existence of kinship relations across the border lessened the difficulties of integration for the emigrants. In fact, for some, it was an additional enticement to move. "As the people over the border are all the same tribe as on this side," wrote the native commissioner for the district of Umtali, "it can easily be understood that there may be cases where the natives themselves do give no reason [for cross-border emigration] except that they wanted to."[60] In fact, it was the colonial border that was dividing kinspeople.

However, the option of migrating across the border was not available to every African living on alienated land in northeastern Zimbabwe. Consequently, many others agreed to pay rent and to remain on settler-owned farms. However, as Inyanga District's native commissioner complained in March 1905, the rents were "not however being paid all too well."[61] Africans perfected the art of passive resistance. By 1909, headman Muparutsa had been "sued three years in succession by Bullock bros. for his private rental but still remain[ed] a staunch passive resister." He, wrote a bewildered native commissioner, "has no stock and a writ cannot be executed."[62] It was highly unlikely that headman Muparutsa did not have any livestock, but like many other Africans, he concealed his wealth.[63] Indeed, not only did the headman occasionally pay his rent when seriously pressed to do so, he also had five wives. Sustaining such a big household surely required some wealth.[64]

"CUSTOMARY" RULE AND THE POLITICS OF TENANTRY

The politics of tenancy became entangled with the colonial state's projects of rural rule. Colonial states in Africa pursued visions of rural rule that differentiated Africans along "tribal" lines. Under this system, Africans not only belonged to different "tribes," but each "tribe" was under the authority of a "tribal" chief, whom the colonial state incorporated as its local representative among his people. For the colonial state, the category of tribe only pertained to the "natives," whom it distinguished from settlers through race.[65] To sustain this vision, colonial officials constructed reserves as bounded spaces inhabited by members of a particular "tribe" where Africans accessed land by virtue of their membership in this corporate body.[66]

Africans threatened by land alienation turned the colonial image of the "tribe" on its head to sustain their own claims to land. In 1912, the owner of the farm Mbombo Flats demanded that Chief Makoni and his subjects pay rent or move off the land. At the time, the chief and a large number of his followers lived on a farm called Mbombovale but had fields on the neighboring farms, including Mbombo Flats. Makoni appealed to the native commissioner, stating that "as he is old and infirm, he did not care to move but preferred to remain on the spot where he had lived all his life and to be buried near the graves of his forefathers."[67] He was supported by the native commissioner, who suggested that the government should allow the chief and his people to occupy the nearby farm, Mt. Zonga, for the balance of his life. Thereafter, the Makoni people were to move into the south end of the Makoni Reserve.[68]

In the event, Chief Makoni and those of his subjects whose villages were enclosed in the farm Mbombovale did not move to the reserve. Instead, in 1922, the chief and his headmen negotiated for the purchase of the farm, arguing that it "contains the ancestral hills and home of the Makoni family and tribe."[69] The argument found purchase with the government, which was keen to keep its vision of a tribal Africa intact and shore up the authority of "customary" leaders as part of its grand scheme of indirect rule. "The main object to be served is to retain this land as the ancestral home of the chief of the Makoni tribe, and as a point of cohesion to hold the tribe together as a tribe," wrote the chief native commissioner in support of Makoni's request.[70]

Makoni's was one of the few cases in which chiefs successfully invoked the politics of graves to hang onto their ancestral lands.[71] Makoni's neighbor,

Chief Chipunza, together with some 405 households under his authority, also found their homes within the boundaries of land claimed by white settlers as farms.[72] In 1934, Chipunza petitioned the chief native commissioner to be allowed to remain on his ancestral lands, saying that his eviction would mean that nobody would tend his ancestors' graves, a key ritual performed by chiefs to request rains from the ancestors and ensure the fertility of the land, thereby legitimating their authority. The chief explained that his father kept him away from the missionary schools because he wanted Chipunza to sweep the graves of his ancestors. He also expressed his wish to be buried alongside his ancestors, whose remains were interred on the hills near his homestead.[73] Chief Chipunza and his people obtained temporary relief, but the colonial state ultimately evicted them.

In pursuing the policy of "tribal" spatial fixing, the colonial state was, however, tying itself in knots. Although in the Southern Rhodesian colonial state's imagination, segregation demarcated both racial and "tribal" lines, in practice, finding land that could accommodate such visions proved impossible. This complicated the colonial state's efforts to relocate Africans from alienated land into the few available reserves. At one time, the native commissioner for the district of Inyanga found himself unable to move Chief Mutasa's subjects from their historic territory of Manyika to Unyama because he believed that the African communities in the district "have to be quite different from each other and their original boundaries are distinct and observed today. Scotsdale," he argued, "is in Saunyama's country and it is no use suggesting to natives from Umtasa's that there is ground on Scotsdale."[74] Likewise, a special land committee set to look into the inadequacy of land for Africans in the Umtali District in 1931 pondered what to do with the people under Chief Zimunya who could not be accommodated on land earmarked for their settlement. The committee weighed the possibilities of moving them into the northeastern portion of the Maranke Reserve. Apart from the difficulty of finding additional land in the area, argued the committee, another factor to consider was "one of tribal mixture."[75] "Maranke Reserve has a chief with a number of headmen under him; each headman has a recognized area for the use of his people; and any people of a new tribe introduced into these areas is a constant source of friction and trouble," the committee argued.[76] The problem the colonial state faced was that a considerable influx of people could not be placed in any one area by themselves. "It follows that they would be placed, if moved into this reserve, into the areas of various headmen and so would accentuate the trouble," the committee concluded, adding that "for some years to come, administratively, it would be unwise to endeavour to force a settlement of this nature."[77] These officials exaggerated the differences—which, in practice, represented political rather than cultural identities—but such views led them to postpone plans to relocate African "squatters."

SEGREGATION, ENVIRONMENTALISM, AND THE CHANGING FORTUNES OF AFRICAN TENANTS, 1930–1950s

Rooted in custom and identity politics, arguments similar to those that Chiefs Makoni and Chipunza employed to retain access to their ancestral lands worked as long as the colonial state's modes of rural rule rested on the "customary" authority of chiefs and headmen. So too were concerns about ethnic spatial mixing. Between the late 1930s and the 1950s, however, colonial states became increasingly critical of "customary" authorities such as chiefs and headmen, whom they characterized as traditional, conservative, and antithetical to development. A 1948 assessment of the chiefs' abilities to carry the message of development by the native commissioner of the district of Inyanga gives us a sense of this attitude. "The four chiefs of the district are very old men, who are unable to give much assistance to the advancement of their people. They have done their best, but belong to the past, and fail to hold the respect of their more-travelled and enlightened subjects."[78] The Southern Rhodesian state, as chapter 5 shows, gradually shifted away from a dependence on "customary" authorities toward a reliance on a technocratic bureaucracy.[79]

The skepticism about chiefs' ability to spearhead colonial development and the shift toward technocrats developed from colonial officials' concerns over environmental degradation and declining productivity in the reserves. Both problems were consequences of colonial land and segregationist policies. The Southern Rhodesian colonial state institutionalized racial segregation through the Land Apportionment Act (LAA). Passed by the colony's legislature in 1930, the LAA, like the shift from "customary" to technocratic modes of rural rule, had far-reaching consequences for African access to land in the colony. Not only did the act enshrine racial segregation as a principle of land distribution in the country's statute books, it also allocated the half of the country's land that was best suited for agriculture to European settlers.[80] The law further abolished rent agreements on white-owned land, effectively making it illegal for Africans to reside in white areas except as laborers.

In the short term, the Land Apportionment Act caused anxieties among Native Affairs Department officials, who had to find land to accommodate thousands of soon-to-be-evicted former tenants and "squatters." Shouldering the burden of finding land for the Africans under their authority, Department of Native Affairs officials operating in northeastern Zimbabwe were quick to point to the difficulties of implementing the act in its 1930 form. "The application of the Land Apportionment Act will probably be more difficult in Umtali district than in any other, for there are 18,000 natives living on alienated land, a huge proportion of whom will have to be moved," wrote the chief native commissioner in March 1931. "The largest reserve in the District, the Maranke," he continued, "is said to be unsuitable for the bulk of people who will have to move. The remaining Reserves are small and, with the exception of Zimunya, thickly populated. The Native Purchase Area is not large."[81] The officials requested that more land in the district should be set aside for African occupation.

In response, the administration set up a Special Native Land Committee later that year to explore the possibilities of acquiring additional land for Africans in Umtali. This committee recommended that the Gilmerton farm be set aside for Africans. The committee invoked the principles of segregation enshrined in the Land Apportionment Act to make their case. "To our mind, it would be unthinkable that 'Stewarton North' and 'Dora Estate' should be created Native Area, leaving 'Gilmerton' as European area. Gilmerton would be in such circumstances an absolute island between the aforementioned two properties and the two native reserves Zimunya and Maranke and this would be the negation of the whole principle on which the policy of land segregation has hitherto been approached," they reasoned.[82]

The same committee pointed to the difficulties of finding land for Africans north of the city of Umtali, the historic territory of the Manyika kingdom, because of the scale of alienations there. It recommended that the administration should purchase privately held land, arguing that many of the farms were, at any rate, already occupied by rent-paying Africans. In 1935, the Umtali native commissioner requested the acquisition of more settler-owned land for African occupation in the historic portions of the Manyika kingdom. W. Selwyn Bazely, the Umtali native commissioner, invoked the familiar arguments about the undesirability of mixing "tribes," as well as the highlanders' reluctance to relocate to low-lying lands, which were hot and malarial. Bazely further invoked history to explain why the Manyika deserved to retain their ancestral lands. "Mutasa, chief of the Manyika tribe, voluntarily granted the use of his country to the BSA Company in preference to the Portuguese in 1890," he said.[83] "Mutasa and the Manyika," Bazely elaborated a year later,

> were in no way subordinate to Lobengula but were entirely independent in 1890. If Mutasa had chosen the Portuguese in preference to the British, the River Odzi would now be the boundary of

> Southern Rhodesia as the Imperial British Government would have insisted on the Portuguese retaining Manicaland. As it was he made a voluntary treaty with the British South Africa Company. Mutasa steadily supported the British South Africa Company in 1893 and 1896 and never rebelled. As a reward for this he was deprived of all his land except Mt Bingaguru (the present tiny Mutasa South Reserve) and the small Manyika reserve in the Inyanga district. About 30,000 to 40,000 Manyika Natives were left to pay rent to landowners who were mostly absentees, or to work in return for the right to live on the land of their ancestors. It is doubtful whether there was ever such another disgraceful breach of faith in the whole history of the British Empire.[84]

Bazely argued that the government could restore this faith by setting aside land for the Manyika. He added the benefits of keeping the Manyika contented. "As loyal subjects," he warned, "they can be most useful; as disaffected ones, they may cause considerable trouble."[85] Bazely's protestations came to naught. The Rhodesian settler state was unwilling to subtract an inch from the vast lands it had set aside for white settlement so as to accommodate landless Africans.

What complicated matters was that while members of the Department of Native Affairs pointed to the challenges of evicting Africans resident on alienated land and requested that more land be set aside for African occupation, a clique within the settler society that included individual settlers and members of the Department of Lands relentlessly pushed for the removal of Africans from settler farms. This push gained traction in the late 1930s when more and more officials raised concerns over environmental degradation on land held by Africans.[86] Opponents of African presence on settler farms used these concerns to call for the eviction of the Africans.[87] In December 1937, the Lands Department pushed for the eviction of African tenants on Yorkshire Estate in Makoni District, arguing that "cultivation by these natives is seriously damaging the farm."[88] Six years later, in 1943, the Natural Resources Board decried what it considered to be severe land degradation caused by African "squatters" on alienated land. "The evils described by the Natural Resources Commission [of 1939] as attendant to so called 'kaffir' farming and squatters on Crown land cannot be strongly emphasized," wrote the board's chairman, Robert McIlwaine.[89] He regretted the limitations imposed on the implementation of the Land Apportionment Act by wartime conditions, adding that "in the meantime, unrestrained destruction of the land, so common among squatters, goes on apace by large numbers of natives who are in occupation contrary to the terms of the Act."[90] The plight of Africans resident on alienated and Crown land was to worsen in the postwar period.[91] Thousands of Africans were forcibly evicted from alienated land to give way to postwar European immigrants, not only in Inyanga and Umtali but elsewhere in Southern Rhodesia.[92] These included people like Chief Chipunza and his subjects, who a decade earlier had deployed ideas of tradition to remain on their ancestral lands.

The discourse of degradation was so powerful that even missionaries adopted it to evict African tenants on mission farms. In 1951, the priest-in-charge at Bonda Mission gave nineteen tenants notice to leave the farm, citing both their unwillingness to fulfill their part of the contract and the threat that their stock caused to the environment. "Yesterday," he wrote, "I counted the tenants' cattle & find that they have one hundred head of cattle more than the agreement allows. This," he continued, "is a very serious matter in view of the drought especially. Something will have to be done immediately to reduce the cattle & to get the tenants off. . . . I really cannot allow them to remain here in view of the damage they are doing."[93] The Anglican missionary at Bonda Mission was not alone in using environmental declensionist arguments to justify the removal of his African tenants. Two elders whose families were tenants at the Roman Catholic mission farm at Chishawasha recounted stories of missionaries who threatened to evict any tenants who refused to undertake environmental conservation measures as prescribed by the Native Land Husbandry Act of 1951.[94]

DISPLACEMENT, RESETTLEMENT, AND THE LOCAL POLITICS OF LAND, CA. 1940–CA. 1955

The colonial state resettled the Africans that were evicted by white landowners in the reserves. By the mid-1940s, these areas were already overpopulated.[95] As we have already seen, in 1946 the Svosve Reserve was "in a very critical condition."[96] It was "46% overstocked and . . . 166% overpopulated."[97] Things were no better in the Zimunya Reserve. There, grazing land was by 1949 "in poor condition . . . despite the fact that approx. ½ of Reserve was rested for 4 months."[98]

The arrival of new families in these overcrowded areas deepened competition for land while producing conflicts over authority. This was born out of the fact that colonial land alienation and displacement produced results that contrasted with what the architects of native policy envisaged. Instead of residing in neatly bounded communities under the leadership of a local leader—kraalhead, headman, or chief—Africans living under conditions of land scarcity defied boundary making and the authority of local officials.

Consider, for example, the case of people under headmen Muponda and Mupotedzi. Following their displacement from Ruunji farm in 1944, Muponda and his people relocated to the Honde valley. There, conflicts with their neighbors, the people under the headman Mupotedzi, soon erupted. Although the boundary between the two communities was fixed, the disputes continued because some of Mupotedzi's people were living in Muponda's area "but pay[ing] tax under Mupotedzi's book and . . . d[id] not listen to Muponda."[99] Moreover, some of Muponda's people had lands in Mupotedzi's area though they lived in Muponda's area.[100] By creating conditions of land scarcity and then forcing Africans to live and farm within customarily defined areas, the colonial state created conflicts not only between itself and its subjects but also among Africans.

The conflicts between people under headmen Mupotedzi and Muponda, then, remind us of the complexities of struggles over land that colonial rule generated in Zimbabwe. By dispossessing Africans of their land and parceling it out to white settlers, the colonial state generated racialized disparities. However, the resultant conflicts quickly cascaded beyond race. They also pitted colonial officials against one another just as they produced conflicts within African communities. This complexity is what I emphasize both in this chapter and throughout the book. As Africans fought to remain on their lands, their struggles became entangled in debates over segregation, modes of rural rule, and environmental change.

Postscript

The Longue Durée, the Recent Past, and the Nexus between Land and Power

THE STORY told in this book revolves around power and land. It is a story of social relations and how they informed access to a crucial productive resource. It is also a story of the place of land in the making of power over territory. The book shows that, by the mid-sixteenth century, the people of northeastern Zimbabwe possessed fine-grained knowledge of land's different qualities. They also recognized differential power relations rooted in kinship, gender, seniority, and status and understood that these forms of power mediated access to good farming land. Colonial rule deepened these inequalities by, for example, assigning land to male heads of households, disenfranchising, in the process, women and junior men.

Locating power at the center of how land was accessed among Africans from precolonial times through the late colonial period illuminates several issues. An extensive literature on land and society in African societies before colonial rule gives the sense that community members accessed land in equal measure. Two long-standing assumptions account for this. The first is the assumption that in precolonial Africa, land was plentiful, and the scarce factors of production were labor and capital. Consequently, so the argument goes, no one, not even the political elites, sought to monopolize land. The second is the idea that in African societies, land was owned communally and membership in the community ensured access to land.

This understanding acknowledges that individuals could be excluded from landownership outside their communities but is oblivious to the fact that unequal power relations created landed inequities within the bounds of community. This book identifies these power relations and demonstrates their central role in shaping how individuals claimed and excluded others from the land in northeastern Zimbabwe from the mid-sixteenth century onward. In the process, it argues that power, rather than availability alone, was pivotal to how resources, including land, were claimed, controlled, and accessed. This remains the case today.

Society, Power, and Land shows how many chiefly lineages living in the shadow of powerful kingdoms from the mid-sixteenth century onward asserted their autonomy and legitimated their power by claiming a landed domain—territory. By explaining how their ancestors acquired land and chieftainships through their relations with subject populations, the traditional histories of these lineages temper standard scholarly accounts that attribute the distribution of political authority on the Zimbabwean plateau after 1500 to the leadership of famed kingdoms such as the Mutapa and Rozvi states. For the leaders of many polities in northeastern Zimbabwe there was no "big brother"; independent dynasties presided over territories of varied sizes.[1] Even those chiefly lineages that justified their claims to land and authority by invoking the support of Rozvi elites did so in furtherance of local politics rather than in reflection of their bigger neighbors' powers. At the same time, the book demonstrates that, beginning even earlier than the sixteenth century, the ability to ensure the land's fertility added another axis of power to life on the plateau. Those seen to wield such were able to rival and limit chiefs' powers. Later, when colonial officials attempted to strengthen the power of chiefs and male elders, authority over land remained contested.

Throughout the period covered in this book, then, unequal power relations produced landed inequalities, but the power that led to such outcomes was always contested. This continued in the decades after 1960. Granted, as the rest of Africa marched toward independence, the settler state entrenched itself in Zimbabwe. It also sought to centralize rural authority in the hands of chiefs whom it portrayed as the authentic representatives of Africans in a wedge strategy intended to divide Africans and undercut the appeal of nationalism.[2] To this end, the Rhodesian Front government granted chiefs some judicial power that preceding regimes had long denied them. But the colonial state was never able to silence those who contested its hegemony. In fact, the racialized inequalities in land that it upheld, and other grievances, drove Africans to swell the ranks of nationalists and to support the liberation struggle.[3] Many Zimbabweans saw through the facade of tradition that the Rhodesian Front government deployed in its attempts to strengthen chiefs' powers.

African experience with colonial racialized dispossession and authoritarianism would inform understandings of land and power in the postcolonial period.[4] Once political independence arrived in 1980, the new government initiated a land resettlement program meant to address colonially induced racialized inequalities. Its initial goal was to settle those displaced by the war of independence and the landless from communal areas.[5] The postcolonial government's ambitions were handicapped by the Lancaster House constitution, which restricted compulsory land acquisition by the state for ten years. The new government was forced to adopt a willing buyer–willing seller model of land acquisition. It could only procure land that was on the market at prevailing prices.

There were several problems with this model, which was clearly meant to protect the interests of large-scale landowners, most of whom were white. The new government lacked financial resources, and land purchases were a significant drain on the treasury. The 1981 Zimbabwe Conference on Reconstruction and Development (ZIMCORD) was intended to raise funds for the reconstruction of the broader economy. Although $1.45 billion in aid was pledged, not all the pledges were honored.[6] Soon, donor fatigue set in, accompanied by accusations of corruption, and foreign aid for land reform was reduced to a trickle. Ultimately, donor funds fell far short of the amounts needed for reconstruction and the acquisition of land for resettlement. Prices tended to rise in response to government interest in acquiring land. And sellers were inclined to offer marginal or inferior land for sale. The government redistributed about three million acres to an estimated 50,000 households during the 1980s.[7] This was a very modest success when measured against the lofty goal of resettling 162,000 families on ten million hectares of land.[8] What is more, most of the land that the government acquired for resettlement was in the poorer agroecological regions (classified three and four), far less suited to crop cultivation than regions one and two.[9]

In the 1990s the pace of land acquisition and resettlement slowed considerably. By the end of the millennium, government had acquired a total of 3.5 million hectares over twenty years. Only 20,000 additional families received land in the 1990s.[10] Several factors account for this slowdown in land acquisition. One was an embrace of "neoliberal, monetarist macro-economic and trade policies as well as export oriented sectorial policies in agriculture," under the Economic Structural Adjustment Program (ESAP) sponsored by the International Monetary Fund (IMF).[11] The Land Acquisition Act of 1992 (passed after the ten-year ban on compulsory land acquisition in the Lancaster House constitution had lapsed) perpetuated the willing buyer–willing seller model of land acquisition at a time when the Zimbabwean economy was slowing down and fiscal space was shrinking. Additional allegations of corruption in the use of previous aid led to a further decline in external financial support for land reform. To compound the problem of limited funds, in 1997, the Zimbabwean economy, which had been slowing down since the late 1980s, slipped into crisis with the government's decision to deploy its army in the Congo and to pay a one-time gratuity of ZW$50,000 to veterans of the war of independence. Neither expenditure was budgeted for. A campaign to raise funds for land acquisition achieved little success, and the state's attempt to expedite compulsory purchase of 1,471 farms was frustrated by litigation initiated by the landowners.

Against this backdrop, grassroots demand for land grew louder. In 1998, peasants from the Svosve communal lands occupied large-scale commercial farms bordering their communities. Things came to a head two years later when the ZANU (PF) government faced the most formidable challenge to its power since independence, the newly formed Movement for Democratic Change (MDC), and Zimbabweans rejected a new constitution that provided for compulsory land acquisition.[12] The outcome of the constitutional referendum was a clear rebuke to the country's leadership. In response ZANU (PF) revisited the land question. Following a wave of farm invasions, the government announced its Fast Track Land Reform Programme (FTLRP). By 2008, it had acquired 6,818,727 hectares of land from white commercial farmers and resettled 163,141 Black indigenous households, effectively doubling in eight years the amount of land acquired and the numbers settled in the preceding two decades.[13] Much criticized for the way it was conducted, the FTLRP undid the racial structure of landholding that had commenced with the arrival of colonial rule in the late nineteenth century.

There was much merit in efforts to address racialized land inequalities. There for all to see, the racialized land disparities were deeply unjust, a stain on the polity and an encumbrance on the future. But a laser-like focus on the colonial legacy of racialized inequality hindered progress toward transcendent justice. Many commentators have criticized the manner in which land reform was implemented, especially the violence that accompanied it. On the hostility and bloodshed that accompanied reform, they certainly had a point. But this was made with little recognition that the resolute focus on colonially induced racial disparities left other old inequities intact. Women reaped few benefits from the reforms of the 1980s and 1990s.[14] As shown in this book, and as a study of landholding patterns at the end of the millennium noted, "patriarchal land tenure systems . . . consistently discriminated against women."[15] Even the FTLRP failed to address these disparities.[16] "Women," Prosper Matondi (the author of a 2012 study of the FTLRP) found, "were the last beneficiaries after men were satisfied with their choice of plots." Even an oft-described "radical" reform program failed women by shunning the need and opportunity to improve their access to land.[17]

The land reform exercise also excluded farmworkers, many of whom were descendants of immigrants from Malawi, Mozambique, and Zambia.[18] This group bore the brunt of the violence that accompanied the FTLRP. Zimbabwe's postcolonial rulers denied these individuals and their families land because their framing of land and belonging was—and continues to be—informed by colonial nativist narratives.[19] These narratives reduced people to "settlers" and "natives" to justify expropriation, exclusion, and racial and ethnic spatial fixing.[20] When the postcolonial state appropriated the categories of "settler" and "native," it excluded from the nation both non-African races and other "subject minorities."[21] Denying these groups land only entrenched the politics and the fact of exclusion, because many of them considered landownership important to their sense of belonging to the country.[22]

Zimbabwe's former president, Robert Mugabe, encapsulated the state's conceptualization of land, race, and belonging. "This country is our country, and this land is our land," he said in a speech that clearly coded "our" to reference Black Zimbabweans. "They," he added, in reference to Zimbabweans of European descent, "think because they are white, they have a divine right to our resources. Not here. The white man is not indigenous to Africa. Africa is for Africans. Zimbabwe is for Zimbabweans."[23] The president also excluded Malawian, Mozambican, and Zambian immigrants and their descendants, Coloureds (those of mixed racial parentage), and urbanites, whom he infamously disparaged as "undisciplined, totemless elements of alien origin," from his conception of true Zimbabweans.[24] This insult, understood by many locals to communicate illegitimacy, meant that members of these groups had no legitimate claims to the land or other resources of Zimbabwe.

Mugabe's characterization of these peoples rested on the understanding that lineage was traced through the father's line. From this it followed that only those sired by Zimbabwean fathers and who knew their totems belonged to Zimbabwe. Immigrants lacked Zimbabwean totems, and "outsiders" (presumably sired by male labor migrants and Zimbabwean women) could not claim the totems of their maternal relatives. Descendants of immigrants and urbanites were further excluded because they did not have a rural home. Ironically, this idea is based in part on the colonial method of demarcating land (native reserves) for specific "tribes."[25] As Phineas Chihota, a deputy minister, told Parliament in 2005, "An indigenous person is one who has a rural home allocated to him by virtue of being indigenous."[26] Section 8(2)(b) of the Communal Lands Act reinforces this point when it states that when granting permission to the occupation of communal lands, "a rural district council shall," among other things, "grant consent only to persons who, according to the customary law of the community that has traditionally and continuously occupied and used land in the area concerned, are regarded as forming part of such community or who, according to such customary law, may be permitted to occupy and use such land."[27] In this conception, immigrants were excluded because as residents of urban townships and farm and mine *komboni*s (compounds), they did not have rural homes.

Ideas of nativity and "tribe" were also used locally to exclude Shona and non-Shona-speaking immigrants from other parts of the Zimbabwean plateau. In fact, when combined with competition for resources, ideas of nativity and "tribe" are a well-tested recipe for racial and ethnic tensions.[28] In 2002, Nobbie Dzinzi, the ZANU (PF) Member of Parliament for Muzarabani, reportedly "ordered all people originally from Masvingo and Buhera districts [Karanga speakers] now living in his constituency to move out."[29] Muzarabani, a district in the Zambezi valley, is mostly inhabited by people who speak the Korekore dialect of Central Shona. Following a cotton boom in the area in the 1980s, this and other parts of northern and northwestern Zimbabwe witnessed an influx of immigrants from south-central Zimbabwe.[30] These people spoke the Chikaranga dialect of Central Shona, and their presence among a majority Korekore-speaking population eventually triggered tensions over land and belonging.[31]

One aim of this book is to highlight how gender, generation, status, and kinship shaped access to land on the Zimbabwean plateau through several centuries and to implore scholars and policy makers to keep these structures of power and the inequities they engender in mind when addressing historical inequalities in resource distribution. The book also partly underscores the point that for at least five centuries, if not longer, the people of the Zimbabwean plateau challenged or subverted their leaders' impulses to concentrate power over land in their own hands. This continued after 1960. To be sure, the colonial state intransigently entrenched itself in the 1960s and 1970s and sought, as it had done before, to concentrate rural authority in the hands of chiefs. Its goal in pursuing the disingenuously named policy of "community development" was to portray chiefs as the authentic representatives of rural Africans and to undercut the appeal of nationalists calling for African liberation.[32] In the end, the colonial scheme came to naught, because Africans understood that many of their chiefs had become colonial functionaries.[33] Deeply aggrieved over the dispossession of their land by the colonial regime, and other factors, they joined the nationalist cause and fought to end colonial rule.

Following Zimbabwe's independence in 1980, the postcolonial government withdrew power over rural land from chiefs and passed it to elected party functionaries.[34] At the same time, the ruling elites sought to centralize power in their hands through a one-party state. But neither effort was successful. The postcolonial state, like its predecessor, the settler state, retained control over land in the communal areas (the reserves of the colonial era), but its party functionaries floundered in their efforts to exercise absolute authority and, like the one-party state, ultimately failed.

Just as prior generations had done, many Zimbabweans flouted increasingly centralized authority by approaching chiefs, headmen, and village heads to access land.[35] But the lingering efficacy of traditional practices that worked to limit the centralization of authority has declined as state institutions have strengthened their power in land matters. Ironically, this concentration of power received a boost with the introduction of the FTLRP. The new Land Acquisition Act (2001), as amended, gives the state president or his appointee power to acquire "(a) any land, where the acquisition is reasonably necessary . . . for a purpose beneficial to the public generally or to any section of the public; (b) any rural land, . . . (i) for settlement for agricultural or other purposes; or (ii) for purposes of land reorganization, forestry, environmental conservation or the utilization of wildlife or other natural resources; or (iii) for the relocation of persons dispossessed pursuant to these provisos."[36]

The implication here is that the president or his appointee can remove rural land users, including beneficiaries of the FTLRP, because they occupy state land. It is precisely for this reason that powerful members of the ruling elite have been emboldened, and able, to displace whole communities to provide senior officials with large landholdings or to convert extensive areas to the production of stock feed.[37] *Society, Power, and Land* reminds Zimbabweans and others concerned with questions of access to land everywhere in the former colonial world that if the quest for equity envisioned in land reforms is to be meaningful, the state needs to democratize this process and to be attentive to the voices and needs of its citizens. States also need to create strong institutions that serve to check the impulses of those in power. And, in addition to addressing racialized inequalities inherited from the colonial experience, land reforms need to overcome old forms of exclusion rooted in ideas of kinship, gender, generation, and status. This is true for Zimbabwe as for other parts of Africa, because power, in these guises, structures how resources are accessed everywhere on the continent.

Appendix A

Language Relationships

TABLE A.1. RATES OF COGNITION BETWEEN DIFFERENT SHONA LANGUAGES AND/OR DIALECTS

	S10_ Nyanga	S15_ Ndau	S16B_ Nambya	S16_ Kalanga	S14_ Karanga	S12_ Zezuru	S13_ Manyika	S11_ Korekore
S10_Nyanga								
S15_Ndau	76%							
S16B_Nambya	63%	66%						
S16_Kalanga	61%	72%	78%					
S14_Karanga	77%	86%	72%	79%				
S12_Zezuru	77%	87%	71%	81%	95%			
S13_Manyika	77%	83%	69%	75%	93%	95%		
S11_Korekore	77%	83%	64%	70%	87%	89%	87%	

Note: Eastern Shona (Nyanga and Ndau) and Western Shona (Kalanga and Nambya) have the lowest number of shared cognates. Central Shona dialects have the highest number of shared cognates, showing a much more recent divergence.

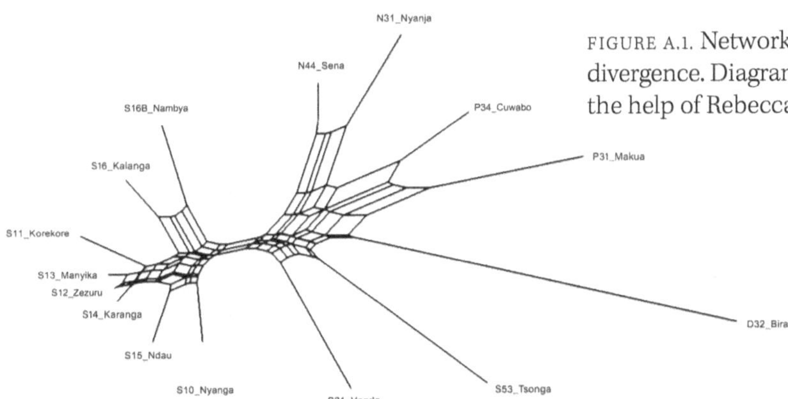

FIGURE A.1. Network sequence of divergence. Diagram created with the help of Rebecca Grollemund.

Appendix B

Lexical Items

The lexical items follow the order in which they appear for the first time in textual material.

Root: **-jícò* (BLR3, 3405)

Gloss: eye

Protolanguage: Bantu

Shona Distribution:

Kalanga: *hhího*
Nambya: *ızhıhso*
Nyanga: *dzıso*
Ndau: *dzıso*
Karanga: *ziso*
Zezuru: *ziso*
Manyika: *ziso*
Korekore: *ziso*

Other Bantu: BLR3 Zones A, B, C, D, E, F, G, H, J, K, L, M, N, P, R, S

Root: **-júbà* (BLR3, 1614; Guthrie, C.S. 955)

Gloss: sun

Protolanguage: Bantu

Shona Distribution:

Kalanga: *hhuba*
Nambya: *ızhuba*
Nyanga: *zuwa*
Ndau: *zuwa*

Karanga: *zuva*
Zezuru: *zuva*
Manyika: *zuwa*
Korekore: *zuva*

Other Bantu: BLR3 Zones A, B, C, D, E, F, G, H, J, K, L, M, N, P, R, S

Root: *-*dímì* (BLR3, 973; Guthrie, C.S. 572)

Gloss: tongue

Protolanguage: Bantu

Shona Distribution:

Kalanga: *lulımı*
Nambya: *lulımı*
Nyanga: *rurumı*
Ndau: *rurumı*
Karanga: *rurimi*
Zezuru: *rurimi*
Manyika: *rurimi*
Korekore: *rurimi*

Other Bantu: BLR3 Zones A, B, C, D, E, F, G, H, J, K, L, M, N, P, R, S

Root: *-*dáad* (BLR3, 795; Guthrie, C.S. 454, C.S. 455, C.S. 456)

Gloss: sleep

Protolanguage: Bantu

Shona Distribution:

Kalanga: *lala*
Nambya: *lala*
Nyanga:
Ndau:
Karanga:
Zezuru: *rara*
Manyika: *rara*
Korekore:

Other Bantu: BLR3 Zones A, B, C, D, E, F, G, H, J, K, L, M, N, P, R, S

Root: *-*jìkà*

Gloss: savanna

Protolanguage: Mashariki

Shona Distribution:

Kalanga: *nyika* (country, territory, land)

Nambya: *nyika*
Nyanga: *nyika*
Ndau: *nyika*
Karanga: *nyika*
Zezuru: *nyika*
Manyika: *nyika*
Korekore: *nyika*

Other Bantu: BLR3 Zones E, G, M, S

Note: De Luna glosses this as "grassland/floodplain," possibly the meaning in Shona too (de Luna, "Collecting Food, Cultivating Persons," 474).

Root: **gùdùbè* (BLR3, 1494; Guthrie, C.S. 888)

Gloss: bushpig

Protolanguage: proto-Savanna

Shona Distribution:
Kalanga: *nguluve*
Nambya: *ingulube*
Nyanga: *nguruwe*
Ndau: *nguruve*
Karanga: *nguruve*
Zezuru: *nguruve*
Manyika: *nguruwe*
Korekore: *nguruve*

Other Bantu: BLR3 Zones A, B, C, D, E, F, G, H, J, K, L, M, N, P, R, S

Root: *-*gùè* (BLR3, 8668; Guthrie, C.S. 834)

Gloss: leopard

Protolanguage: proto-Bantu

Shona Distribution:
Kalanga: *ŋgwe*
Nambya *ingwe*
Nyanga: *parugwe*
Ndau:
Karanga: *ngwe*
Zezuru: *ingwe*
Manyika: *ingwe*
Korekore:

Other Bantu: The authors of BLR 3 point out that this is a reflex of *-*gòì*, which has a wider distribution in Zones A, B, C, D, E, H, J, K, M, N, R, S.

Note: Ndau dropped this root and replaced it with *khamba*. However, like Central Shona dialects, Ndau uses *dindingwe* for "cheater."

Root: *-*pembele* (BLR3, 1754)

Gloss: black rhinoceros

Protolanguage: Mashariki

Shona Distribution:

Kalanga:
Nambya:
Nyanga:
Ndau: *chipembere*
Karanga: *chipembere*
Zezuru: *chipembere*
Manyika: *chipembere*
Korekore: *chipembere*

Other Bantu: BLR3 Zones M and S

Note: Karanga, Manyika, and Zezuru also retain *nhema* for the rhinoceros. The identification of this item as a proto-Mashariki root is based on Ehret, *An African Classical Age*, 42.

Root: *-*gululu*

Gloss: klipspringer

Protolanguage: Mashariki

Shona Distribution:

Kalanga: *ngululu*
Nambya: *ingululu*
Nyanga: *ngururu*
Ndau: *ngururu*
Karanga: *ngururu*
Zezuru: *nguruu*
Manyika:
Korekore: *nguruu*

Note: The identification of this item as a proto-Mashariki root is based on Ehret, *An African Classical Age*, 42.

Root: **-pàdá* (BLR3, 2355; Guthrie, C.S. 1411)

Gloss: antelope impala

Protolanguage: Bantu?

Shona Distribution:

Kalanga: *mhala*
Nambya: *imhalapala*
Nyanga: *mhara*
Ndau: *mhara*
Karanga: *mhara*
Zezuru: *mhara*
Manyika:
Korekore: *mhara*

Other Bantu: BLR3 Zones C, E, F, G, J, L, M, P, R, S

Root: **-tùìgà* (BLR3, 3028; Guthrie, P.S. 468)

Gloss: giraffe

Protolanguage: Mashariki

Shona Distribution:

Kalanga: *khwiza*
Nambya: *inhwizha*
Nyanga: *inwizha*
Ndau: *hushu*
Karanga: *twiza*
Zezuru: *twiza*
Manyika: *twiza*
Korekore: *twiza*

Other Bantu: BLR3 Zones E, F, G, J, S

Root: *gìdì*

Gloss: warthog

Protolanguage: proto-Mashariki (BLR3, 1376; Guthrie, C.S. 814)

Shona Distribution:

Kalanga:
Nambya: *injili*
Nyanga:
Ndau:
Karanga: *njiri*
Zezuru: *njiri*

Manyika: *njiri/njidi*
Korekore: *njiri*

Other Bantu: BLR3 Zones E, F, G, J, K, M, N, S

Root: *-*sịumba* (BLR3, 616)

Gloss: lion

Protolanguage: Mashariki

Shona Distribution:

Kalanga: *humba*
Nambya: *isumba*
Nyanga: *shumba*
Ndau: (dropped *shumba* for *mbhondoro/mphondoro*)
Karanga: *shumba*
Zezuru: *shumba* (also uses *mhondoro* but continues to use *shumba*)
Manyika: *shumba*
Korekore: *shumba* (for the most part uses *mhondoro*)

Other Bantu: BLR3 Zones A, C, D, E, F, G, H, J, K, L, M, N, P, R, S

Note: BLR 3 gives this root as *-*címbà.*

Root: *-*poku* (BLR3, 2601; Guthrie, C.S. 1574)

Gloss: eland

Protolanguage: Mashariki

Shona Distribution:

Kalanga:
Nambya: *imhofu*
Nyanga:
Ndau: *mpofu*
Karanga: *mhofu*
Zezuru: *mhofu*
Manyika: *mhofu*
Korekore: *mhofu*

Other Bantu: BLR 3 Zones F, G, S

Note: The identification of the protolanguage is based on Ehret, *An African Classical Age,* 42.

Root: *-*biji*

Gloss: zebra

Protolanguage: Kusi

Shona Distribution:

Kalanga: *mbizi*
Nambya: *imbizi*
Nyanga:
Ndau: *mbizi/mbhizi*
Karanga: *mbizi*
Zezuru: *mbizi*
Manyika: *mbizi*
Korekore: *mbizi*

Note: This identification of the protolanguage is based on Ehret, *An African Classical Age*, 42. It should be noted that de Luna suggests this might be an older Savanna term. She explains that "Botatwe attestations follow the expected sound correspondences" (de Luna, "Collecting Food, Cultivating People," 473).

Root: **-jògù* (BLR3, 1607; Guthrie, C.S. 951)

Gloss: elephant

Protolanguage: proto-Bantu

Shona Distribution:

Kalanga: *hhou*
Nambya: *izhou*
Nyanga:
Ndau: *nzou*
Karanga: *zhou*
Zezuru: *nzou*
Manyika: *nzou*
Korekore: *nzou*

Other Bantu: BLR3 Zones A, B, C, D, E, F, G, J, K, L, M, N, R, S

Root: **-játì* (BLR3, 1569; Guthrie, C.S. 927)

Gloss: buffalo

Protolanguage: proto-Bantu

Shona Distribution:

Kalanga: *nyathi*
Nambya: *inyati*
Nyanga:
Ndau:
Karanga: *nyati*

Zezuru: *nyati*
Manyika: *nyati*
Korekore: *nyati*

Other Bantu: BLR3 Zones A, B, C, E, G, M, N, P, R, S

Root: *-*kongoni* (BLR3, 6862)

Gloss: large antelope

Protolanguage: Mashariki

Shona Distribution:

Kalanga: *nkonkoni*
Nambya: *inkolomu*
Nyanga: *ngongoni*
Ndau:
Karanga: *ngongoni*
Zezuru:
Manyika: *ngongoni,* hartebeest
Korekore:

Other Bantu: BLR3 Zones G and S

Note: This identification of the protolanguage is based on Ehret, *An African Classical Age,* 300.

Root: *pogu(e/a)*

Gloss: ostrich

Protolanguage: Kusi

Shona Distribution:

Kalanga: *mhowu*
Nambya: *imhou/impou*
Nyanga:
Ndau: *mphowani*
Karanga: *mhou*
Zezuru: *mhou*
Manyika: *mhowani*
Korekore: *mhowani*

Other Bantu: BLR3 Zones R and S

Note: This identification of the protolanguage is based on Ehret, *An African Classical Age,* 300. It also appears to be the same root as *-*pòí* (BLR3, 7163).

Root: *-*káŋgà* (BLR3, 1720; Guthrie, C.S. 1010)

Gloss: guineafowl

Protolanguage: Bantu

Shona Distribution:

Kalanga: *hhanga*
Nambya: *ihanga*
Nyanga: *hanga*
Ndau: *hanga/ganga*
Karanga: *hanga*
Zezuru: *hanga*
Manyika: *hanga*
Korekore: *hanga*

Other Bantu: BLR3 Zones A, B, C, D, E, F, G, H, J, K, L, M, N, P, R, S

Root: *-*gúim-* (BLR 3, 1525; Guthrie, C.S. 904)

Gloss: to hunt

Protolanguage: proto–Eastern Savanna

Shona Distribution:

Kalanga: *vima*
Nambya: *kuvwima*
Nyanga:
Ndau:
Karanga: *vhima*
Zezuru: *vhima*
Manyika: *vhima*
Korekore: *vhima*

Other Bantu: BLR3 Zones E, F, G, M, S

Root: *-*tég-* (BLR3, 2825; Guthrie, C.S. 1698)

Gloss: to set trap

Protolanguage: Bantu

Shona Distribution:

Kalanga: *teya*
Nambya: *teya*
Nyanga: *teya*
Ndau: *teya*
Karanga: *teya*
Zezuru: *teya*

Manyika: *teya*
Korekore: *teya*

Other Bantu: BLR 3 Zones B, D, E, F, G, H, J, L, M, P, S

Root: *-*ta* (BLR3, 9207; Guthrie, C.S. 1631)

Gloss: bow

Protolanguage: proto-Bantu

Shona Distribution:

Kalanga:
Nambya:
Nyanga: *uta*
Ndau: *uta*
Karanga: *vuta*
Zezuru: *uta*
Manyika: *wuta*
Korekore: *wuta*

Other Bantu: BLR 3 Zones A, B, C, D, E, F, G, H, K, L, M, N, P, R, S

Note: BLR3 has this root as *-*táà.*

Root: *-*cèbè* (BLR3, 503; Guthrie, P.S. 82)

Gloss: arrow

Protolanguage: Eastern Sahelian loan in Kusi

Shona Distribution:

Kalanga: *nsebe*
Nambya: *unsebe*
Nyanga: *museve*
Ndau: *musee*
Karanga: *museve*
Zezuru: *museve*
Manyika: *museve*
Korekore: *museve*

Other Bantu: BLR 3 Zones N and S

Root: *-*túmò* (BLR 3, 3109 and 3110)

Gloss: spear

Protolanguage: proto-Bantu

Shona Distribution:

Kalanga: *thumo*

Nambya: *ifhumo*
Nyanga:
Ndau:
Karanga: *pfumo*
Zezuru: *pfumo*
Manyika: *pfumo*
Korekore: *pfumo*

Other Bantu: BLR 3 Zones D, E, G, J, L, M, N, S

Root: *-*bùjú* (BLR 3, 354; Guthrie, C.S. 214)

Gloss: baobab tree

Protolanguage: Savanna

Shona Distribution:

Kalanga: *mbuyu*
Nambya: *umbuyu/ibuyu*
Nyanga:
Ndau:
Karanga: *vuyu*
Zezuru: *uyu*
Manyika: *wuyu*
Korekore:

Other Bantu: BLR 3 Zones C, G, M, N, S

Root: *-*júkì* (BLR 3, 3350 and 6225; Guthrie, C.S. 962)

Gloss: bee, honey

Protolanguage: proto-Bantu

Shona Distribution:

Kalanga: *nyúchi*
Nambya: *buchi*
Nyanga:
Ndau: *uchi*
Karanga: *vuchi*
Zezuru: *uchi*
Manyika: *uchi*
Korekore: *wuchi, nyuchi*

Other Bantu: BLR3 Zones A, B, C, D, E, F, G, H, J, K, L, M, N, P, R, S

Note: According to BLR3, 6225 is a derivative of 3350.

Root: *-*gùndà* (BLR 3, 1509; Guthrie, C.S. 897)

Gloss: cultivated field

Protolanguage: Bantu

Shona Distribution:

Kalanga: *nnda*
Nambya: *unda*
Nyanga: *munda*
Ndau: *munda*
Karanga: *munda*
Zezuru: *munda*
Manyika: *munda*
Korekore: *munda*

Other Bantu: BLR3 Zones A, B, C, D, E, F, G, K, M, N, R, S

Root: *-*bègú* (BLR3, 140; Guthrie, C.S. 96)

Gloss: seed

Protolanguage: Mashariki

Etymology: proto-Bantu verb *-*bèg-*, "to snap/break (off)"

Shona Distribution:

Kalanga: *mbewu*
Nambya: *imbeyu*
Nyanga: *mbeyu*
Ndau: *mbeu*
Karanga: *mbewu*
Zezuru: *mbeu*
Manyika: *mbewu*
Korekore: *mbeyu*

Other Bantu: BLR3 Zones E, G, J, N, S

Note: The etymology is based on Ehret, *An African Classical Age,* 128. Guthrie reconstructs this root as *-*béyù.*

Root: *-*tem-* (BLR3, 2832; Guthrie, C.S. 1703)

Gloss: to cut (vegetation in clearing for cultivation)

Protolanguage: Bantu

Shona Distribution:

Kalanga: *tema*
Nambya: *tema*

Nyanga: *tema*
Ndau: *tema* (to cut)
Karanga: *tema*
Zezuru: *tema*
Manyika: *tema*
Korekore: *tema*

Other Bantu: BLR3 Zones A, B, E, F, G, J, K, L, M, N, P, S

Root: *témò* (BLR 3, 2836; Guthrie, C.S. 1706)

Gloss: ax/hoe

Protolanguage: Mashariki

Etymology: proto-Mashariki verb, "to cut down"

Shona Distribution:

Kalanga:
Nambya: *idemo*
Nyanga: *demo*
Ndau:
Karanga: *demo*
Zezuru: *demo*
Manyika: *demo*
Korekore: *demo*

Other Bantu: BLR3 Zones B, D, E, H, K, L, M, N, R, S

Note: The etymology and gloss are based on Ehret, *An African Classical Age*, 267.

Root: *-*lìm*- (BLR 3, 968)

Gloss: to cultivate

Protolanguage: Bantu

Shona Distribution:

Kalanga: *lima*
Nambya: *lima*
Nyanga: *rima*
Ndau: *rima*
Karanga: *rima*
Zezuru: *rima*
Manyika: *rima*
Korekore: *rima*

Other Bantu: BLR3 Zones B, C, E, F, G, J, K, L, M, N, P, R, S

Root: *-*bíad-* (BLR3, 165; Guthrie, C.S. 99)

Gloss: to sow

Protolanguage: Mashariki

Shona Distribution:

Kalanga: *dzwala*
Nambya: *kubyala*
Nyanga: *kuzvara*
Ndau:
Karanga: *dzvara*
Zezuru: *dyara*
Manyika: *zhara/dyara*
Korekore: *jara/dyara*

Other Bantu: BLR 3 Zones A, G, J, L, M, N, S

Root: *-*pànd-* (BLR3, 2387; Guthrie, C.S. 1434)

Gloss: to plant

Protolanguage: Mashariki

Etymology: proto-Bantu verb, "to split"

Shona Distribution:

Kalanga: *pandila*
Nambya:
Nyanga:
Ndau: *panda*
Karanga: *pandira*
Zezuru: *pandira*
Manyika: *pandira*
Korekore:

Other Bantu: BLR 3 Zones L, M, S

Note: The etymology and gloss are based on Ehret, *An African Classical Age*, 28.

Root: *-*càkud* (BLR 3, 429; Guthrie, C.S. 263)

Gloss: weed

Protolanguage: Savanna

Etymology: proto-Savanna noun, "-*càká*, thicket"

Shona Distribution:

Kalanga: *shakula*
Nambya: *kushakula*

Nyanga: *tsakura*
Ndau: *shakura*
Karanga: *shakura*
Zezuru: *sakura*
Manyika: *sakura*
Korekore: *sakura*

Other Bantu: BLR3 Zones E, F, G, H, J, L, M, N, S

Root: *-*púúd* (BLR3, 2628; Guthrie, C.S. 1590)

Gloss: to thresh

Protolanguage: proto-Mashariki

Shona Distribution:

Kalanga: *-pula*
Nambya: *-bhula*
Nyanga:
Ndau:
Karanga: *-pura*
Zezuru: *-pura*
Manyika:
Korekore:

Other Bantu: BLR3 Zones D, E, F, G, J, L, M, N, S

Root: *-*pepet* (BLR3, 2465; Guthrie, C.S. 1488a)

Gloss: to winnow

Protolanguage: proto-Mashariki?

Shona Distribution:

Kalanga:
Nambya: *kupyeka*
Nyanga: *pepeta*
Ndau:
Karanga: *pepeta/peya*
Zezuru: *pépeta*
Manyika:
Korekore:

Other Bantu: BLR 3 Zones A, B, J, K, L, R, S

Root: *-*selo* (BLR 3, 7851 as *-*cèdò*)

Gloss: winnowing tray

Protolanguage: Mashariki

Shona Distribution:

Kalanga: *luselo*
Nambya:
Nyanga: *rusero*
Ndau: *rutsero*
Karanga: *rusero*
Zezuru: *rusero*
Manyika: *rutsero*
Korekore:

Other Bantu: BLR3 Zones J and S

Root: *-*pùdį* (BLR3, 2631; Guthrie, C.S. 1593)

Gloss: pumpkin

Protolanguage: Mashariki?

Shona Distribution:

Kalanga: *mahhudzi*
Nambya: *izhuji*
Nyanga: *budzi*
Ndau: *budzi*
Karanga: *budzi*
Zezuru: *budzi*
Manyika: *budzi*
Korekore: *budzi*

Other Bantu: BLR3 Zones E, L, M, N, S

Root: *-*tùdì* (BLR3, 3042; Guthrie, C.S. 1820)

Gloss: mortar

Protolanguage: Eastern Sahelian loanwords in proto-Mashariki

Replaces: *nú?*

Shona Distribution:

Kalanga: *duni*
Nambya: *iduri*
Nyanga: *duri*
Ndau: *duri*
Karanga: *duri*
Zezuru: *duri*
Manyika: *duri*
Korekore: *duri*

Other Bantu: BLR3 Zones E, L, M, N, S

Note: The identification of this root's protolanguage follows Ehret, *An African Classical Age*, 51.

Root: **-jìcì* (BLR3, 6054)

Gloss: pestle

Protolanguage: Mashariki?

Shona Distribution:

Kalanga: *mwisi*
Nambya: *nsi*
Nyanga: *mutwi*
Ndau: *mutço*
Karanga: *musi*
Zezuru: *mutsi*
Manyika: *mutwo*
Korekore: *mutsi*

Other Bantu: BLR3 Zones D, E, G, K, L, N, P, R, S

Root: **-gòmbè* (BLR3, 1434; Guthrie, C.S. 849)

Gloss: cow/cattle

Protolanguage: Mashariki

Shona Distribution:

Kalanga: *n'ombe*
Nambya: *in'ombe*
Nyanga: *n'ombe*
Ndau: *n'ombe*
Karanga: *n'ombe*
Zezuru: *mombe*
Manyika: *n'ombe*
Korekore: *n'ombe*

Other Bantu: BLR3 Zones C, D, E, F, G, H, J, K, L, M, N, P, R, S

Root: **-tàngá* (BLR3, 2795; Guthrie, C.S. 1679)

Gloss: herd; cattle pen

Protolanguage: Eastern Sahelian loanword to Kusi

Shona Distribution:

Kalanga: *dhanga*
Nambya: *idanga*

Nyanga: *danga*
Ndau: *danga*
Karanga: *danga*
Zezuru: *danga*
Manyika: *danga*
Korekore: *danga*

Other Bantu: BLR 3 Zones G, K, L, M, N, S

Note: The identification of this root's protolanguage follows Ehret, *An African Classical Age*, 135, 212.

Root: *-*kám*- (BLR3, 1688; Guthrie, C.S. 994)

Gloss: to milk

Protolanguage: Mashariki

Etymology: old [Bantu] verb for squeezing

Shona Distribution:

Kalanga: *kama*
Nambya: *kama*
Nyanga: *kama*
Ndau: *kama*
Karanga: *kama*
Zezuru: *kama*
Manyika: *kama*
Korekore: *kama*

Other Bantu: BLR3 Zones, B, C, D, E, F, G, H, J, K, L, M, N, P, R, S

Note: The identification of this root's protolanguage is based on Ehret, *An African Classical Age*, 134.

Root: *-*pulu*

Gloss: calf

Protolanguage: Kusi

Shona Distribution:

Kalanga: *mhulu*
Nambya:
Nyanga: *mhuru*
Ndau: *mphuru*
Karanga: *mhuru*
Zezuru: *mhuru*
Manyika: *mhuru*

Korekore: *mhuru*

Note: The identification of this root's protolanguage is based on Ehret, *An African Classical Age,* 67.

Root: *-*liis-*

Gloss: to herd (literally 'to feed')

Protolanguage: Mashariki

Etymology: proto-Bantu verb *-*lì-*, "to eat"

Shona Distribution:

Kalanga: *lisa*
Nambya: *kuembela*
Nyanga: *utsa*
Ndau: *usha*
Karanga: *risa*
Zezuru: *risa*
Manyika: *risa*
Korekore: *risa*

Note: The identification of this root's protolanguage and etymology is based on Ehret, *An African Classical Age,* 68.

Root: *-*búdì* (BLR3, 303; Guthrie, C.S. 185)

Gloss: goat

Protolanguage: proto-Bantu

Shona Distribution:

Kalanga: *mbúdzi*
Nambya: *imbuji*
Nyanga: *mbuzi*
Ndau: *mbudzi*
Karanga: *mbudzi*
Zezuru: *mbudzi*
Manyika: *mbudzi*
Korekore: *mbudzi*

Other Bantu: BLR 3 Zones A, B, C, D, E, F, G, J, L, M, N, P, S

Note: The identification of this root's protolanguage is based on Ehret, *An African Classical Age,* 105.

Root: *-*bùbo* (BLR3, 1530; Guthrie, C.S. 907)

Gloss: bellows

Protolanguage: Mashariki?

Shona Distribution:

Kalanga: *buto*
Nambya: *ivuto*
Nyanga: *pfuto/mvuto*
Ndau: *mvuto*
Karanga: *mvuto*
Zezuru: *mvuto*
Manyika: *mvuto*
Korekore: *mvuto*

Note: Guthrie reconstructs this root as *-*gùbò*.

Root: *jùndò* (BLR 3, 1628; Guthrie, C.S. 2171)

Gloss: hammer, anvil

Protolanguage: proto-Bantu

Shona Distribution:

Kalanga: *sando*
Nambya: *insando*
Nyanga: *nyundo*
Ndau: *nyundo*
Karanga: *nyundo*
Zezuru: *nyundo*
Manyika: *nyundo*
Korekore:

Other Bantu: BLR 3 Zones A, B, C, D, E, G, H, J, K, L, M, N, P, R, S

Root: *-*búmb* (BLR 3, 333; Guthrie, C.S. 199)

Gloss: to make pot

Protolanguage: proto-Bantu

Shona Distribution:

Kalanga: *bumba*
Nambya: *bumba*
Nyanga: *umba*
Ndau: *umba*
Karanga: *vumba*
Zezuru: *umba*
Manyika: *wumba*
Korekore: *wumba*

Other Bantu: BLR3 Zones B, C, D, E, F, G, H, J, K, L, M, N, P, S

Note: The identification of this root's protolanguage is based on Ehret, *An African Classical Age*, 121; Vansina, *How Societies Are Born*, 45.

Root: *-*limo*

Gloss: rainy season, "season at which cultivation commenced"

Etymology: *-*dim-*, "to cultivate"

Shona Distribution:

Kalanga: *chilimo* (summer season)
Nambya:
Nyanga: *shirimo*
Ndau: *chirimo*
Karanga: *chirimo*
Zezuru: *chirimo*
Manyika: *chirimo* (springtime)
Korekore: *chirimo*

Note: Both the gloss and the etymology are based on Ehret, *An African Classical Age*, 38.

Root: *-*saano*

Gloss: dry, possibly cool season, June to September

Protolanguage: Mashariki

Shona Distribution:

Kalanga:
Nambya:
Nyanga:
Ndau: *chando*
Karanga: *chando*
Zezuru: *chando*
Manyika: *chandu*
Korekore: *chando*

Note: The identification of this root's protolanguage is based on Ehret, *An African Classical Age*, 40.

Root: *-*cángó*

Gloss: forest, bush country, veld (uninhabited)

Protolanguage: Kusi?

Shona Distribution:

Kalanga: *hango* (country, earth, land)
Nambya: *ishango*
Nyanga:
Ndau: *shango* (veld, wilderness)
Karanga: *sango*
Zezuru: *sango*
Manyika: *sango*
Korekore: *sango*

Other Bantu: BLR3, Zones P and S

Root: **-tondo*

Gloss: thicket

Protolanguage: Kusi

Shona Distribution:

Kalanga:
Nambya: *ibhote*
Nyanga: *dondo*
Ndau: *dondo*
Karanga: *dondo*
Zezuru: *dondo*
Manyika: *dondo*
Korekore: *dondo*

Note: The identification of this root's protolanguage is based on Ehret, *An African Classical Age*, 38.

Root: **-toolo*

Gloss: bog, muddy place

Protolanguage: Eastern Sahelian loanwords in proto-Mashariki

Shona Distribution:

Kalanga:
Nambya:
Nyanga: *toro*
Ndau: *mutoro*
Karanga: *dóró*
Zezuru: *dóró*
Manyika: *dóró*
Korekore: *dóró*

Note: The identification of this root's protolanguage is based on Ehret, *An African Classical Age*, 51.

Root: *-*tòpè* (BLR3, 3002; Guthrie, C.S. 1797)

Gloss: mud

Protolanguage: Eastern Sahelian loanwords in proto-Mashariki

Shona Distribution:

Kalanga: *dope*
Nambya: *idope*
Nyanga: *matope*
Ndau: *matope*
Karanga: *dope*
Zezuru: *dope*
Manyika: *dope*
Korekore: *dope*

Other Bantu: BLR3 Zones A, B, G, J, N, P, S

Note: The identification of this root's protolanguage is based on Ehret, *An African Classical Age*, 51.

Root: *-*bú* (BLR3, 355; Guthrie, C.S. 215)

Gloss: soil

Protolanguage: Bantu

Shona Distribution:

Kalanga: *vhu*
Nambya: *ivu*
Nyanga: *ivhu*
Ndau: *ivhu*
Karanga: *vhu*
Zezuru: *ivhu*
Manyika: *ivhu*
Korekore: *ivhu*

Other Bantu: BLR 3 Zones A, C, D, E, F, G, J, K, L, M, P, R, S

Root: *-*dòngó* (BLR3 1138; Guthrie, C.S. 667)

Gloss: clay soil

Protolanguage: Savanna?

Shona Distribution:

Kalanga:

Nambya:
Nyanga: *dongo,* dark clay soil
Ndau: *dongo,* clay soil
Karanga:
Zezuru:
Manyika: *dongo,* clay soil
Korekore:

Other Bantu: BLR3 Zones E, F, G, J, L, M, N, S

Root: *gova*

Gloss: low-lying land/valley

Protolanguage: proto-Shona

Shona Distribution:

Kalanga: *goba*
Nambya: *igoba*
Nyanga: *gova*
Ndau: *mugova*
Karanga: *gova*
Zezuru: *gova*
Manyika:
Korekore: *gova*

Note: The presence of this word in all the Shona languages and/or dialects except for Manyika suggests that it might have been a proto-Shona innovation.

Root: *pani*

Gloss: wide, level land between hills

Protolanguage: proto-Shona

Shona Distribution:

Kalanga:
Nambya: *ibhani*
Nyanga: *pani*
Ndau: *bani* (valley)
Karanga: *bani*
Zezuru: *bani*
Manyika:
Korekore:

Note: The presence of this word in Western, Eastern, and Central Shona languages suggests that it might have been a proto-Shona innovation.

Root: **-céké*

Gloss: sand

Protolanguage: Bantu

Shona Distribution:

Kalanga: *nsetje*
Nambya: *unsechelele*
Nyanga:
Ndau: *sheshe*
Karanga: *jecha*
Zezuru: *jecha*
Manyika: *jecha*
Korekore: *jecha*

Other Bantu: BLR3 Zones A, B, C, D, H, J, K, L, M, N, R, S

Root: *-shapa*

Gloss: sandy soils of low fertility

Protolanguage: proto–East Central Shona

Shona Distribution:

Kalanga:
Nambya:
Nyanga: *mutsapa*
Ndau: *mushapa*
Karanga: *mushapa*
Zezuru: *mutsapa*
Manyika: *mutsapa; sapa*
Korekore: *mutsapa*

Note: This item is restricted to Eastern and Central Shona languages. It seems to have emerged only after East-Central Shona had diverged from Western Shona.

Root: *jiho*

Gloss: red clay soil country

Protolanguage: proto–East Central Shona

Shona Distribution:

Kalanga:
Nambya:
Nyanga: *jiho*
Ndau: *jiho*
Karanga: *jiho*

Zezuru:
Manyika: *jiho*
Korekore:

Note: This item is restricted to Eastern and Central Shona languages. It seems to have emerged only after East-Central Shona had diverged from Western Shona.

Root: *mhukutu*

Gloss: soil on side of a hill, mixed with detritus; any red soil

Protolanguage: proto–East Central Shona

Shona Distribution:

Kalanga:
Nambya:
Nyanga:
Ndau: *mphukutu*
Karanga: *mhukutu*
Zezuru: *mhukutu*
Manyika: *mhukutu*
Korekore:

Note: This item is restricted to Eastern and Central Shona languages. It seems to have emerged only after East-Central Shona had diverged from Western Shona.

Root: *dofo*

Gloss: soft, fertile vlei

Protolanguage: proto–Central Shona

Shona Distribution:

Kalanga:
Nambya:
Nyanga:
Ndau:
Karanga: *dofo*
Zezuru: *dofo*
Manyika:
Korekore:

Note: This item is restricted to dialects of Central Shona. It seems to have emerged only after Central Shona had diverged from Eastern Shona.

Root: *wova*

Gloss: rich red soils

Protolanguage: proto–Central Shona

Shona Distribution:

Kalanga:
Nambya:
Nyanga:
Ndau:
Karanga:
Zezuru: *wova/gova*
Manyika: *wowa/gova*
Korekore: *gova*

Note: This item is restricted to dialects of Central Shona. It seems to have emerged only after Central Shona had diverged from Eastern Shona.

Root: *bomho*

Gloss: narrow valley but open veld; grassy plain; treeless veld

Protolanguage: proto–East Central Shona

Shona Distribution:

Kalanga:
Nambya:
Nyanga:
Ndau: *bompho* (treeless veld; prairie)
Karanga:
Zezuru: *bomho*
Manyika: *bomho* (plain open veld)
Korekore:

Note: This item is restricted to Eastern and Central Shona languages. It seems to have emerged only after East-Central Shona had diverged from Western Shona.

Root: *gan'a*

Gloss: dry barren land

Protolanguage: proto–Central Shona?

Shona Distribution:

Kalanga:
Nambya:

Nyanga:
Ndau:
Karanga: *gan'a*
Zezuru: *gan'a*
Manyika: *gan'a*
Korekore: *gan'a*

Note: This item is restricted to dialects of Central Shona. It seems to have emerged only after Central Shona had diverged from Eastern Shona.

Root: *huludza*

Gloss: outstandingly successful farmer

Protolanguage: Shona

Shona Distribution:
Kalanga: *huludza*
Nambya:
Nyanga: *hurudza*
Ndau:
Karanga: *hurudza*
Zezuru: *hurudza*
Manyika: *hurudza*
Korekore: *hurudza*

Note: This root is a compounding of *kúdú* 'big' and **-dúsa,* another root for winnowing; its emergence may have to be understood in the context of small grains cultivation.

Root: **-kúdú* (BLR3, 2003; Guthrie, C.S. 1194, 1195, 1196, 1197, 1198)

Gloss: elder/senior, big, mature, adult, big, important

Protolanguage: Bantu

Shona Distribution:
Kalanga: *nkulu basekulu,* grandfather
Nambya: *nkulwana*
Nyanga:
Ndau:
Karanga: *mukuru,* elder, senior; *sekuru,* grandfather
Zezuru: *mukuru,* elder, senior; *sekuru,* grandfather
Manyika:
Korekore:

Other Bantu: BLR3 Zones B, D, E, G, H, J, K, L, N, R, S

Root: *-*dusa*

Gloss: to winnow

Protolanguage: Shona

Shona Distribution:

Kalanga: *wulusa*
Nambya:
Nyanga:
Ndau:
Karanga: *rudza*
Zezuru: *rudza*
Manyika: *wurusa*
Korekore:

Note: This item is found in Western and Central Shona. It is possible that the term was in use in proto-Shona times.

Root: *hombarume*

Gloss: expert hunter

Protolanguage: proto–Central Shona?

Etymology: unclear etymology

Shona Distribution:

Kalanga:
Nambya:
Nyanga:
Ndau:
Karanga: *hombarume*
Zezuru: *hombarume*
Manyika: *hombarume*
Korekore: *hombarume*

Note: This term is only found in the dialects of Central Shona, suggesting that it may be a Central Shona innovation. A variation, *nkombalume*, is found in Botatwe languages; as de Luna suggests, it is possible that it is a borrowing from Shona (see de Luna, "Collecting Food, Cultivating Persons," 594–96).

Root: *-*júbò/jú/jó* (BLR3, 1615/1610; Guthrie, C.S. 956/C.S. 953)

Gloss: house (rectangular, gabled)

Protolanguage: Bantu

Shona Distribution:

Kalanga: *hhuvo* (rendered by Masola [*Nau DzabaKalanga,* 176] as *xubo*)
Nambya: *nkoba* (reflex for this is *mukova*)
Nyanga:
Ndau: *musiwo* (door)
Karanga: *suwo* (doorway, entrance)
Zezuru: *suo* (doorway, entrance)
Manyika: *musuwo*
Korekore:

Other Bantu: BLR3 Zones B, J, H, L, S

Note: The identification of this root's protolanguage is based on Ehret, *An African Classical Age,* 152.

Root: *-*jùmbá* (BLR3, 3628)

Gloss: lineage

Protolanguage: Mashariki

Replaces: *-*gàndà;* *-*júbò/jú/jó*

Shona Distribution:

Kalanga: *n'umba*
Nambya: *ingumba*
Nyanga: *umba,* the kitchen
Ndau: *nyumba*
Karanga: *imba*
Zezuru: *imba*
Manyika: *nyumba*
Korekore: *imba*

Other Bantu: BLR3 Zones C, E, F, G, J, N, P, S

Root: *-*jooto* (BLR3, 2584)

Gloss: hearth

Protolanguage: Bantu?

Etymology: proto-Bantu *-*jot,* "to warm oneself"

Shona Distribution:

Kalanga:
Nambya: *choto*
Nyanga:
Ndau:
Karanga: *choto*

Zezuru: *choto*
Manyika:
Korekore:

Other Bantu: BLR3 Zones B, C, E, F, G, H, J, K, L, M, N, P, R, S

Note: Among Central Shona dialects, *choto* refers to the hearth but may also reference individual households in polygynous families. Each wife has a hearth, *choto,* from which she prepares food for her children. According to Vansina, among speakers of Njila languages in west-central Africa, **-jóoto* refers to "council house" as well as household or descent group. Vansina points out that the proto-Bantu **-jot* 'to warm oneself' "referred to all the inhabitants of a village" (Vansina, *How Societies Are Born,* 47).

Root: *-*bánjá* (BLR 3, 97 as a derivative of 8591)

Gloss: meeting place of men at a village

Shona Distribution:

Kalanga: *lubahe*
Nambya: *lubazhe*
Nyanga: *banze*
Ndau:
Karanga: *ruvazhe,* courtyard
Zezuru: *ruvanze,* courtyard
Manyika: *banze*
Korekore:

Other Bantu: BLR3 Zones B, C, D, E, F, G, H, J, K, L, M, N, S

Root: *-*kócì* (BLR3, 1871; Guthrie, C.S. 1101)

Gloss: "strong or mature person, extended family head; in this sense also an institution of political authority"

Protolanguage: Mashariki

Shona Distribution:

Kalanga: *bahosi/vawosi,* senior wife
Nambya:
Nyanga: *nyahotsi,* clan leader
Ndau: *vahosi*
Karanga: *vahosi,* senior wife
Zezuru: *vahosi,* senior wife
Manyika:
Korekore:

Other Bantu: BLR3, Zones G, L, M, N, S

Note: The gloss is based on Ehret, *An African Classical Age,* 146, 148–50.

Root: *-*dongo* (BLR3, 1135; Guthrie, C.S. 657, C.S. 658, C.S. 659)

Gloss: lineage

Protolanguage: Bantu

Shona Distribution:

Kalanga: *nlongo* (bride, daughter-in-law)
Nambya:
Nyanga: *murongoti* (sibling of the opposite sex)
Ndau: *murongo* (chief's wife)
Karanga: *murongo* (junior wife)
Zezuru: *murongo*
Manyika: *murongo* (king's/chief's wife)
Korekore:

Other Bantu: BLR3 Zones A, B, C, D, E, F, G, H, J, K, L, M, N, P, R, S

Note: Guthrie glosses C.S. 657 as "arrange," C.S. 659 as "heap up," and C.S. 659 as "pack carefully."

Root: *-*zìmù* (BLR3, 1050; Guthrie, C.S. 619)

Gloss: ancestral spirit

Protolanguage: Bantu

Etymology: dim, to extinguish

Shona Distribution:

Kalanga: *ndzimu* (God); *badzimu* (spirits of dead ancestors)
Nambya: *injimu*
Nyanga: *muzimu*
Ndau: *mudzimu* (Wilder [*Chindau-English Vocabulary*] glossed this as "personal ancestral spirit")
Karanga: *mudzimu*
Zezuru: *mudzimu*
Manyika: *mudzimu*
Korekore: *mudzimu*

Other Bantu: BLR3 Zones A, C, D, E, F, G, K, M, N, S

Root: *-*kúmù* (BLR3, 218)

Gloss: big man/ritual leader

Protolanguage: Bantu

Etymology: *-*kúm-*

Shona Distribution:

Kalanga: *mfumi*
Nambya: *umfumbu*
Nyanga:
Ndau: *mufumi* (rich person)
Karanga: *mufumi* (rich person)
Zezuru: *mufumi* (rich person)
Manyika: *mufumi* (rich person)
Korekore: *mufumi* (rich person)

Other Bantu: BLR 3 Zones A, B, C, G, H, J, K, L, M, N, P, R, S

Note: BLR3 linguists identify this as a derivative of **-kúm* (BLR3, 2113) and gloss it as "to be honored, to be rich." This meaning is found in the Shona nouns *mupfumi,* a rich person, and *pfuma,* wealth.

Root: **lobol-*

Gloss: bridewealth

Protolanguage: unclear, but the word has distribution in Shona and Nguni languages

Shona Distribution:

Kalanga:
Nambya: *ualoboli* (grooms); *balobolwa* (brides)
Nyanga:
Ndau: *roorgwa* (be married)
Karanga: *rovora* (bridewealth), *murovora* (daughter-in-law)
Zezuru: *roora* (bridewealth), *muroora* (daughter-in-law)
Manyika: *-roora* (bridewealth, be a partner in marriage)
Korekore: *-roora* (be a partner in marriage)

Other Bantu: Swati, Ndebele (Zimbabwe), Ndebele (South Africa), Bhaca, Mpondo, Zulu, Xhosa, Phuthi (Jimenez, "Rights of Reproduction")

Note: The root might date back to a time before proto-Shona emerged from its shared ancestor with Southeastern Bantu. It is shared across Shona and Nguni languages.

Root: *-padza*

Gloss: hoe

Protolanguage: proto-Shona

Replaces: **-gèmbè*

Shona Distribution:

Kalanga: *bhadza*
Nambya: *ibhaja*
Nyanga: *badza*
Ndau: *badza*
Karanga: *badza*
Zezuru: *badza*
Manyika: *badza*
Korekore: *badza*

Note: This word is found in all the Shona languages, suggesting that it is a proto-Shona innovation which replaced the old root *-*gèmbè*.

Root: *júmà* (BLR3, 3618)

Gloss: bead

Protolanguage: proto-Bantu

Shona Distribution:

Kalanga:
Nambya:
Nyanga:
Ndau:
Karanga: *chuma*
Zezuru: *chuma*
Manyika: *huma*
Korekore:

Other Bantu: BLR3 A, B, C, D, E, F, G, H, J, K, L, M, N, P, R, S

Root: *-ronzer*

Gloss: entrust livestock to another's care

Protolanguage: proto–Central Shona

Shona Distribution:

Kalanga:
Nambya:
Nyanga:
Ndau:
Karanga: *ronza*
Zezuru: *ronza*
Manyika:
Korekore:

Note: This root, with this precise meaning, is only found in Central Shona dialects, suggesting that the concept might have emerged after Central Shona diverged from Eastern Shona.

Root: **-éné* (BLR3, 3928)

Gloss: owner, master, chief, king

Protolanguage: Bantu

Shona Distribution:

Kalanga: *mweni*
Nambya: *mweni*
Nyanga:
Ndau: *mune* (owner)
Karanga: *mwene* (owner)
Zezuru: *mwene* (owner)
Manyika: *mwene* (owner)
Korekore: *Mwene* (title of the rulers of the Mutapa state)

Other Bantu: BLR3 Zones E, F, G, H, J, K, L, M, N, P, R, S

Root: *mhondoro*

Gloss: lion, especially one possessed by a territorial spirit; territorial spirit, one that possessed a human medium but also lived in a lion and medium of a territorial spirit

Protolanguage: Central Shona

Shona Distribution:

Kalanga:
Nambya:
Nyanga: *mhondoro*
Ndau: *mphondoro*
Karanga:
Zezuru: *mhondoro*
Manyika: *mhondoro*
Korekore: *mhondoro*

Note: This term's distribution is restricted to the northern dialects of Central Shona. Its variation, *mphondoro,* is found in Eastern Shona. It appears to me to be a Central Shona innovation that extended to Eastern Shona and nearby Nyanja-Sena languages (e.g., Chibaruwe) with the expansion of the influence of the Mutapa state.

Root: **tòngò* (BLR3, 6820)

Gloss: deserted hut

Protolanguage: Eastern Savanna?

Shona Distribution:

Kalanga: *dongo,* ruin, deserted house or home
Nambya: *idongo*
Nyanga: *dongo,* deserted village
Ndau: *dongo,* deserted hut
Karanga: *dongo*
Zezuru: *dongo*
Manyika: *dongo*
Korekore:

Other Bantu: BLR3 suggests that this item's distribution is limited to Zones J, L, and M in the Central and Northeastern regions, but in fact it extends to the Southeastern Bantu languages including Venda, Zulu, and Shona.

Root: **-bùè*

Gloss: stone

Protolanguage: Bantu

Shona Distribution:

Kalanga: *bgwe*
Nambya: *ibwe*
Nyanga: *ibwe*
Ndau: *buwe*
Karanga: *bwge*
Zezuru: *ibwge*
Manyika: *zihwe/ibwe*

Other Bantu: BLR3 Zones C, D, E, F, G, J, K, L, M, N, P, R, S

Root: **-yadi* (BLR3, 3158 [as **-jàdí*]; Guthrie, C.S. 1896)

Gloss: girl at puberty (but in Shona speech communities, this root has taken the meaning of God)

Protolanguage: Bantu

Shona Distribution:

Kalanga: *mwali*
Nambya: *mwali*
Nyanga:

Ndau: *mwari*
Karanga: *mwari*
Zezuru: *mwari*
Manyika: *mwari*
Korekore: *mwari*

Other Bantu: BLR3 Zones C, E, F, G, J, K, L, M, N, P, R, S

Note: For Zezuru, Manyika, and Korekore, George Fortune points out that this term as a reference to the creator God is a result of missionary interventions (Fortune, "Who Was Mwari?"). Northern Zimbabwean communities had neither such a concept nor a term for it. The term may have existed previously, however, because it appears among the Sabi languages as well as the Nyasa languages in East-Central Africa, referencing a different set of rituals (and ritual actors).

Root: *-tunhu*

Gloss: ward

Protolanguage: proto-Shona

Shona Distribution:

Kalanga: *dúthu* (low hill, heap), *ntunhu*
Nambya: *idunhu* (mountain, not hill)
Nyanga: *mutanha*
Ndau: *dunthu, mutunthu* (mountain, hill)
Karanga: *dunhu*
Zezuru: *dunhu*
Manyika: *dunhu*
Korekore: *dunhu*

Note: This same root is used for hill, mountain, lower open slopes of hill or mountain, and distance between places. *Dunhu* seems to have also meant a place, a piece of land to which one could make a claim. A Kalanga (South-West Shona) tradition on the construction of a family has the following injunction: "*kawana ntunhu unodan'wa ngezina lile, kalima, kawana zwidlo zwinji*" (and he should get a place which is called by his name, and he must plow [grow crops / cultivate] and get plenty of food) (Masola, *Nau DzabaKalanga*, 32–33).

Root: *gula*

Gloss: fallow field

Protolanguage: proto-Shona

Shona Distribution:

Kalanga: *gula*
Nambya:
Nyanga: *gura*
Ndau: *gura*
Karanga: *gura*
Zezuru: *gura*
Manyika: *gura*
Korekore: *gura*

Note: The item with this particular meaning appears to be a proto-Shona innovation from *-*càkud* (BLR3, 429), to weed. *Càkud* is itself a derivation of *-*càká* (BLR3, 423), bush or thicket. The act of clearing thickets, like weeding, appears to have legitimated claims to a piece of land even when it was left to fallow.

Notes

PREFACE

1. Jocelyn Alexander, "The Historiography of Land in Zimbabwe: Strengths, Silences and Questions," *Safundi: The Journal of South African and American Studies* 8, no. 2 (2007): 190–91.
2. Robin Palmer, *Land and Racial Domination in Rhodesia* (Berkeley: University of California Press, 1977); Henry V. Moyana, *The Political Economy of Land in Zimbabwe* (Gweru: Mambo Press, 2002); Ian R. Phimister, *An Economic and Social History of Zimbabwe, 1890–1948: Capital Accumulation and Class Struggle* (London: Longman, 1988).
3. Terence O. Ranger, *Peasant Consciousness and Guerrilla War in Zimbabwe: A Comparative Study* (London: James Currey, 1985); Terence O. Ranger, *Voices from the Rocks: Nature, Culture and History in the Matopos Hills of Zimbabwe* (Oxford, UK: James Currey, 1999); Ngwabi Bhebe, *Benjamin Burombo: African Politics in Zimbabwe* (Harare: College Press, 1989).
4. Jocelyn Alexander, *The Unsettled Land: State-Making and the Politics of Land in Zimbabwe, 1893–2003* (Oxford, UK: James Currey, 2006); William A. Munro, *The Moral Economy of the State: Conservation, Community Development and State-Making in Zimbabwe* (Athens: Ohio University Center for International Studies, 1998); George Hamandishe Karekwaivanane, *The Struggle over State Power in Zimbabwe: Law and Politics since 1950* (Cambridge: Cambridge University Press, 2017).
5. David Lan, *Guns and Rain: Guerrillas and Spirit Mediums in Zimbabwe* (London: James Currey, 1985).
6. Donald S. Moore, *Suffering for Territory: Race, Place and Power in Zimbabwe* (Durham, NC: Duke University Press, 2005); Joost Fontein, *Remaking Mutirikwi: Landscape, Water and Belonging in Southern Zimbabwe* (Woodbridge, UK: James Currey, 2015).

INTRODUCTION

1. Statement by His Excellency the President of the Republic of Zimbabwe Comrade R. G. Mugabe, on the Occasion of the World Summit on Sustainable Development, Johannesburg, 2 September 2002, http://www.un.org/events/wssd/statements/zimbabweE.htm.

2. Joseph Hanlon, Jeannette Manjengwa, and Theresa Smart, *Zimbabwe Takes Back Its Land* (Boulder, CO: Kumarian Press, 2013), 160.
3. Prosper B. Matondi, *Zimbabwe's Fast Track Land Reform* (London: Zed Books, 2012), 185.
4. Jocelyn Alexander, "The Historiography of Land in Zimbabwe: Strengths, Silences and Questions," *Safundi: The Journal of South African and American Studies* 8, no. 2 (2007): 190–91; Donald S. Moore, *Suffering for Territory: Race, Place and Power in Zimbabwe* (Durham, NC: Duke University Press, 2005); Joost Fontein, *Remaking Mutirikwi: Landscape, Water and Belonging in Southern Zimbabwe* (Woodbridge, UK: James Currey, 2015).
5. Elizabeth Schmidt, *Peasants, Traders and Wives: Shona Women in the History of Zimbabwe* (Portsmouth, NH: Heinemann, 1992); Diana Jeater, *Marriage, Perversion and Power: The Construction of a Moral Discourse in Southern Rhodesia, 1894–1930* (Oxford, UK: Clarendon Press, 1993); Teresa Barnes, *"We Women Worked So Hard": Gender, Urbanization and Social Reproduction in Colonial Harare, Zimbabwe, 1930–1956* (Portsmouth, NH: Heinemann, 1992).
6. Martha Kaplan, *Neither Cargo nor Cult: Ritual Politics and the Colonial Imagination in Fiji* (Durham, NC: Duke University Press, 1995), 2.
7. See, for example, the discussion in Jeater, *Marriage, Perversion and Power.*
8. Eugenia W. Herbert, *Iron, Gender and Power: Rituals of Transformation in African Societies* (Bloomington: Indiana University Press, 1993), 1.
9. Herbert, *Iron, Gender and Power,* 2.
10. Steven Feierman, *Peasant Intellectuals: Anthropology and History in Tanzania* (Madison: University of Wisconsin Press, 1990).
11. Pauline E. Peters, "Revisiting the Social Bedrock of Kinship and Descent in the Anthropology of Africa," in *A Companion to the Anthropology of Africa,* ed. Roy Richard Grinker, Steven C. Lubkemann, Christopher B. Steiner, and Euclides Gonçalves (Oxford, UK: John Wiley and Sons, 2019), 33–62; Alfred R. Radcliffe-Brown, introduction to *African Systems of Kinship and Marriage,* ed. Alfred R. Radcliffe-Brown and Daryll Forde (New York: Routledge, 2015), 1–85; Schmidt, *Peasants, Traders and Wives.*
12. Terence Ranger, "The Communal Areas of Zimbabwe," in *Land in African Agrarian Systems,* ed. Thomas J. Bassett and Donald E. Crummey (Madison: University of Wisconsin Press, 1993), 354–85; Angela P. Cheater, "The Ideology of 'Communal' Land Tenure in Zimbabwe: Mythogenesis Enacted?," *Africa: Journal of the International African Institute* 60, no. 2 (1990): 188–206.
13. Native Commissioner, Chibi District, Written Evidence, N3/6/3, NAZ; J[on] F. Holleman, *Chief, Council and Commissioner: Some Problems of Government in Rhodesia* (Assen: Royal VanGorcum, 1969), 62.
14. Holleman, *Chief, Council and Commissioner,* 62.
15. W. H. Stead, "The Clan Organization and Kinship System of Some Shona Tribes," *African Studies* 5, no. 1 (1946): 1–20; Peters, "Social Bedrock of Kinship," 34.
16. Peters, "Social Bedrock of Kinship," 36.

17. Marshall Sahlins, *What Kinship Is—And Is Not* (Chicago: University of Chicago Press, 2013), ix.
18. Sahlins, *What Kinship Is*, 1–2.
19. The quotation comes from Sahlins, *What Kinship Is*, 2. For conflict and hierarchies in kinship groups, see Robert Brightman, "Hierarchy and Conflict in Mutual Being," *HAU: Journal of Ethnographic Theory* 3, no. 2 (2013): 260.
20. William P. Murphy and Caroline H. Bledsloe, "Kinship and Territory in the History of a Kpelle Chiefdom (Liberia)," in *The African Frontier: The Reproduction of Traditional Societies*, ed. Igor Kopytoff (Bloomington: Indiana University Press, 1987), 127–28; Liazzat J. K. Bonate, "The Ascendance of Angoche: The Politics of Kinship and Territory in Nineteenth Century Northern Mozambique," *Lusotopie* 10 (2003): 115–40; Schmidt, *Peasants, Traders and Wives*, 17.
21. Schmidt, *Peasants, Traders and Wives*, 17.
22. Schmidt, 17.
23. Jack Goody, *Technology, Tradition and the State in Africa* (London: Oxford University Press, 1971); Gareth Austin, *Labour, Land and Capital in Ghana: From Slavery to Free Labor in Asante, 1807–1956* (Rochester: University of Rochester Press, 2005).
24. The quotation is from Goody, *Technology, Tradition*, 29–30. See also Paul Bohannan, "'Land,' 'Tenure' and Land Tenure," in *African Agrarian Systems*, ed. Daniel Biebuyck (New York: Oxford University Press, 1963), 101–15; Elizabeth Colson, "Land Rights and Land Use among the Valley Tonga of the Rhodesian Federation: The Background to the Kariba Resettlement Scheme," in Biebuyck, *African Agrarian Systems*, 137–56; Elizabeth Colson, "The Impact of the Colonial Period on the Definition of Land Rights," in *Colonialism in Africa*, vol. 3, *Profiles of Change: African Society and Colonial Rule*, ed. Victor Turner (Cambridge: Cambridge University Press, 1971), 193–215. The wealth in people thesis has its origins in studies of slavery and other social relations such as marriage in Africa. It emerges from scholars' efforts to understand why Africans enslaved other Africans before the rise of the Transatlantic Slave Trade or why they practiced polygamy. Igor Kopytoff and Suzzaine Miers, "Introduction: African Slavery as an Institution of Marginality," in Suzzaine Miers and Igor Kopytoff, eds., *Slavery in Africa: Historical and Anthropological Perspectives* (Madison: University of Wisconsin Press, 1977); Paul E. Lovejoy, *Transformations in Slavery: A History of Slavery in Africa* (Cambridge: Cambridge University Press, 2000); Joseph Miller, *Way of Death: Merchant Capitalism and the Angolan Slave Trade* (Madison: University of Wisconsin Press, 1988); Jan Vansina, *Paths in the Rain Forest: Toward a History of Political Tradition in Equatorial Africa* (Madison: University of Wisconsin Press, 1990).
25. Terence O. Ranger, *Peasant Consciousness and Guerrilla War in Zimbabwe: A Comparative Study* (London: James Currey, 1985), 28.
26. Colson, "Definition of Land Rights," 196.

27. Austin, *Labour, Land and Capital;* Sara Berry, *No Condition Is Permanent: The Social Dynamics of Agrarian Change in Sub-Saharan Africa* (Madison: University of Wisconsin Press, 1993), 22; David McDermott Hughes, *From Enslavement to Environmentalism: Politics on a Southern African Frontier* (Seattle: University of Washington Press, 2006).
28. Jane Guyer, "Wealth in People and Self-Realization in Equatorial Africa," *Man* 28, no. 2 (1993): 244.
29. Jane I. Guyer, "Wealth in People, Wealth in Things—Introduction," *Journal of African History* 36, no. 1 (1995): 84.
30. Jane I. Guyer and Samuel M. Eno Belinga, "Wealth in People as Wealth in Knowledge: Accumulation and Composition in Equatorial Africa." *Journal of African History* 36, no. 1 (1995): 93; Mariana P. Candido, *Wealth, Land and Property in Angola: A History of Dispossession, Slavery and Inequality* (Cambridge: Cambridge University Press, 2022).
31. Carola Lentz, *Land, Mobility and Belonging in West Africa* (Bloomington: Indiana University Press, 2013), 9.
32. Candido, *Wealth, Land, and Property,* 1.
33. Candido, 4.
34. Lentz, *Land, Mobility and Belonging,* 18.
35. Lentz, 19.
36. Gerald Chikozho Mazarire, "The *Gadzingo:* Towards a Karanga Expansion Matrix in 18th- and 19th-Century Southern Zimbabwe," *Critical African Studies* 5, no. 1 (2013): 4–16.
37. Mazarire.
38. Mazarire, 5.
39. Mazarire, 8.
40. See Martinus Daneel, *God of the Matopo Hills: An Essay on the Mwari Cult of Rhodesia* (The Hague: Mouton, 1970); Ngwabi Bhebe, "The Ndebele and Mwari before 1893: A Religious Conquest of the Conquerors by the Vanquished," in *Guardians of the Land: Essays on Central African Territorial Cults,* ed. Mathew J. Schoffeleers (Gweru: Mambo Press, 1979), 287–95; Mathew J. Schoffeleers and R. Mwanza, "An Organizational Model for the Mwari Shrines," in Schoffeleers, *Guardians of the Land,* 297–315; Terence O. Ranger, *Voices from the Rocks: Nature, Culture and History in the Matopos Hills of Zimbabwe* (Oxford, UK: James Currey, 1999).
41. Peter Fry, *Spirits of Protest: Spirit Mediums and the Articulation of Consensus among the Zezuru of Southern Rhodesia (Zimbabwe)* (Cambridge: Cambridge University Press, 1976); Michael Gelfand, "The Mhondoro—Chaminuka," *Native Affairs Department Annual* 36 (1959): 6–10; David Lan, *Guns and Rain: Guerrillas and Spirit Mediums in Zimbabwe* (London: James Currey, 1985).
42. In some parts of the British Empire, the colonial state attempted to use chiefs in urban governance. See, for example, Naaborko Sackeyfro, *The Politics of Chieftaincy: Authority and Property in Colonial Ghana, 1920–1950* (Rochester: University of Rochester Press, 2014).

43. Murray C. Steele, "The Foundations of a 'Native' Policy in Southern Rhodesia, 1923–1933" (PhD diss., Simon Fraser University, 1972).
44. Mahmood Mamdani, *Citizen and Subject: Contemporary Africa and the Legacy of Late Colonialism* (Princeton: Princeton University Press, 1996). See also Mahmood Mamdani, *When Victims Became Killers: Colonialism, Nativism, and the Genocide in Rwanda* (Princeton: Princeton University Press, 2001); Mahmood Mamdani, *Define and Rule: Native as Political Identity* (Cambridge, MA: Harvard University Press, 2012).
45. Terence O. Ranger, "Invention of Tradition in Colonial Africa," in *The Invention of Tradition,* ed. Eric J. Hobsbawm and Terence O. Ranger (Cambridge, Cambridge University Press, 1983), 211–62; Martin Chanock, *Law, Custom and Social Order: The Colonial Experience in Malawi and Zambia* (Cambridge: Cambridge University Press, 1985).
46. Terence Ranger, "The Invention of Tradition Revisited: The Case of Colonial Africa," in *Legitimacy and the State in Twentieth Century Africa,* ed. Terence Ranger and O. Vaughan (Houndsmills, UK: Macmillan, 1993), 81.
47. Sara Berry, "Hegemony on a Shoestring: Indirect Rule and Access to Agricultural Land," *Africa* 62, no. 3 (1992): 327–55; Berry, *No Condition Is Permanent.*
48. Steven Feierman, quoted in Thomas T. Spear, "Neo-traditionalism and the Limits of Invention in British Colonial Africa," *Journal of African History* 44, no. 1 (2003): 6; see also Feierman, *Peasant Intellectuals.*
49. Michael Drinkwater, *The State and Agrarian Change in Zimbabwe's Communal Areas* (Houndsmills, UK: Macmillan, 1991); Moore, *Suffering for Territory;* Jocelyn Alexander, *The Unsettled Land: State-Making and the Politics of Land in Zimbabwe, 1893–2003* (Oxford, UK: James Currey, 2006); George Hamandishe Karekwaivanane, *The Struggle over State Power in Zimbabwe: Law and Politics since 1950* (Cambridge: Cambridge University Press, 2017), 47–80.
50. Karekwaivanane, *Struggle over State Power.*
51. Christopher Ehret and Margaret Kinsman, "Shona Dialect Classification and Its Implications for Iron Age History in Southern Africa," *International Journal of African Historical Studies* 14, no. 3 (1981): 401–43. See also C. H. Borland, "Conflicting Methodologies of Shona Dialect Classification," *South African Journal of African Languages* 4, no. 1 (1984): 1–12; George M. Fortune, "Linguistics and Prehistory," in *Essays in Shona Dialects,* ed. George Fortune (Harare: University of Zimbabwe, 2004), http://www.edd.uio.no/allex/ibooks/fortune/index.html.
52. Terence Ranger, "Missionaries, Migrants and the Manyika: The Invention of Ethnicity in Zimbabwe," African Studies Seminar Paper, African Studies Institute, University of the Witwatersrand (1984), 1–38; Terence Ranger, *The Invention of Tribalism in Zimbabwe* (Gweru: Mambo Press, 1985); Herbert Chimhundu, "Early Missionaries and the Ethnolinguistic Factor during the Invention of Tribalism in Zimbabwe." *Journal of African History* 33, no. 1 (1992): 87–109.
53. David N. Beach, "History and Archaeology in Nyanga," annex in Robert C. Soper, *Nyanga: Ancient Fields, Settlements and Agricultural History in*

Zimbabwe (London: British Institute in Eastern Africa, 2002), 227; Gerald Chikozho Mazarire, "Reflections on Precolonial Zimbabwe, *c.* 850–1880s," in *Becoming Zimbabwe: A History from the Precolonial Period to 2008,* ed. Brian Raftopoulos and Alois S. Mlambo (Harare: Weaver Press, 2009), 3–5.

54. Sixteenth-century Portuguese documents record the language spoken in the Mutapa state as Mokaranga. Joao Dos Santos, "Eastern Ethiopia," in *Records of South-Eastern Africa,* vol. 7, ed. George M. Theal (Cape Town: C. Struik, 1964), 274.
55. David N. Beach, *A Zimbabwean Past: Shona Dynastic Histories and Oral Traditions* (Gweru: Mambo Press, 1994), xv.
56. George Kay, *Rhodesia: A Human Geography* (New York: African Publishing Corporation, 1970), 16–21.
57. Robert Soper, *Nyanga: Ancient Fields, Settlements and Agricultural History in Zimbabwe* (London: British Institute in Eastern Africa, 2002).
58. The quotation is from Hoyini H. K. Bhila, *Trade and Politics in a Shona Kingdom: The Manyika and Their Portuguese and African Neighbours* (London: Longman, 1983), 6; see also James Goldsmith Thompson, "The Soils of Rhodesia and Their Classification" (PhD thesis, University of Natal, 1965), 2–3; Assistant Native Commissioner, Umtali, to Chief Native Commissioner, 22 December 1896, NUA2/1/1, NAZ.
59. For the Shawasha immigration, see Joshua Chidziva, "History of the VaShawasha," *Native Affairs Department Annual* 9, no. 1 (1964): 16–33. Gerald Chikozho Mazarire, "A Social and Political History of Chishanga: South-Central Zimbabwe, *c.*1750–2000" (DPhil thesis, University of Zimbabwe, 2009).
60. Interview with Chief Muchenje Chinamhora, AOH 73, NAZ.
61. Chinamhora interview.
62. Bhila, *Trade and Politics;* Antonio Bocarro, "Decade of the Performances of the Portuguese in the East," in Theal, *Records of South-Eastern Africa,* vol. 3, 355–56; Pedro Baretto de Rezende, "Of the State of India," in Theal, *Records of South-Eastern Africa,* vol. 2, 414; Donald P. Abraham, "The Principality of Maungwe: Its History and Traditions," *Native Affairs Department Annual* 28 (1951): 56; Beach, *The Shona and Zimbabwe: An Outline of Shona History* (Gweru: Mambo Press, 1980), 166.
63. Alexander, *Unsettled Land,* 7.
64. Alexander; William A. Munro, *The Moral Economy of the State: Conservation, Community Development and State-Making in Zimbabwe* (Athens: Ohio University Center for International Studies, 1998); Karekwaivanane, *Struggle over State Power.*
65. Ben Cousins and Steven Robins, "Institutions for Land Redistribution and Management: The Zimbabwean Experience," *South African Sociological Review* 6, no. 2 (1994): 32–55; Alexander, *Unsettled Land;* Drinkwater, *State and Agrarian Change.*
66. Karekwaivanane, *Struggle over State Power,* 47.

67. See, among others, Alexander, *Unsettled Land;* Munro, *Moral Economy;* Moore, *Suffering for Territory;* Fontein, *Remaking Mutirikwi;* Karekwaivanane, *Struggle over State Power.*
68. Paul J. Sinclair, *Space, Time and Social Formation: A Territorial Approach to the Archaeology and Anthropology of Zimbabwe and Mozambique, c.0–1700 AD* (Uppsala: Societas Archaeologica Upsaliensis, 1987); James Denbow, "A New Look at the Later Prehistory of the Kalahari," *Journal of African History* 27, no. 1 (1986): 10–25.
69. For a study that focuses on non-elite sites, see Gilbert Pwiti, *Continuity and Change: An Archaeological Study of Farming Communities in Northern Zimbabwe, AD 500–1700,* Studies in African Archaeology 13 (Uppsala: Department of Archaeology and Ancient History, Uppsala University, 1996). For the recent shift from well-known elite sites, see Shadreck Chirikure, Munyaradzi Manyanga, A. Mark Pollard, Foreman Bandama, Godfrey Mahachi, and Innocent Pikirayi, "Zimbabwe Culture before Mapungubwe: New Evidence from Mapela Hill, South-Western Zimbabwe," *PLoS One* 9, no. 10 (2014): 1–18.
70. Christopher Ehret, *Southern Nilotic History: Linguistic Approaches to the Study of the Past* (Evanston, IL: Northwestern University Press, 1971); Christopher Ehret, *An African Classical Age: Eastern and Southern Africa in World History* (Charlottesville: University of Virginia Press, 1998); Christopher Ehret, *History and the Testimony of Language* (Berkeley: University of California Press, 2011); Jan Vansina, *Paths in the Rain Forest: Toward a History of Political Tradition in Equatorial Africa* (Madison: University of Wisconsin Press, 1990); Jan Vansina, *How Societies Are Born: Governance in West Central Africa before 1600* (Charlottesville: University of Virginia Press, 2004); David L. Schoenbrun, *A Green Place, A Good Place: Agrarian Change, Gender and Social Identity in the Great Lakes Region to the 15th Century* (Heinemann, NH: Portsmouth, 1998); Kathryn M. de Luna, *Collecting Food, Cultivating People: Subsistence and Society in Central Africa* (New Haven, CT: Yale University Press, 2016); Kathryn M. de Luna and Jeffrey B. Fleisher, *Speaking with Substance: Methods of Language and Materials in African History* (Cham, Switzerland: Springer, 2019).
71. Vansina, *Paths in Rain Forest,* 12. See also Ehret, *History and Testimony of Language,* 3–4.
72. David L Schoenbrun, "Early African Pasts: Sources, Interpretations, and Meanings," in *The Oxford Research Encyclopedia, African History* (Oxford: Oxford University Press, 2018), 6.
73. Vansina, *Paths in Rain Forest,* 13.
74. Vansina, 13.
75. Ehret, *History and Testimony of Language,* 30.
76. Christopher Ehret, "Outlining Southern African History: A Re-evaluation, AD 100–1500," *Ufahamu: A Journal of African Studies* 3, no. 1 (1972): 9–28; Ehret and Kinsman, "Shona Dialect Classification."

77. This is usually done with a list of hundred words that are assumed to be resistant to cultural influence.
78. Vansina, *Paths in Rain Forest,* 12.
79. Ehret, *History and Testimony of Language,* 28. For the Shona languages, a few words illustrate this point. The proto-Bantu "j" becomes "hh" or "zh" in Western Shona, "dz" in Eastern Shona, and "z" in Central Shona. The proto-Bantu **-jícò* (eye) becomes *hhiho* in Kalanga (Western Shona), *izhıso* in Nambya, *dziso* in Nyanga and Ndau, and *ziso* in the Central Shona dialects of Karanga, Korekore, Manyika, and Zezuru. Similarly, the proto-Bantu **-júbà* (sun) becomes *hhuba* in Kalanga, *izhuba* in Nambya, and *zuva* in Eastern and Central Shona languages. Likewise, the proto-Bantu "d" becomes "l" in Western Shona and "r" in Eastern and Central Shona. Thus, the proto-Bantu **-dímì* (tongue) becomes *lulimi* in Kalanga and Nambya, *rurumi* in Ndau and Nyanga, and *rurimi* in the Central Shona dialects of Karanga, Korekore, Manyika, and Zezuru. And the proto-Bantu **-dáad* (sleep) becomes *lala* in Western Shona and *rara* in Central Shona.
80. I am grateful to Rebecca Grollemund, my former colleague at the University of Missouri–Columbia, for helping me with figure A.1.
81. Rebecca Grollemund, David Schoenbrun, and Jan Vansina, "Moving Histories: Bantu Language Expansions, Eclectic Economies, and Mobilities," *Journal of African History* 64 (2023): 1–25.
82. Terry Crowley and Claire Bowern, *An Introduction to Historical Linguistics,* 4th ed. (Oxford, Oxford University Press, 2010), 148; Vansina, *How Societies Are Born;* Ehret, *History and Testimony of Language,* 105–7; de Luna, *Collecting Food, Cultivating People.*
83. Vansina, *Paths in Rain Forest,* 16; Schoenbrun, "Early African Pasts," 6; Ehret, *History and Testimony of Language.*
84. Ehret and Kinsman, "Shona Dialect Classification," 402.
85. See, e.g., Neil Kodesh, *Beyond the Royal Gaze: Clanship and Public Healing in Buganda* (Charlottesville: University of Virginia Press, 2010); Neil Kodesh, "History from the Healer's Shrine: Genre, Historical Imagination and Early Ganda History," *Comparative Studies in Society and History* 49, no. 3 (2007): 527–52.
86. Mathew J. Schoffeleers, *River of Blood: The Genesis of a Martyr Cult in Southern Malawi, c. AD 1600* (Madison: University of Wisconsin Press, 1992).
87. The manuscript, which was never published, is cataloged under the National Archives of Zimbabwe's Historical Manuscripts. See MA 14/1/1 and MA 14/1/2, NAZ.
88. Interviews with Simboti, 8 March 2017; Soko, 8 and 9 March 2017; Toto Tangwena, 10 March 2017; Mutyawasara, 10 March 2017; Chikonamombe, 11 March 2017; *mbuya* Gededza, 29 June 2013; *ambuya* Chikonzo, 25 April 2014.
89. Elizabeth Tonkin, *Narrating Our Pasts: The Social Construction of Oral History* (Cambridge: Cambridge University Press, 1992).
90. Joseph C. Miller, "Introduction: Listening for the African Past," in *The African Past Speaks: Essays on Oral Tradition and History,* ed. Joseph C. Miller

(Kent: W. M. Dawson and Sons, 1980), 5–10; Jan Vansina, *Oral Tradition as History* (Madison: University of Wisconsin Press, 1985); Jan Bender Shetler, *Imagining Serengeti: A History of Landscape and Memory in Tanzania from Earliest Times to the Present* (Athens: Ohio University Press, 2007), 18–21.

91. Miller, "Introduction," 8–10.
92. Shetler, *Imagining Serengeti,* 19. See also Vansina, *Oral Tradition as History,* 21; Miller, "Introduction."
93. David Beach raises this issue with regard to the genealogy of Mutapa kings reconstructed by Donald P. Abraham. See Beach, *Zimbabwean Past,* 211–43.
94. Bhila, *Trade and Politics.*
95. Native Commissioner, Umtali, to Chief Native Commissioner, 31 March 1898, NUA2/1/3, NAZ; Ernest W. Morris, "'Marondella's District': History of Native Tribes and Chiefs; Information Supplied to the South African Native Affairs Commission, 1903," *Native Affairs Department Annual* 9, no. 4 (1977): 436. This exercise followed a request by the South African Native Affairs Commission.
96. Diana Jeater, *Law, Language and Science: The Invention of the "Native" Mind in Southern Rhodesia, 1890–1930* (Portsmouth, NH: Heinemann, 2007), xvi.
97. See, e.g., Schmidt, *Peasants, Traders and Wives,* 7; Chanock, *Law, Custom.*
98. See, e.g., the characterization of early farming communities in Pwiti, *Continuity and Change.*

CHAPTER 1: KNOWING THE LAND, MARKING SOCIAL HIERARCHIES, AND LEGITIMATING CLAIMS TO LAND AND POWER

1. Some scholars have suggested that people speaking the language ancestral to Shona languages arrived on the Zimbabwean plateau around AD 1000. See, e.g., Christopher Ehret, *An African Classical Age: Eastern and Southern Africa in World History* (Charlottesville: University of Virginia Press, 1998); Christopher Ehret, *History and the Testimony of Language* (Berkeley: University of California Press, 2011); Carolan Postma Ownby, "Early Nguni History: The Linguistic Evidence and Its Correlation with Archaeology and Oral Tradition" (PhD diss., University of California–Los Angeles, 1985); Thomas N. Huffman, "The Origins of Leopard's Kopje: An 11th Century Difaquane," *Arnoldia* 23, no. 8 (1978): 1–23. The archaeological evidence does not support this argument. See Tim Maggs, "The Iron Age South of the Zambezi," in *Southern African Prehistory and Paleoenvironments,* ed. Richard G. Klein (Rotterdam: A. A. Balkema, 1984), 345; Gilbert Pwiti, *Continuity and Change: An Archaeological Study of Farming Communities in Northern Zimbabwe, AD 500–1700,* Studies in African Archaeology 13 (Uppsala: Department of Archaeology and Ancient History, Uppsala University, 1996), 148–49. Historical linguists who rode on Huffman's hypothesis rely on M. Hannan's *Standard Shona Dictionary,* rev. ed. (Harare: College Press, 2000), which is essentially a dictionary of Central Shona. It excludes Eastern Shona (Ndau, Nyanga) and Western Shona (Kalanga and Nambya), all of which have a

longer history on the Zimbabwean plateau than Central Shona and its dialects of Karanga, Zezuru, Manyika, and Korekore. See Herbert Chimhundu, "Some Problems Relating to the Incorporation of Loanwords in the Lexicon," *Zambezia* 7 (1979): 81.

2. Robert Soper, *Nyanga: Ancient Fields, Settlements and Agricultural History in Zimbabwe* (London: British Institute in Eastern Africa, 2002); Roger Summers, *Inyanga: Prehistoric Settlements in Southern Rhodesia.*
3. The savanna landscape, **-jika,* teemed with animals known to the early farmers' linguistic ancestors, including bushpig, **-gùdùbè;* leopard, **-gùè;* rhinoceros, **-pembele;* klipspringer, **-gululu;* impala, **-pàdá;* giraffe, **-tùìgà;* warthog, *gìdì;* lion, **-sįumba;* eland, **-poku;* zebra, **-biji;* elephant, **-jògù;* buffalo, **-játì;* a large antelope species known to these people as **-kongoni;* ostrich, *pogu(e/a);* and guinea fowl, **-kángà.* My identification of most of these terms in protolanguages is informed by the work of Christopher Ehret and Kathryn de Luna. See Ehret, *African Classical Age;* Kathryn de Luna, "Collecting Food, Cultivating Persons: Wild Resources Use in Central African Political Culture, c. 1000 B.C.E. to c. 1900 C.E." (PhD diss., Northwestern University, 2008); Kathryn M. de Luna, *Collecting Food, Cultivating People: Subsistence and Society in Central Africa* (New Haven, CT: Yale University Press, 2016).
4. For the idea of **nyika* and what it meant, see de Luna, *Collecting Food, Cultivating People,* 250. Linguistic evidence of familiar economic activities includes inherited words for (a) hunting: **-gúim* (to hunt), **-tég-* (to set a trap), **-ta* (bow), **-cèbè* (arrow), and **-túmò* (spear); (b) food collection: **-bùjú* (baobab tree and fruit) and **-júkì* (honey, bee); (c) the agricultural economy, particularly cereal production: **-gùndà* (cleared field), **-bègú* (seed), **-tem-* (to cut), *témò* (ax/hoe), **-dìm-* (to cultivate), **-bíad-* (to sow), **-pànd-* (to plant; in this case, dry planting), **-càkud* (to weed), **-púúd* (to thresh), **-pepet* (to winnow), **-selo* (winnowing tray), and **-pùdį,* pumpkin; (d) tools to prepare cereal and vegetable foods: **-tùdì* (mortar) and **-jìcì* (pestle); (e) livestock production: **-gòmbè* (cattle), **-tàngá* (cattle pen/herd), **-kám-* (to milk), **-pulu* (calf), **-liis-* (to herd), and **-búdì* (goat); and (f) crafting, iron working: **-bùbo* (bellows), *jùndò* (hammer, anvil), and **-búmb* (to make pottery).
5. Ehret, *African Classical Age,* 39.
6. Ehret, 39.
7. Rhonda M. Gonzalez, *Societies, Religion, and History: Central East Tanzanians and the World They Created, c. 200 BCE to 1800 CE* (New York: Columbia University Press, 2009), 59.
8. Ehret, *African Classical Age,* 39; Gonzalez, *Societies, Religion, and History,* 59.
9. Ehret, *African Classical Age,* 39.
10. Pwiti, *Continuity and Change;* Paul J. Sinclair, *Space, Time and Social Formation: A Territorial Approach to the Archaeology and Anthropology of Zimbabwe and Mozambique, c.0–1700 AD* (Uppsala: Societas Archaeologica

Upsaliensis, 1987); Ina Plug, "Early Iron Age Buffalo Hunters on the Kadzi River, Zimbabwe," *African Archaeological Review* 14, no. 2 (1997): 85–105; Jimmy Jonsson, *Early Plant Economy in Zimbabwe* (Uppsala: Societas Archaeologica Upsaliensis, 1998).

11. Jonsson, *Early Plant Economy*, 34. See also Summers, *Inyanga*, 261–62.
12. In addition to these soils, proto–Central Shona speakers also identified and then named *bomho* (narrow valley, but open veld; grassy plain; treeless veld) and *gan'a* (dry barren land).
13. This would change later, when farmers on the Zimbabwean plateau incorporated rice in their repertoire of crops. Rice was grown in these **-toolo* landscapes.
14. Soper, *Nyanga*, 2.
15. David N. Beach, *The Shona and Zimbabwe: An Outline of Shona History* (Gweru: Mambo Press, 1980), 186. See also J. G. Storry, "The Settlement and Territorial Expansion of the Mutasa Dynasty," *Rhodesian History* 7 (1976): 15.
16. Innocent Pikirayi, "Archaeological, Historical and Anthropological Sources on Great Zimbabwe and the Nyanga Archaeological Complex," *Aluka Technical Report* (2008): 35.
17. Heike Schmidt, *Colonialism and Violence in Zimbabwe: A History of Suffering* (Woodbridge, UK: Boydell & Brewer, 2013), 45.
18. Lowe Börjeson, "A History under Siege: Intensive Agriculture in the Mbulu Highlands, Tanzania, 19th Century to the Present" (PhD thesis, Stockholm University, 2004).
19. Mats Widgren, "Towards an Historical Geography of Intensive Farming in Eastern Africa," in *Islands of Intensive Agriculture in Eastern Africa: Past and Present*, ed. Mats Widgren and John E. G. Sutton (Oxford, UK: James Currey, 2004), 15.
20. Soper, *Nyanga*.
21. George Kay, *Rhodesia: A Human Geography* (New York: African Publishing Corporation, 1970), 21.
22. See the discussion of the physical geography of the eastern highlands in Soper, *Nyanga*, 13–21; Steven Chirawu, "The Archaeology of the Ancient Agricultural and Settlement Systems in Nyanga Lowland" (MPhil thesis, University of Zimbabwe, 1999), 55; Seke Katsamudanga, "Environment and Culture: A Study of Prehistoric Settlement Patterns in the Eastern Highlands of Zimbabwe" (DPhil thesis, University of Zimbabwe, 2007), 36–39.
23. Soper, *Nyanga*, 35.
24. Pikirayi, "Archaeological, Historical," 35.
25. Barry N. Floyd, "Changing Patterns of African Land Use in Southern Rhodesia" (PhD diss., Syracuse University, 1959). As Paul Sinclair points out, the idea that precolonial African societies practiced shifting cultivation was based on a selective reading of Audrey Richards's work on *Chitemene* among the Bemba of northeastern Zambia. This selective reading ignored the fact that Richards indicated that the move to open new lands was one

of three ways of utilizing land that went together concurrently. See Sinclair, *Space, Time*. For a detailed discussion of this point, see Henrietta L. Moore and Meghan Vaughan, *Cutting Down Trees: Gender, Nutrition and Agricultural Change in the Northern Province of Zambia, 1890–1990* (Portsmouth, NH: Heinemann, 1994).

26. Kenneth D. Manungo, "The Role Peasants Played in the Zimbabwean War of Liberation with Special Emphasis on Chiweshe" (PhD diss., Ohio University, 1991), 22–42; Terence O. Ranger, *Peasant Consciousness and Guerrilla War in Zimbabwe: A Comparative Study* (London: James Currey, 1985).
27. Interview with Svongore, 28 June 2013; discussion with Svongore brothers, 28 June 2013; interview with Charova, 28 June 2013.
28. Francisco de Souza, "Oriente Conquistado a Jesu Christo pelos Padres da Campanhia de Jesua da Provincia de Goa," in "The Shona and the Portuguese," ed. David N. Beach and H. de Noronha (unpublished ms., University of Zimbabwe, 1980), vol. 1, 260; Hoyini H. K. Bhila, *Trade and Politics in a Shona Kingdom: The Manyika and Their Portuguese and African Neighbours* (London: Longman, 1983), 62.
29. For constructions of some environments as dangerous elsewhere on the Zimbabwean plateau, see Jocelyn Alexander, JoAnn McGregor, and Terence Ranger, *Violence and Memory: One Hundred Years in the "Dark Forests" of Matabeleland* (Portsmouth, NH: Heinemann, 2000).
30. In addition to **-dusa,* Shona languages have retained **-pepet,* the Mashariki Bantu word for "to winnow."
31. The word for hunter in all the three subgroups—Western, Eastern, and Central Shona—is *muvhimi.*
32. Kathryn M. de Luna, "Collecting Food, Cultivating Persons: Wild Resources Use in Central African Political Culture, c. 1000 B.C.E. to c. 1900 C.E." (PhD diss., Northwestern University, 2008), 594.
33. Shadreck Chirikure, "Iron Production in Iron Age Zimbabwe: Stagnation or Innovation?" (PhD thesis, University College London, 2005), 76. See also Peter S. Garlake, *Great Zimbabwe: Described and Explained* (Harare: Zimbabwe Publishing House, 1985), 8; Summers, *Inyanga.*
34. For the point about fame and social standing among hunters elsewhere in South-Central Africa, see de Luna, *Collecting Food, Cultivating People,* esp. chap. 3.
35. David L. Schoenbrun, *A Green Place, a Good Place: Agrarian Change, Gender and Social Identity in the Great Lakes Region to the 15th Century* (Portsmouth, NH: Heinemann, 1998), 92–93. See also Ehret, *African Classical Age;* Jan Vansina, *Paths in the Rain Forest: Toward a History of Political Tradition in Equatorial Africa* (Madison: University of Wisconsin Press, 1990).
36. David Schoenbrun makes the same observation for East Nyanza societies. See Schoenbrun, *Green Place, Good Place,* 98.
37. Among the various Shona speech communities in which this root was retained, **-jooto* refers to the hearth. It is also used as a reference to individual

households in polygynous families. Each wife has a hearth, *choto,* from where she prepares food for her children.

38. In the Bantu Lexical Reconstruction database (hereinafter BLR3), linguists suggest that this is a derivation of 8591, "plot of ground prepared for building house" (BLR3 97); see Yvonne Bastin and Thilo Schadeberg, eds., Bantu Lexical Reconstruction 3, Truven, Belgium, Musée Royale de l'Afrique Centrale, https://www.africamuseum.be/en/research/discover/human_sciences/culture_society/blr/bantou_history. See also Malcom Guthrie, *Comparative Bantu: An Introduction to the Comparative Linguistics and Prehistory of the Bantu Languages,* vol. 4 (Hants, UK: Gregg International Publishers, 1970), C.S. 55.
39. David L. Schoenbrun, "The (In)visible Roots of Bunyoro-Kitara and Buganda in the Lakes Region, AD 800–1300," in *Beyond Chiefdoms: Pathways to Complexity in Africa,* ed. Susan Keech McIntosh (Cambridge: Cambridge University Press, 1999), 41.
40. Kumile Masola, *Nau DzabaKalanga / A History of the Kalanga,* vol. 1, trans. Petrus Johannes Wentzel (Pretoria: University of South Africa, 1983).
41. The quotation comes from David L. Schoenbrun, *The Historical Reconstruction of Great Lakes Bantu Cultural Vocabulary: Etymologies and Distributions* (Köln: Rüdiger Köppe Press, 1997), 75. See also Ehret, *African Classical Age,* 146, 148–50.
42. That Eastern Shona speakers understood **-kosi*'s older meaning as clan leader is shown by the fact that its reflex remains with that meaning within the Nyanga speech communities. For the reconstruction of **-dòngó,* and its meaning to proto-Bantu times, see Schoenbrun, *Historical Reconstruction,* 75.
43. Shona speech communities distinctly lack the terminology for matrilineality that characterizes their northern matrilineal neighbors, indicating, if indirectly, that those who spoke proto-Shona's recent linguistic ancestor might not have organized their societies along matrilineal lines. If they did, proto-Shona speakers replaced the terms for matrilineages with ones for patrilineages before the language evolved into its daughter dialects. For the terminology for matrilineality in neighboring societies, see Christine Saidi, *Women's Authority and Society in Early East-Central Africa* (Rochester: University of Rochester Press, 2010). For a discussion of the dynamics of power in the twentieth century, see Diana Jeater, *Marriage, Perversion and Power: The Construction of a Moral Discourse in Southern Rhodesia, 1894–1930* (Oxford, UK: Clarendon Press, 1993).
44. See Vansina, *Paths in Rain Forest,* 95; Ehret, *African Classical Age,* 159; Schoenbrun, *Historical Reconstruction,* 182–83; Gonzalez, *Societies, Religion and History,* 95.
45. Vansina, *Paths in Rain Forest,* 95.
46. Ehret, *African Classical Age,* 159.
47. Vansina, *Paths in Rain Forest,* 95; Ehret, *African Classical Age,* 159.

48. Manyikeni is a good example of a site where cattle were slaughtered for beef in their prime. See Peter S. Garlake, "Pastoralism and Zimbabwe," *Journal of African History* 19, no. 4 (1978): 479–93; Pwiti, *Continuity and Change;* Gilbert Pwiti, "Peasants, Chiefs and Kings: A Model of the Development of Cultural Complexity in Northern Zimbabwe," *Zambezia* 23, no. 1 (1996): 31–52; Sinclair, *Space, Time;* Munyaradzi Manyanga and Plan Shenjere, "The Archaeology of the Northern Nyanga Lowlands and the Unfolding Farming Community Sequence in Northeastern Zimbabwe," *South African Archaeological Bulletin* 67, no. 196 (2012): 244–55; Plan Shenjere, "The Animal Economy of Prehistoric Farming Communities in Manicaland, Eastern Zimbabwe" (PhD thesis, University of Dar es Salaam, 2011). However, at Tsindi, the cattle bones were of somewhat older cattle. See Kevin Mukabeta, "Does Similarity Equal Relationship? An Archaeological Study of Tsindi, a Dzimbabwe Site in North-Eastern Zimbabwe" (MPhil thesis, University of Cape Town, 2018).
49. Garlake, "Pastoralism and Zimbabwe."
50. The trappings of power include the dry-stone structures widely understood to have been the abode of ruling families. For transhumance, see Garlake, "Pastoralism and Zimbabwe." The absence of cattle kraals in these settlements is also the basis of Huffman's argument for a Zimbabwe Pattern (ZP) that he suggests was different from what he has called the Central Cattle Pattern. See Thomas N. Huffman, *Handbook to the Iron Age: The Archaeology of Precolonial Farming Societies in Southern Africa* (Scottsville: University of Kwazulu Natal Press, 2007); Thomas N. Huffman, *Snakes and Crocodiles: Power and Symbolism in Ancient Zimbabwe* (Johannesburg: Witwatersrand University Press, 1996); Thomas N. Huffman, "Snakes and Birds: Expressive Space at Great Zimbabwe," *African Studies* 40, no. 2 (1981): 131–50; Thomas N. Huffman, "Expressive Space in the Zimbabwe Culture," *Man* 194, no. 4 (1984): 593–612.
51. Abigail Joy Moffett and Shadreck Chirikure, "Exotica in Context: Reconfiguring Prestige, Power and Wealth in the Southern African Iron Age," *Journal of World Prehistory* 29, no. 4 (2016): 337–82.
52. Soper, *Nyanga,* 125.
53. Saidi, *Women's Authority,* 138. See also Eugenia W. Herbert, *Iron, Gender and Power: Rituals of Transformation in African Societies* (Bloomington: Indiana University Press, 1993), 116; Weber Ndoro, "Why Decorate Her?," *Zimbabwea* 3 (1991): 60–65; Chirikure, "Iron Production," 90.
54. Herbert, *Iron, Gender and Power,* 116; Ndoro, "Why Decorate Her?"; F. O. Bernhard, "Two Types of Iron Smelting Furnaces on Ziwa Farm (Inyanga)," *South African Archaeological Bulletin* 17, no. 68 (1962): 235.
55. Anders Lindahl and Innocent Pikirayi, "Ceramics and Change: An Overview of Pottery Production Techniques in Northern South Africa and Eastern Zimbabwe during the First and Second Millennium AD," *Archaeological and Anthropological Sciences* 2, no. 3 (2010): 141; Innocent Pikirayi and Anders

Lindahl, "Ceramics, Ethnohistory and Ethnography: Locating the Meaning in Southern African Iron Age Ceramic Assemblages," *African Archaeological Review* 30, no. 4 (2013): 11; Ndoro, "Why Decorate Her?"; Saidi, *Women's Authority,* 137.

56. Pwiti, *Continuity and Change,* 148.
57. Innocent Pikirayi, *The Zimbabwe Culture: The Origins and Decline in Southern Zambezian States* (Walnut Creek, CA: AltaMira Press, 2001), 97.
58. Lindahl and Pikirayi, "Ceramics and Change," 133.
59. The rise of the Toutswe chiefdom is itself linked to the emergence of a cattle-rich elite. Peter Mitchel, *The Archaeology of Southern Africa* (Cambridge: Cambridge University Press, 2002), 307–9. See also Stanislus Isack Mudenge, "The Rozvi and the Feira of Zumbo" (PhD Thesis, University of London, 1972); Stanislus I. G. Mudenge, "The Role of Foreign Trade in the Rozvi Empire: A Reappraisal," *Journal of African History* 15, no. 3 (1974): 373–91.
60. "Father Antonio Gomes to Father João Marachi, 2 January 1648," in Beach and de Noronha, "The Shona and the Portuguese," vol. 1, 129–30; Innocent Pikirayi, *The Archaeological Identity of the Mutapa State: Towards an Historical Archaeology of Northern Zimbabwe,* Studies in African Archaeology 6 (Uppsala: Department of Archaeology and Ancient History, Uppsala University, 1993), 110, 112.
61. Father Monclaro, "Account of the Journey Made by Fathers of the Company of Jesus with Francisco Barreto in the Conquest of Monomotapa in the Year 1569," in *Records of South-Eastern Africa,* ed. George M. Theal (Cape Town: C. Struik, 1964), vol. 3, 227. See also Francisco de Monclaro, "Narrative by Father Francisco de Monclaro of the Society of Jesus of the Expedition to Monomutapa, Led by Francisco Barreto," in *Documents on the Portuguese in Mozambique and Central Africa,* ed. T. W. Baxter and A. da Silva Rego (Salisbury: National Archives of Rhodesia, 1975), vol. 8, 379; "Father Antonio Gomes," in Beach and de Noronha, "The Shona and the Portuguese," vol. 1, 92; Clement Doke, *A Comparative Study in Shona Phonetics* (Johannesburg: University of the Witwatersrand Press, 1931), appendix IV(a); Clement Doke, "The Earliest Records of Bantu," *African Studies* 19, no. 1 (1960): 30.
62. Vansina, *Paths in Rain Forest,* 74; Ehret, *African Classical Age,* 146–49. For the most recent periodization of proto-Bantu, see Rebecca Grollemund, David Schoenbrun, and Jan Vansina, "Moving Histories: Bantu Language Expansions, Eclectic Economies, and Mobilities," *Journal of African History* 64 (2023): 1–25.
63. Vansina, *Paths in Rain Forest,* 74.
64. Ehret, *African Classical Age,* 147.
65. The dating of *mhondoro* to the ninth century and beyond is based on the fact that the term and the institution are found only among linguistic descendants of proto–East Central Shona in northern and eastern Zimbabwe. *Mhondoro* is not found among speakers of proto-Western Shona and those

speakers of proto–Eastern Shona dialects closest to them. These are Karanga speakers who turned to the Mwari cult rather than to the *mhondoro*.

66. Father Monclaro, "Account of the Journey," 227.
67. "Father Antonio Gomes," in Beach and de Noronha, "The Shona and the Portuguese," vol. 1, 92.
68. Ehret, *African Classical Age*, 148–49.
69. Ehret, 148.
70. Ehret, 148.
71. This linkage between **-éné*, the title of a leader, and "Mwenemutapa," the title of the rulers of the Mutapa state, escaped Hoyini Bhila when he argued that "Mwenemutapa" was a misspelling of the Shona word "Munhumutapa." Here, David Beach's interpretation of the term is closer to its historical meaning than that of Bhila. See Hoyini H. K. Bhila, "The History and Misspelling of a Shona Term," *Rhodesian History* 5 (1974): 79–80; David N. Beach, "Mutapa: An Alternative Approach to the Study of Titles," *Rhodesian History* 6 (1975): 98.
72. Shadreck Chirikure et al., "Decisive Evidence for Multidirectional Evolution of Sociopolitical Complexity in Southern Africa," *African Archaeological Review* 33, no. 1 (2016): 75–95; Shadreck Chirikure et al., "Zimbabwe Culture before Mapungubwe: New Evidence from Mapela Hill, South-Western Zimbabwe," *PLoS One* 9, no. 10 (2014): 1–18; Shadreck Chirikure et al., "No Big Brother Here: Heterarchy, Shona Political Succession and the Relationship between Great Zimbabwe and Khami, Southern Africa," *Cambridge Archaeological Journal* 28, no. 1 (2017): 45–66.
73. Schoenbrun, *Green Place, Good Place*, 13.
74. Schoenbrun.
75. The quotation is from Thomas N. Huffman, "Revisiting Great Zimbabwe," *Azania: Archaeological Research in Africa* 45, no. 3 (2010), 325. See also Huffman, "Snakes and Birds"; Huffman, "Expressive Space"; Huffman, *Snakes and Crocodiles*.
76. Huffman, "Revisiting Great Zimbabwe," 325.
77. Huffman, 325.
78. Huffman, "Expressive Space"; Huffman, "Snakes and Birds"; Huffman, *Snakes and Crocodiles*, 321–28; Huffman, "Leopard's Kopje."
79. David Beach, "Cognitive Archaeology and Imaginary History at Great Zimbabwe," *Current Anthropology* 39, no. 1 (1998): 49; David Beach et al., "Reviews of *Snakes and Crocodiles: Power and Symbolism in Ancient Zimbabwe* by Thomas N. Huffman," *South African Archaeological Bulletin* 52, no. 166 (1997): 135–43; Shadreck Chirikure and Innocent Pikirayi, "Inside and Outside the Dry Stone Walls: Revisiting the Material Culture of Great Zimbabwe," *Antiquity* 82 (2008): 976–93; Innocent Pikirayi and Shadreck Chirikure, "Debating Great Zimbabwe," *Azania: Archaeological Research in Africa* 46, no. 2 (2011): 221–31; Innocent Pikirayi, "Stone Architecture and the Development of Power in the Zimbabwe Tradition, AD 1270–1830," *Azania: Archaeological*

Research in Africa 48, no. 2 (2013): 282–300; Shadreck Chirikure, *Great Zimbabwe: Reclaiming a Confiscated Past* (London: Routledge, 2021).

80. Chirikure et al., "Decisive Evidence," 90.
81. Steven Feierman, *Peasant Intellectuals: Anthropology and History in Tanzania* (Madison: University of Wisconsin Press, 1990); Chirikure et al., "Decisive Evidence," 89–91.
82. Chirikure, *Great Zimbabwe*, 16; Gerald Chikozho Mazarire, "The *Gadzingo:* Towards a Karanga Expansion Matrix in 18th- and 19th-Century Southern Zimbabwe," *Critical African Studies* 5, no. 1 (2013): 10.
83. Martinus Daneel, *God of the Matopo Hills: An Essay on the Mwari Cult of Rhodesia* (The Hague: Mouton, 1970); Terence Ranger, "The Meaning of Mwari," *Rhodesian History* 5 (1974): 5–17; Terence Ranger, *Voices from the Rocks: Nature, Culture and History in the Matopos Hills of Zimbabwe* (Oxford, UK: James Currey, 1999); George Fortune, "Who was Mwari?," *Rhodesian History* 4 (1973): 1–20; Richard M. G. Mtetwa, "The Relationship between Gutu Dynasties and the Mwari Cult," *Rhodesian History* 6 (1975): 89–95.
84. John K. Rennie, "From Zimbabwe to a Colonial Chieftaincy: Four Transformations of the Musikavanhu Territorial Cult in Rhodesia," in *Guardians of the Land: Essays on Central African Territorial Cults*, ed. Mathew J. Schoffeleers (Gweru: Mambo Press, 1979), 257–85; Mtetwa, "Gutu Dynasties and Mwari Cult"; Michael Bourdillon, *The Shona Peoples: An Ethnography of the Contemporary Shona, with Special Reference to Their Religion* (1976; Gweru: Mambo Press, 1987), 253–73; Michael F. C. Bourdillon, "The Cults of Dzivaguru and Karuva amongst the North Eastern Shona Peoples," in Schoffeleers, *Guardians of the Land*, 235–55; Joseph Mujere, "The Marumbi Rain Cult: Gender and the Interface between Rain Making and the Politics of Water in Gutu" (paper presented at The Power of Water: Landscape, Water and the State in Southern and Eastern Africa conference, CAS, University of Edinburgh, Scotland, 28–29 March 2007).
85. See the appendix in Doke, *Comparative Study.* See also Allen Isaacman, "Madzi-Manga, Mhondoro and the Use of Oral Traditions: A Chapter in Barue Religious and Political History," *Journal of African History* 14, no. 3 (1973): 395–409.
86. De Almeida to the Viceroy, 23 June 1687, in Beach and de Noronha, "The Shona and the Portuguese," vol. 1, 105.
87. For the relationship between climate change and politics across southern Africa, see Mathew J. Hannaford, "The Consequences of Past Climate Change for State Formation and Security in Southern Africa" (PhD thesis, University of Sheffield, 2015); Mathew J. Hannaford and David J. Nash, "Climate, History, Society over the Last Millennium in Southeast Africa," *Wiley Interdisciplinary Reviews: Climate Change* 7, no. 3 (2016): 370–92.
88. Bourdillon, *Shona Peoples*, 253.
89. Mazarire, "The *Gadzingo*"; Gerald Chikozho Mazarire, "Changing Landscapes and Oral Memory in South-Central Zimbabwe: Towards a Historical

Geography of Chishanga, c. 1850–1990," *Journal of Southern African Studies* 29, no. 3 (2003): 701–15.

CHAPTER 2: IN THE SHADOW OF KINGDOMS

1. Shadreck Chirikure, T. Mukwende, A. J. Moffett, R. T. Nyamushosho, F. Bandama, and M. House, "No Big Brother Here: Heterarchy, Shona Political Succession and the Relationship between Great Zimbabwe and Khami, Southern Africa," *Cambridge Archaeological Journal* 28, no. 1 (2017): 45–66; Shadreck Chirikure and Innocent Pikirayi, "Inside and Outside the Dry Stone Walls: Revisiting the Material Culture of Great Zimbabwe," *Antiquity* 82 (2008): 989.
2. Kevin Mukabeta, "Does Similarity Equal Relationship? An Archaeological Study of Tsindi, a Dzimbabwe Site in North-Eastern Zimbabwe" (MPhil thesis, University of Cape Town, 2018).
3. Francisco de Monclaro, "Narrative by Father Francisco de Monclaro, of the Society of Jesus of the Expedition to Monomutapa, Led by Francisco Barreto," in *Documents on the Portuguese in Mozambique and Central Africa,* ed. T. W. Baxter and A. da Silva Rego (Salisbury: National Archives of Rhodesia, 1975), vol. 8, 379; Antonio Bocarro, "Decade of the Performances of the Portuguese in the East," in *Records of South-Eastern Africa,* ed. George M. Theal (Cape Town: C. Struik, 1902), vol. 3, 227; Pedro Baretto de Rezende, "Of the State of India," in Theal, *Records of South-Eastern Africa,* vol. 2, 414; Diogo do Couto, "Chapters XX–XXV of 9th Decada Da Asia," in Baxter and da Silva Rego, *Documents on the Portuguese,* vol. 8, 321. The same account is found in Theal, *Records of South-Eastern Africa,* vol. 6, 357–42.
4. "João de Sepúlveda to the King of Portugal, 10 August 1542," in Baxter and da Silva Rego, *Documents on the Portuguese,* vol. 7, 137.
5. Monclaro, "Narrative," 379.
6. António da Conceição to Diogo da Conceição, "Treatise on the Rivers of Cuama, 12 December 1696," in "The Shona and the Portuguese," ed. David N. Beach and H. de Noronha (unpublished ms., University of Zimbabwe, 1980), vol. 1, 207.
7. Anonymous, "Chorographic Description of the Kingdom of Manhica, Its Customs and Laws," in Beach and de Noronha, "The Shona and the Portuguese," vol. 2, 1.
8. "João Vaz d'Almada to the King [of Portugal]," in Baxter and da Silva Rego, *Documents on the Portuguese,* vol. 4, 277–79.
9. "De Sepúlveda to the King," 139.
10. "De Sepúlveda to the King," 139.
11. António Alberto de Andrade, *Relações de Moçambique Setecentista* (Lisbon: Agencia Geral do Ultramar, Divisão de Publicações e Biblioteca, 1955), 55. See also Allen Isaacman, *Mozambique, the Africanization of a European Institution: The Zambezi Prazos, 1750–1902* (Madison: University of Wisconsin Press, 1972), 8.

12. David N. Beach, *The Shona and Zimbabwe: An Outline of Shona History* (Gweru: Mambo Press, 1980), 121–54; Stanislus Isack G. Mudenge, *A Political History of Munhumutapa, c1400–1902* (Harare: Zimbabwe Publishing House, 1988); Gerald Chikozho Mazarire, "Reflections on Precolonial Zimbabwe, c. 850–1880s," in *Becoming Zimbabwe: A History from the Precolonial Period to 2008,* ed. Brian Raftopoulos and Alois S. Mlambo (Harare: Weaver Press, 2009), 14–17; Innocent Pikirayi, *The Zimbabwe Culture: The Origins and Decline in Southern Zambezian States* (Walnut Creek, CA: AltaMira Press, 2001), 229; Innocent Pikirayi, *The Archaeological Identity of the Mutapa State: Towards an Historical Archaeology of Northern Zimbabwe,* Studies in African Archaeology 6 (Uppsala: Department of Archaeology and Ancient History, Uppsala University, 1993), 116–17.
13. Albino Manoel Pacheco, "A Voyage from Tete to Zumbo," in Beach and de Noronha, "The Shona and the Portuguese," vol. 2, 21–23; Herbert Chitepo, "Soko Risina Musoro," in H. Chitepo et al., *Nduri DzeZimbabwe* (Harare: Longman Zimbabwe, 1983); interview with SaMuponda, 24 June 2013; Ignasiyo M. Zvarevashe, *Dzinza RaVagovera VaChirumhanzu NaMutasa* (Gweru: Mambo Press, 1998), 1–4; "History of the Mashona Tribes," N3/33/8, NAZ; Native Commissioner, Umtali, to the Chief Native Commissioner, 3 May 1906, NUA2/1/6, NAZ; [Jason Takafa] Machiwenyika, "History and Customs of the Manyika," Lesson 68, unpublished ms., MA14/1/1; J. Thokozane, "A Short History of Chipunza," *Native Affairs Department Annual* 9, no. 2 (1965): 59–60; Donald P. Abraham, "The Principalities of Maungwe: Its History and Traditions," *Native Affairs Department Annual* 28 (1951): 56–83; T. E., "The Story of the Origin of the Name 'Makoni,'" *Native Affairs Department Annual* 14 (1937): 76–78; L. V. Jowett, "The Hungwe People of the Makoni District," *Native Affairs Department Annual* 11, no. 5 (1968): 54–55; Nhira Nzvere Chinhoyi, AOH 39, NAZ; Chikwaka Chief Marufu, AOH 34, NAZ; Kapiro Chisvo, AOH 31, NAZ; interview with SaMuponda, 1 July 2013; group interview between George Bishi and members of the Mutsago clan, 29 June 2013.
14. Interviews with SaMuponda, 24 June 2013 and 1 July 2013; "History of the Mashona Tribes," N3/33/8, NAZ; Native Commissioner, Umtali, to the Chief Native Commissioner, 3 May 1906, NUA2/1/6, NAZ.
15. Kathryn M. de Luna, *Collecting Food, Cultivating People: Subsistence and Society in Central Africa* (New Haven, CT: Yale University Press, 2016), 93.
16. For this argument being made with reference to neighboring Botatwe-speaking peoples, see de Luna, *Collecting Food, Cultivating People,* 93.
17. Machiwenyika, "History and Customs of the Manyika," Lesson 68.
18. Fr. Antonio Gomes to Fr. João Marachi, "Voyage Made by Fr. Antonio Gomes of the Society of Jesus to the Monomutapa Empire and His Work There for Several Years, 2 January 1648 (with notes by E. A. Axelson)," in Beach and de Noronha, "The Shona and the Portuguese," vol. 1, 91.
19. Thokozane, "Short History of Chipunza," 59.

20. Interview with Mutsago, 28 June 2013; interviews with SaMuponda, 24 June 2013 and 1 July 2013. In the Mutsago oral traditions, for example, Mutsago is portrayed as a brave hunter who killed elephants that were destroying people's crops.
21. Interviews with SaMuponda, 24 June 2013 and 1 July 2013.
22. For a discussion of the idea of children and the political message it conveyed on the Zimbabwean plateau after 1450, see David N. Beach, "Cognitive Archaeology and Imaginary History at Great Zimbabwe," *Current Anthropology* 39, no. 1 (1998): 47–72; Chirikure and Pikirayi, "Inside and Outside"; Shadreck Chirikure, *Great Zimbabwe: Reclaiming a Confiscated Past* (London: Routledge, 2021), 43.
23. Francisco de Sousa, "Oriente Conquistado a Jesu Christo pelos Padres da Campanhia de Jesua da Provincia de Goa," in Beach and de Noronha, "The Shona and the Portuguese," vol. 1, 232.
24. Duarte Barbosa, "Extracts from a Book Written by Duarte Barbosa, 1516," in Theal, *Records of South-Eastern Africa,* vol. 1, 96. See also Hoyini H. K. Bhila, *Trade and Politics in a Shona Kingdom: The Manyika and Their Portuguese and African Neighbours* (London: Longman, 1983), 12.
25. Da Conceição, "Treatise on the Rivers," 222.
26. Da Conceição, 222.
27. Chikwaka Chief Marufu, AOH 34, NAZ; Aaron Jacha, AOH 14, NAZ; Chief Chiduku's installation, Makoni District, 13 June 1989, PER/Chiduku, Makoni District Council Files; Provincial Commissioner Manicaland to District Commissioner, Rusape, 1 December 1976, PER/Chiduku, Makoni District Council Files. For the South African highveld, see Paul Landau, *Popular Politics in the History of South Africa, 1400–1948* (Cambridge: Cambridge University Press, 2010), 53–59. For the contemporary utility of these myths, see Joost Fontein, *The Silence of Great Zimbabwe: Contested Landscapes and the Power of Heritage* (New York: UCL Press, 2006).
28. Aaron Jacha, AOH 14, NAZ.
29. Stanislus Isack G. Mudenge, "The Rozvi Empire and the Feira of Zumbo" (PhD thesis, University of London, 1972), 141.
30. See Friedrich Wilhelm Traugott Posselt, *Fact and Faction* (Bulawayo: Books of Rhodesia, 1935).
31. Mudenge, "Rozvi Empire," 141; See also Mazarire, "The *Gadzingo:* Towards a Karanga Expansion Matrix in 18th- and 19th-Century Southern Zimbabwe," *Critical African Studies* 5, no. 1 (2013): 4–16.
32. Mazarire, "The *Gadzingo,*" 6. It is worth noting that Mazarire cites Mudenge on this point.
33. Mudenge, "Rozvi Empire," 141.
34. Bhila, *Trade and Politics,* 98.
35. Landau, *Popular Politics,* 58.
36. Bhila, *Trade and Politics,* 97.
37. Bhila, 102.

38. Mudenge, "Rozvi Empire," 141.
39. Bhila, *Trade and Politics,* 98. The quotation about the instruction given to Chikanga comes from Manoel Galvão da Silva, "A Journal of Manoel Galvão da Silva's Travels through the Territory of Manica in 1790," trans. and ed. H. H. K. Bhila, in *Monumenta: Publicacão dos Monumentos Nacionals de Moçambique* 8 (1972), 82.
40. Bhila, *Trade and Politics,* 104.
41. Mudenge, "Rozvi Empire," 148.
42. Mudenge, 148.
43. Malyn Newitt, introduction to *Treatise in the Rivers of Cuama* by António da Conceição, ed. and trans. Malyn Newitt (Oxford: Oxford University Press, 2009), xxv.
44. E. W. Morris, "Marondella's District," N3/33/8, NAZ; David N. Beach, *A Zimbabwean Past: Shona Dynastic Histories and Oral Traditions* (Gweru: Mambo Press, 1994), 91.
45. Bhila, *Trade and Politics,* 102–3.
46. Bhila, 103.
47. Residents of Sena, "Minutes of a Meeting, 5 July 1795," in Beach and de Noronha, "The Shona and the Portuguese," vol. 2, 1–2.
48. Diego de Souza to Joao de Souza e Brito, 8 September 1795, in Beach and de Noronha, "The Shona and the Portuguese," vol. 2.
49. Pacheco, "Voyage from Tete to Zumbo," 27.
50. Although the traditional accounts do not allow us to date this with any specificity, in all likelihood it happened in the early nineteenth century. The traditions suggest that the four were Nyarumwe's sons, who (as discussed earlier) rose to the throne of the Manyika chieftainship in 1796. See Machiwenyika, "History and Customs of the Manyika," Lessons 103 and 104.
51. Machiwenyika, "History and Customs of the Manyika," Lessons 103 and 104.
52. Machiwenyika, Lesson 89.
53. Machiwenyika, Lesson 89.
54. Indeed, Manyika oral traditions recall that in the late nineteenth century, these headmen became important in parrying attacks from Makoni and the Gaza Nguni. See Machiwenyika, "History and Customs of the Manyika," Lesson 82; H. Franklin, "'The War of the Tale-Tale' between Chiefs Makoni and Mutasa," *Native Affairs Department Annual* 15 (1938): 39–40; Abraham, "Principality of Maungwe"; J. G. Storry, "The Settlement and Territorial Expansion of the Mutasa Dynasty," *Rhodesian History* 7 (1976): 19. For the attacks from the Gaza Nguni, see Heike Schmidt, *Colonialism and Violence in Zimbabwe: A History of Suffering* (Woodbridge, UK: Boydell & Brewer, 2013), 41–46.
55. Igor Kopytoff, "The Internal African Frontier: The Making of African Political Culture," in *The African Frontier: The Reproduction of Traditional African Societies,* ed. Igor Kopytoff (Bloomington: Indiana University Press, 1987), 3–84.

56. Thokozane, "Short History of Chipunza."
57. Kopytoff, "Internal African Frontier."
58. Interviews with Makanya, 29 June 2013, and James Charova, 28 June 2013; David Kamusoko, AOH 79, NAZ.
59. Madzivanyika Bvudzijena, Taonezvi Mazivei, and Simon Zhuwarara, AOH 81, NAZ; Rwambiwa Chari, AOH 37, NAZ; Makutu Taonezvi, AOH 80, NAZ.
60. "Record of the Enquiry Made by Command of the Governor Francisco Barreto, Post 1573 May 1," in Baxter and da Silva Rego, *Documents on the Portuguese,* vol. 8, 239. The actual testimony was recorded from Symão d'Abreu.
61. For a discussion of wealth in things and wealth in people, see Jane I. Guyer, "Wealth in People, Wealth in Things—Introduction," *Journal of African History* 36, no. 1 (1995): 83–90; Jane I. Guyer, "Wealth in People and Self-Realization in Equatorial Africa," *Man* 28, no. 2 (1993): 243–65; Jane I. Guyer and Samuel M. Eno Belinga, "Wealth in People as Wealth in Knowledge: Accumulation and Composition in Equatorial Africa," *Journal of African History* 36, no. 1 (1995): 91–120; Igor Kopytoff and Suzzaine Miers, "Introduction: African Slavery as an Institution of Marginality," in *Slavery in Africa: Historical and Anthropological Perspectives,* ed. Suzzaine Miers and Igor Kopytoff (Madison: University of Wisconsin Press, 1977); Paul E. Lovejoy, *Transformations in Slavery: A History of Slavery in Africa* (Cambridge: Cambridge University Press, 2000); Joseph C. Miller, *Way of Death: Merchant Capitalism and the Angolan Slave Trade* (Madison: University of Wisconsin Press, 1988); Jan Vansina, *Paths in the Rain Forest: Toward a History of Political Tradition in Equatorial Africa* (Madison: University of Wisconsin Press, 1990).
62. Bhila, *Trade and Politics,* 62.
63. De Souza, "Oriente Conquistado," 260. The Portuguese who recounted this famine believed it was God's punishment to the people of Mukaranga for the killing at the court of the Mwenemutapa of the missionary Gonçalo da Silveira that year.
64. Newitt, introduction, xiii.
65. Antonio Pinto de Miranda, "Report on the Coast of Africa," in Beach and de Noronha, "The Shona and the Portuguese," vol. 2, 89. For a broader discussion of slavery in this region, see Allen E. Isaacman and Barbra S. Isaacman, *Slavery and Beyond: The Making of Men and Chikunda Ethnic Identities in the Unstable World of South-Central Africa, 1750–1920* (Portsmouth, NH: Heinemann, 2004).
66. David Maxwell, *Christians and Chiefs in Zimbabwe: A Social History of the Hewsa People, c.1870s–1990s* (Edinburgh: Edinburgh University Press, 1999), 12.
67. Bocarro, "Decade of the Portuguese," 358.
68. Ruramisai Charumbira, "Over Her Dead Body: The Gendered Exercise of Power in a Sixteenth Century Southern African Kingdom," unpublished ms. (n.d.), 27.
69. Charumbira, 27.

70. De Andrade, *Relações de Moçambique Setecentista,* 312.
71. Manoel Galvão da Silva, "A Journal," 82.
72. "History of Native Tribes," N3/33/8, NAZ; Ernest W. Morris, "'Marondella's District': History of Native Tribes and Chiefs; Information Supplied to the South African Native Affairs Commission, 1903," *Native Affairs Department Annual* 9, no. 4 (1977): 440–41.
73. "History of Native Tribes," N3/33/8, NAZ; Native Commissioner, Marandellas, to Chief Native Commissioner; Morris, "Marondella's District," 440–41.
74. "Antonio Caiado to a Friend, 1561," in Baxter and da Silva Rego, *Documents on the Portuguese,* vol. 8, 5. See also Luiz Froes, "Of the Voyage of the Father Dom Gonçalo to the Kingdom of Monomutapa and of His Happy Passing Away," in Theal, *Records of South-Eastern Africa,* vol. 2, 124.
75. "Record of the Enquiry Made by Command of the Governor Francisco Barreto," in Baxter and da Silva Rego, *Documents on the Portuguese,* vol. 8, 235. The actual testimony was recorded from Álvaro Fernandez. See also "Fr. Antonio Gomes to Fr. João Marachi, January 2, 1648," in Beach and de Noronha, "The Shona and the Portuguese," vol. 1, 36.
76. Mazarire, "The *Gadzingo.*"
77. Mazarire; Chirikure, *Great Zimbabwe;* Chirikure and Pikirayi, "Inside and Outside."
78. Anonymous, "Chorographic Description," 10.
79. Anonymous, "Chorographic Description," 10.
80. "Fr. Antonio Gomes to Fr. João Marachi, January 2, 1648," 92.
81. "Fr. Antonio Gomes to Fr. João Marachi, January 2, 1648," 92.
82. "Fr. Antonio Gomes to Fr. João Marachi, January 2, 1648," 93.
83. Mudenge, *Political History of Munhumutapa,* 127.
84. Feierman, *Peasant Intellectuals,* 96.
85. "Narrative by Father Francisco de Monclaro," 389.
86. Mudenge, *Political History of Munhumutapa,* 125.
87. William Edwards, "Sacred Places," *Native Affairs Department Annual* 6 (1928): 23–24. The oral tradition on the origins of Dziva Ranyamhita recalls a tradition of the founding of a Tavara ritual center related to Manual Pacheco by people in Chidima in 1861. See Pacheco, "Voyage from Tete to Zumbo," 22.
88. Lan, *Guns and Rain: Guerrillas and Spirit Mediums in Zimbabwe* (London: James Currey, 1985); Ruramisai Charumbira, *Imagining a Nation: History and Memory in Making Zimbabwe* (Charlottesville: University of Virginia Press, 2015).
89. For Charwe's association with anticolonial resistance and postcolonial nation-making, see, e.g., Terence O. Ranger, *Revolt in Southern Rhodesia, 1896–7: A Study of African Resistance* (London: Heinemann, 1967); David N. Beach, "An Innocent Women Unjustly Accused? Charwe, Medium of the Nehanda Mhondoro Spirit, and the 1896–97 Central Shona Rising in Zimbabwe," *History in Africa* 25 (1998): 27–54; Charumbira, *Imagining a Nation.*

For the Spirit of Nyamhita Nehanda and its importance in fertility, see Lan, *Guns and Rain.*

90. Interview with Soko, 9 March 2017; Lan, *Guns and Rain.*
91. Lan, *Guns and Rain,* 86.
92. Edwards, "Sacred Places," 23–24; David Chanaiwa, "A History of Nhowe before 1900" (PhD diss., University of California, Los Angeles, 1971), 110–13.
93. Mudenge, *Political History of Munhumutapa,* 127.
94. Bhila, *Trade and Politics,* 10–12.
95. Feierman, *Peasant Intellectuals: Anthropology and History in Tanzania* (Madison: University of Wisconsin Press, 1990), 69–93.
96. For the Matopos shrines, see Martinus Daneel, *God of the Matopo Hills: An Essay on the Mwari Cult of Rhodesia* (The Hague: Mouton, 1970); Ngwabi Bhebe, "The Ndebele and Mwari before 1893: A Religious Conquest of the Conquerors by the Vanquished," in *Guardians of the Land: Essays on Central African Territorial Cults,* ed. Mathew J. Schoffeleers (Gweru: Mambo Press, 1999), 287–95; Mathew J. Schoffeleers and R. Mwanza, "An Organizational Model for Mwari Shrines," in Schoffeleers, *Guardians of the Land,* 297–315; Terence O. Ranger, *Voices from the Rocks: Nature, Culture and History in the Matopos Hills of Zimbabwe* (Oxford, UK: James Currey, 1999). For Musikavanhu, see John K. Rennie, "From Zimbabwe to a Colonial Chieftaincy: Four Transformations of the Musikavanhu Territorial Cult," in Schoffeleers, *Guardians of the Land,* 257–85. For the Cult of Dzivaguru, see Bourdillon, "The Cults of Dzivaguru and Karuva amongst the North Eastern Shona Peoples," in Schoffeleers, *Guardians of the Land,* 235–55. For Marumbi Karivara, see Joseph Mujere, "The Marumbi Rain Cult: Gender and the Interface between Rain Making and the Politics of Water in Gutu" (paper presented at The Power of Water: Landscape, Water and the State in Southern and Eastern Africa conference, CAS, University of Edinburgh, Scotland, 28–29 March 2007).
97. Interview between Esther Chipashu and Gatsi elders. I am grateful to Esther Chipashu for giving me her transcripts of these interviews. Interview transcripts do not contain the date that she held these interviews. See also interview between author and Gatsi elders, 11 March 2017.
98. Bhila, *Trade and Politics,* 24.
99. Anonymous, "Chorographic Description," 12.
100. Denys Shropshire, "The Crocodile Ceremony of the Mutasa Dynasty," *Man* 30 (1930): 6; Denys Shropshire, "The Mifananidzo of the Mutasa Dynasty," *Man* 30 (1930): 4–5.
101. Bhila, *Trade and Politics,* 24–25. Wyatt McGaffey discusses similar relations in northern Ghana in West Africa. While this should not be read as evidence of cultural continuity between societies in West Africa and those in southern Africa, both cases allude to how power over land was contested among precolonial African societies. In both cases, ritual claims served as political rhetoric and performance to challenge chiefly claims to authority over land. See Wyatt McGaffey, *Chiefs, Priests and Praise-Singers: History,*

Politics and Land Ownership in Northern Ghana (Charlottesville: University of Virginia Press, 2013).

102. Shropshire, "Crocodile Ceremony," 6.
103. Da Conceição, "Treatise on the Rivers," 208.
104. "The Ritual Murders," report accompanying correspondence about ritual murders in Mount Darwin, 1923, N3/31/2, NAZ.

CHAPTER 3: CHANGING GEOGRAPHIES AND OLD REGISTERS OF POWER

1. Thomas Baines, *The Gold Regions of South Eastern Africa* (London: Edward Stanford, 1877), 26.
2. Frederick Courteney Selous, *Travel and Adventure in Southeast Africa* (1893; New York: Arno Press, 1967), 100.
3. W. Alfred Eckersley, "Notes in Eastern Mashonaland," *Geographic Journal* 5, no. 1 (1895): 39.
4. Eckersley, 39; Walter Montagu Kerr, *The Far Interior: A Narrative of Travel and Adventure from the Cape of Good Hope across the Zambezi to the Lake Regions of Central Africa,* vol. 1 (London: Sampson, Low, Martson, Searle and Rivington, 1887), 102.
5. Kerr, *Far Interior,* 103.
6. Kerr, 137–38.
7. Thomas N. Huffman, "Snakes and Birds: Expressive Space at Great Zimbabwe," *African Studies* 40, no. 2 (1981): 131–50; Thomas N. Huffman, *Snakes and Crocodiles: Power and Symbolism in Ancient Zimbabwe* (Johannesburg: Witwatersrand University Press, 1996).
8. Clapperton Chakanetsa Mavhunga, *The Mobile Workshop: The Tsetse Fly and African Knowledge* (Cambridge, MA: MIT Press, 2018), 30–35.
9. Edmund E. Burke, ed., *The Journals of Karl Mauch, 1869–1872* (Salisbury: National Archives of Rhodesia, 1969), 224.
10. Selous, *Travel and Adventure,* 93.
11. Selous, 94.
12. Burke, ed., *Journals of Karl Mauch,* 226. The addition in parentheses is from the original.
13. Eckersley, "Notes in Eastern Mashonaland," 39.
14. Mavhunga, *Mobile Workshop,* 30–35; Gerald Chikozho Mazarire, "Defence Consciousness as a Way of Life: The 'Refuge Period' and Karanga Defense Strategies in the 19th Century," *Zimbabwean Prehistory* 25 (2005): 19–26.
15. Innocent Pikirayi, *The Archaeological Identity of the Mutapa State: Towards an Historical Archaeology of Northern Zimbabwe,* Studies in African Archaeology 6 (Uppsala: Department of Archaeology and Ancient History, Uppsala University, 1993), 70.
16. David N. Beach, *The Shona and Their Neighbours* (Oxford, UK: Blackwell, 1994); David N. Beach, *A Zimbabwean Past: Shona Dynastic Histories and Oral Traditions* (Gweru: Mambo Press, 1994), 94; David N. Beach, "'Refugee' Archaeology, Trade and Gold Mining in Nineteenth Century Zimbabwe:

Izidoro Correia Pereira's List of 1857," *Zimbabwean Prehistory* 20 (1988): 3–8; Allen E. Isaacman and Barbara S. Isaacman, *Slavery and Beyond: The Making of Men and Chikunda Ethnic Identities in the Unstable World of South-Central Africa, 1750–1920* (Portsmouth, NH: Heinemann, 2004), 242. For the Portuguese meddling in the affairs of the Mutapa state, see Stanislus Isack G. Mudenge, *A Political History of Munhumutapa, c1400–1902* (Harare: Zimbabwe Publishing House, 1988), esp. chaps. 6 and 7, 201–84.

17. For Kanyemba's activities, see Isaacman and Isaacman, *Slavery and Beyond,* 241–43. For Gouveia, see David N. Beach, "The Origins of Mozambique and Zimbabwe: Paiva de Andrada, the Companhia de Moçambique and African Diplomacy, 1881–91," History Seminar Paper no. 89, Department of History, University of Zimbabwe, 1992 (unpublished ms.); see also Admire Mseba, "Late Precolonial Struggles, European Expansion, and the Making of Colonial Authority in Northeastern Zimbabwe, ca. 1840–1903," *International Journal of African Historical Studies* 51, no. 2 (2018): 243–62.
18. Burke, *Journals of Karl Mauch,* 232.
19. Jera Chanji, AOH 84, NAZ. Chanji's narrative might have been influenced by the immediate postindependence polarization between ZANU (PF) and (Patriotic Front) Zimbabwe African People's Union ([PF] ZAPU) and the government propaganda about dissidence. Later in the interview he adds that the historical Ndebele raids are the reason why the people in his area opposed Nkomo's ZAPU.
20. David N. Beach, *War and Politics in Zimbabwe, 1840–1900* (Gweru: Mambo Press, 1986), 33–37; David N. Beach, "Ndebele Raiders and Shona Power," *Journal of African History* 15, no. 4 (1974): 633–51.
21. George Wyndham Hamilton Knight-Bruce, *Journals of the Mashonaland Mission, 1888–1892* (London: Society for the Propagation of the Gospel in Foreign Parts, 1892), 31.
22. Beach, *Zimbabwean Past,* 94.
23. Beach, *Shona and Their Neighbours,* 45.
24. Gerald Chikozho Mazarire, "Defence Consciousness as a Way of Life: The 'Refuge Period' and Karanga Defence Strategy in the 19th Century," typescript, March 2005, 14.
25. Beach, *Zimbabwean Past,* 32–33.
26. Selous, *Travel and Adventure,* 90.
27. George Wyndham Hamilton Knight-Bruce, *Memories of Mashonaland* (London: Edward Arnold, 1895), 98.
28. Baines, *Gold Regions,* 27.
29. Kerr, *Far Interior,* 136, 206.
30. For a discussion of dynasties that had disappeared by the time of colonial rule, see Gerald Chikozho Mazarire, "A Social and Political History of Chishanga: South-Central Zimbabwe, *c.*1750–2000" (DPhil thesis, University of Zimbabwe, 2009); Mazarire, "Changing Landscapes." See also Beach, *Zimbabwean Past,* especially chap. 4, 133–88.

31. Gerald Chikozho Mazarire, "Reflections on Colonial Zimbabwe, *c.* 850–1880s," in *Becoming Zimbabwe: A History from the Precolonial Period to 2008,* ed. Brian Raftopoulos and Alois S. Mlambo (Harare: Weaver Press, 2009), 22–23.
32. David N. Beach, "The Rozvi in Search of Their Past," *History in Africa* 10 (1983): 14, 18. See also Beach, *Zimbabwean Past,* 126, 188–210; Elaine M. Lloyd, "Mbava," *Native Affairs Department Annual* 3 (1925): 62–64; "Speech: Chief Chiduku's Installation," Makoni District, 13 June 1987, PER/Chiduku; Innocent Dande and Joseph Mujere, "Contested Histories and Contested Land Claims: Traditional Authorities and the Fast Track Land Reform Programme in Zimbabwe, 2000–2017," *Review of African Political Economy* 46 (2019): 86–100.
33. See, for example, documents in Makoni District Files, PER/Chiduku, including a document titled "Speech: Chief Chiduku's Installation," Makoni District, 13 June 1987.
34. Beach, *Zimbabwean Past,* 126–27.
35. Lloyd, "Mbava," 62. See also Samuel Muhlanga (with Elaine M. Lloyd), "In the Early Days," *Native Affairs Department Annual* 4 (1926): 109.
36. See, for example, Hoyini H. K. Bhila, *Trade and Politics in a Shona Kingdom: The Manyika and Their Portuguese and African Neighbours* (London: Longman, 1983), 98.
37. Beach, *Zimbabwean Past,* 126–27.
38. George Fortune, "A Rozvi Text with Translation and Notes," *Native Affairs Department Annual* 33 (1956): 81. The Rozvi ruling houses living in Jiri in the Duma country in 1950 were resettled in Gokwe by the colonial government later that decade.
39. Igor Kopytoff, "The Internal African Frontier: The Making of African Political Culture," in *The African Frontier: The Reproduction of Traditional African Societies,* ed. Igor Kopytoff (Bloomington: Indiana University Press, 1987), 3–84.
40. Native Commissioner, Umtali, to Chief Native Commissioner, 21 December 1896, NUA2/1/1, NAZ.
41. David N. Beach, "From Heroism to History: Mapondera and the Northern Shona Plateau, 1840–1904," *History in Africa* 15 (1988): 85–161.
42. Beach, *Shona and Their Neighbours,* 45.
43. These are the positions that the colonial state came to call headmenships.
44. David Maxwell, *Christians and Chiefs in Zimbabwe: A Social History of the Hwesa People, c.1870s–1990s* (Edinburgh: Edinburgh University Press, 1999), 14.
45. Maxwell, 14.
46. W. S. Bazely, "Manyika Headwomen," *Native Affairs Department Annual* 17 (1940): 3.
47. Bazely, 3; Knight-Bruce, *Journals.*
48. Rose Blennerhassett and Lucy Sleeman, *Adventure in Mashonaland* (London: Macmillan, 1893), 151–52.

49. Blennerhassett and Sleeman, 239.
50. Knight-Bruce, *Journals,* 58.
51. Knight-Bruce, 58.
52. Albino Manoel Pacheco, "A Journey from Tete to Zumbo," in "The Shona and the Portuguese," ed. David N. Beach and H. de Noronha (unpublished ms., University of Zimbabwe, 1980), vol. 2, 31.
53. Blennerhassett and Sleeman, *Adventure in Mashonaland,* 243.
54. Blennerhassett and Sleeman, 246.
55. Blennerhassett and Sleeman, 254.
56. J. G. Storry, "The Settlement and Territorial Expansion of the Mutasa Dynasty," *Rhodesian History* 7 (1976): 26.
57. Kerr, *Far Interior,* 206.
58. Blennerhassett and Sleeman, *Adventure in Mashonaland,* 151–52, 246–55.
59. Kerr, *Far Interior,* 206.
60. Blennerhassett and Sleeman, *Adventure in Mashonaland,* 255.
61. Blennerhassett and Sleeman, 255.
62. Bazely, "Manyika Headwomen," 3–5. For connections between marriage and power among the Shona, see Diana Jeater, *Marriage, Perversion and Power: The Construction of a Moral Discourse in Southern Rhodesia, 1894–1930* (Oxford, UK: Clarendon Press, 1993).
63. Elizabeth Schmidt, *Peasants, Traders and Wives: Shona Women in the History of Zimbabwe, 1870–1939* (Portsmouth, NH: Heinemann, 1992), 16–19. See also Jeater, *Marriage, Perversion and Power,* 1–22.
64. Bazely, "Manyika Headwomen," 3–4.
65. Admire Mseba, "Narratives, Rituals and Political Imaginations: The Social and Political World of the Vashona of North-Eastern Zimbabwe from the 16th to the 19th Centuries," *Journal of Southern African Studies* 46, no. 3 (2020): 435–54.
66. Group discussion with Svongore brothers, 28 June 2012; interviews with Mutsago, 28 June 2013, and SaMuponda, 1 July 2013.
67. Bernard Kusena, pers. comm., 24 March 2017. Kusena, a longtime colleague who teaches in the Department of History, Heritage and Knowledge systems at the University of Zimbabwe, first related this story to me after he listened to my seminar presentation of an earlier draft of this chapter at the University of Zimbabwe in 2017. He then sent the same information as a text message.
68. Francis Musoni, "Cross-Border Mobility, Violence and Spiritual Healing in Beitbridge District, Zimbabwe," *Journal of Southern African Studies* 42, no. 2 (2016): 318.
69. Musoni, 317.
70. Musoni, 325. See also Heike Schmidt, "Healing the Wounds of War: Memories of Violence and the Making of History in Zimbabwe's Most Recent Past," *Journal of Southern African Studies* 33, no. 2 (1997): 301–10.
71. Albina Manoel Pacheco, *A Journey from Tete to Zumbo,* ed. and trans. Malyn Newitt (Oxford: Oxford University Press, 2013), 91.

72. G. Kingsley Garbett, "Religious Aspect of Political Succession among the Valley Korekore (N. Shona)," in *The Zambezian Past: Studies in Central African History,* ed. Eric Stokes and Richard Brown (Manchester: Manchester University Press, 1966), 141.
73. Garbett, 141. See also the discussion in Michael F. C. Bourdillon, *The Shona Peoples: An Ethnography of the Contemporary Shona, with Special Reference to Their Religion* (Gweru: Mambo Press, 1987).
74. Pacheco, *Journey from Tete to Zumbo,* 91.
75. Frederick Courteney Selous, *A Hunter's Wanderings in Africa: Being a Narrative of Nine Years Spent amongst the Game of the Far Interior of South Africa* (London: Richard Bentley & Son, 1881), 331.
76. Selous, 331.
77. The available sources do not mention the name of this medium. She might have been the medium of Goronga. Of this medium, Beach writes, the "cult had become powerful by at least the last half of the nineteenth century, and in the 1920s, there was a particularly influential medium of the Goronga spirit—so influential that at the time he was thought to be closely linked to, if not identical with, the Chaminuka spirit." Beach, "Rozvi," 19.
78. Frederic William Macdonald, *The Story of Mashonaland and the Missionary Pioneers* (London: Wesleyan Mission House, 1893), 44.
79. Macdonald, 43. Shimmin was clearly accompanied by an Isizulu- or Isindebele-speaking translator because the Shona title of this medium would have been *samukadzi.*
80. F. C. Selous to the Administrator, 25 January 1891, SE1/1/1, NAZ.
81. Pacheco, *Journey from Tete to Zumbo,* 93.
82. Friedrich Wilhelm Traugott Posselt, "Chaminuka the Wizard," *Native Affairs Department Annual* 4 (1926): 35.
83. Posselt, 37.
84. Macdonald, *Story of Mashonaland,* 43.
85. Schmidt, *Peasants, Traders and Wives,* 6; Jeater, *Marriage, Perversion and Power.*
86. Schmidt, *Peasants, Traders and Wives,* 14.
87. Schmidt, 16–19.
88. Madzivanyika Bvudzijena, Taonezvi Mazivei, and Simon Zhuwarara, AOH 81, NAZ; interviews with Svongore, 28 June 2013; Charova, 28 June 2013; *mbuya* Shava, 26 June 2013; *mbuya* Mashizha, 26 June 2013. The specific day of *mushumo* (also known as *chisi*) differed depending on the area. In the areas of Mberengwa, southern Zimbabwe, where I grew up, this day is a Wednesday. In the neighboring area of Chivi, the day is a Thursday.
89. Interviews with Makanya, 29 June 2013; Charova, 28 June 2013.
90. Interviews with Makanya, 29 June 2013; SaMuponda, 24 June 2013 and 1 July 2013; Mutsago, 28 June 2013.
91. Robert Soper, *Nyanga: Ancient Fields, Settlements and Agricultural History in Zimbabwe* (London: British Institute in Eastern Africa, 2002), 129.
92. Soper, 130.

93. Interview with Charova, 28 June 2013.
94. Rwambiwa Chari, AOH 37, NAZ.

CHAPTER 4: IMAGINING TRADITIONS, MAKING AUTHORITY

1. Jon F. Holleman, *Chief, Council and Commissioner: Some Problems of Government in Rhodesia* (Assen: Royal VanGorcum, 1969).
2. A large corpus of literature has shown that the colonial invention and imagination of customary authority and communal land tenure was meant to strengthen the patriarchal power of chiefs and male heads of households. An equally large number of studies has shown that this was not always successful. See, e.g., Terence O. Ranger, "Invention of Tradition in Colonial Africa," in *The Invention of Tradition,* ed. Eric J. Hobsbawm and Terence O. Ranger (Cambridge: Cambridge University Press, 1983), 211–62; Martin Chanock, *Law, Custom and Social Order: The Colonial Experience in Malawi and Zambia* (Cambridge: Cambridge University Press, 1985); Terence O. Ranger, "The Invention of Tradition Revisited: The Case of Colonial Africa," in *Legitimacy and the State in Twentieth Century Africa,* ed. Terence Ranger and O. Vaughan (Houndsmills, UK: Macmillan, 1993), 62–111; Sara Berry, "Hegemony on a Shoestring: Indirect Rule and Access to Agricultural Land," *Africa* 62, no. 3 (1992): 327–55; Sara Berry, *No Condition Is Permanent: The Social Dynamics of Agrarian Change in Sub-Saharan Africa* (Madison: University of Wisconsin Press, 1993); Sara Berry, *Chiefs Know Their Boundaries: Essays on Property, Power, and the Past in Asante, 1896–1996* (Portsmouth, NH: Heinemann, 2001); Thomas T. Spear, "Neo-traditionalism and the Limits of Invention in British Colonial Africa," *Journal of African History* 44, no. 1 (2003): 3–27; Thomas T. Spear, *Mountain Farmers: Moral Economies of Land and Agricultural Development in Arusha and Meru* (Berkeley: University of California Press, 1997).
3. This point is broadly made in Eric J. Hobsbawm and Terence O. Ranger, eds., *The Invention of Tradition* (Cambridge: Cambridge University Press, 1983).
4. Pennefather to Forbes, 28 September 1890, A1/6/1, NAZ.
5. The British South Africa Company, "Reports on the Native Disturbances in Rhodesia, 1896–97," March 1898, 79 (unpublished ms.). I am aware of the debate over the role of religious leaders in the 1896–97 Chimurenga uprisings. This debate does not concern us here. The colonial state, which is our focus in this section, was unambiguously convinced that the religious leaders had fomented and led the rebellions. For the debate, see, e.g., Terence O. Ranger, *Revolt in Southern Rhodesia, 1896–7: A Study in African Resistance* (London: Heinemann, 1967); Julian Cobbing, "The Absent Priesthood: Another Look at the Rhodesian Risings of 1896–1897," *Journal of African History* 18, no. 1 (1977): 61–84; David N. Beach, "An Innocent Woman Unjustly Accused? Charwe, Medium of the Nehanda Mhondoro Spirit, and the 1896–97 Central Shona Rising in Zimbabwe," *History in Africa* 25 (1998): 27–54; David N. Beach, "'Chimurenga': The Shona Rising of 1896–7," *Journal of African History* 20, no. 3 (1979): 395–420; Ruramisai Charumbira, "Nehanda and Gender

Victimhood in the Central Mashonaland 1896–97 Rebellions: Revisiting the Evidence," *History in Africa* 35 (2008): 103–31.

6. See correspondence in NAZ: N3/31/4, Witchcraft: Nyamhita alias Nyanda; N3/31/3, Witchcraft: Mlimo Worship; N3/1/13, Native Department: Interdepartmental Correspondence. See also Ruramisai Charumbira, *Imagining a Nation: History and Memory in Making Zimbabwe* (Charlottesville: University of Virginia Press, 2015), 67–74; Admire Mseba, "Environmental Phenomena, Colonial Injustices and Vernacular Discourse in Early Colonial Zimbabwe, 1895–c.1935," in *Environment, Power and Justice: Southern African Histories,* ed. Graeme Wynn, Jane Caruthers, and Nancy J. Jacobs (Athens: Ohio University Press, 2022), 193–220.
7. See Ranger, *Revolt in Southern Rhodesia;* David N. Beach, *War and Politics in Zimbabwe, 1840–1900* (Gweru: Mambo Press, 1986); Beach, "Innocent Woman Unjustly Accused?"; Charumbira, "Nehanda and Gender Victimhood"; Charumbira, *Imagining a Nation.*
8. Mahmood Mamdani, *Citizen and Subject: Contemporary Africa and the Legacy of Late Colonialism* (Princeton: Princeton University Press, 1996); Chanock, *Law, Custom,* 32–36.
9. Elizabeth Colson, *Marriage and Family among the Plateau Tonga* (Manchester: Manchester University Press, 1958); Chanock, *Law, Custom,* 35.
10. Chanock, *Law, Custom,* 35.
11. Mamdani, *Citizen and Subject,* 52.
12. Mamdani, 50.
13. W. H. Stead, "Concepts and Controls in Native Life: Elements of a Sociological Analysis," *Native Affairs Department Annual* 13 (1935): 6–13; Charles Bullock, "Can a Native Make a Will? Concepts of Testate Succession in Native Law," *Native Affairs Department Annual* 7 (1929): 104–9; Holleman, *Chief, Council and Commissioner.*
14. Native Commissioner, Chibi District, Written Evidence to the South African Native Affairs Commission, 1903, N3/6/3, NAZ.
15. Stead, "Concepts and Control"; Bullock, "Can a Native Make a Will?"
16. Bullock, "Can a Native Make a Will?" 106.
17. Stead, "Concepts and Control," 9.
18. Stead, 8. See also W. H. Stead, "The Clan Organization and Kinship System of Some Shona Tribes," *African Studies* 5, no. 1 (1946): 1–20.
19. Bullock, "Can a Native Make a Will?," 106.
20. Bullock, 106.
21. Native Commissioner, Chibi District, Written Evidence to the South African Native Affairs Commission, 1903, N3/6/3, NAZ.
22. Stead, "Concepts and Control"; Bullock, "Can a Native Make a Will?"; Elizabeth Schmidt, *Peasants, Traders and Wives: Shona Women in the History of Zimbabwe, 1870–1939* (Portsmouth, NH: Heinemann, 1992), 14–42.
23. W. S. Bazely, "Manyika Law and Custom Regarding Inheritance of Wives and Property and the Guardianship of Children," *Native Affairs Department Annual* 7 (1929): 110.

24. According to Terence Ranger, when one colonial official wrote that under the so-called communal land tenure all the land was vested in the chief, who held it in trust for the whole "tribe," the colonial official "emphasized the power of Makoni because he wanted the chief to impose agricultural and conservation rules on his people." Ranger, "The Communal Areas of Zimbabwe," in *Land in African Agrarian Systems,* ed. Thomas J. Bassett and Donald E. Crummey (Madison: University of Wisconsin Press, 1993), 355. See also Angela Cheater, "The Ideology of 'Communal' Land Tenure in Zimbabwe: Mythogenesis Enacted?," *Africa: Journal of the International African Institute* 60, no. 2 (1990): 188–206.
25. Land (Morris Carter) Commission, Final Report, para. 252, ZAH1/1/1, NAZ.
26. The oral evidence provided to the commission by the Africans, in fact, suggests that many Africans preferred to pull their resources together, purchase the land, and divide it into individual holdings. See Kadzima Mutasa (Chief Mutasa's brother), headman Chitombo, headman Munyarara, Chief Maranke, Hama (son of chief), headman Muchenje, headman Matanda, headman Mutsayo (Mutsago?), Chief Zimunya, headman Munyarari, headman Hukuimwe and headman Chigodora, Materi, Hama, Tapei, Chiwezhe, Mahuwe, Tsekwa, Gatawa, Munema, Taurwi, Mambudzi, Karuma, and Masukuta, pp. 1014–1024, ZAH1/1/3, NAZ.
27. Arthur S. Cripps, "African Land Tenure (A Plea for Tolerance)," *Native Affairs Department Annual* 4 (1926): 98.
28. Leroy Vail and Langdeg White, "Tribalism in the Political History of Malawi," in *The Creation of Tribalism in Southern Africa,* ed. Langdeg White (Berkeley: University of California Press, 1989), 163.
29. Attorney General to Chief Native Commissioner, 25 June 1904, N3/1/3, NAZ.
30. Attorney General to Chief Native Commissioner, 25 June 1904, N3/1/3, NAZ.
31. The Witchcraft Suppression Act of 1899 made witchcraft accusations and presiding over such cases a criminal offense.
32. In 1899, for example, colonial courts convicted Chief Kunzvi Nyandoro and three of his people (including the chief's brother) for contravening the Witchcraft Suppression Act (1899); a man from Makumbe's village was likewise convicted under the same law. In subsequent years, colonial courts prosecuted many chiefs, healers (*n'anga*), and commoners alike for their participation in African ritual practices classified by the colonial state as witchcraft. See Annual Report, Native Commissioner, Salisbury, 31 March 1899, N9/1/5, NAZ; Regina vs. Kunzvi Nyandoro, D3/5/1, NAZ; Annual Report, Native Commissioner, Salisbury, 31 March 1899, N9/1/5, NAZ; Native Commissioner, Umtali, to Chief Native Commissioner, 14 December 1900, NUA2/2/1, NAZ; Half Year Report, Native Commissioner and Superintendent of Natives, Umtali, 30 September 1903, NUA2/1/4, NAZ.
33. For a similar formulation about the ritual politics of power elsewhere in Africa, see Steven Feierman, *Peasant Intellectuals: Anthropology and History in Tanzania* (Madison: University of Wisconsin Press, 1990); Randall

Packard, *Chiefship and Cosmology: An Historical Study of Political Competition* (Bloomington: Indiana University Press, 1981).

34. Native Commissioner, Inyanga, to Native Commissioner, Umtali, 23 August 1904, NUC2/3/1, NAZ.
35. Native Commissioner, Inyanga, to Acting Chief Native Commissioner, 16 November 1904, NUC2/3/1, NAZ.
36. Superintendent of Natives, Umtali, to Chief Native Commissioner, 11 July 1917, NUA2/1/12, NAZ.
37. Makoni's claim that his fathers had appointed headmen under Chipunza was a fabrication. The Chipunza dynasty was older than that of Makoni. See discussion in chapter 2. See also David N. Beach, *The Shona and Zimbabwe: An Outline of Shona History* (Gweru: Mambo Press, 1980), 160.
38. For the transformation of the Rhodesian economy, see Giovani Arrighi, *The Political Economy of Rhodesia* (The Hague: Mouton, 1967).
39. Mamdani, *Citizen and Subject,* 96.
40. Donald S. Moore, *Suffering for Territory: Race, Place and Power in Zimbabwe* (Durham, NC: Duke University Press, 2005), 153–83. See also Eric Worby, "Maps, Names and Ethnic Games: The Iconography and Epistemology of Colonial Power in Northwestern Zimbabwe," *Journal of Southern African Studies* 20, no. 3 (1994): 371–92; Pius S. Nyambara, "*Madheruka* and *Shangwe:* Ethnic Identity and the Culture of Modernity in Gokwe, Northwestern Zimbabwe, 1963–1979," *Journal of Africa History* 43, no. 2 (2002): 287–306.
41. Superintendent of Natives, Umtali, Report on Staff of Division III, 1 July 1908, NUA2/2/1, NAZ.
42. "Forget me not re the difficulties of the early days," Box 196, Jesuit Archives Harare.
43. "Forget me not," Box 196, Jesuit Archives Harare. See also Schmidt, *Peasants, Traders and Wives,* 92–97.
44. Quoted in David Maxwell, *Christians and Chiefs in Zimbabwe: A Social History of the Hwesa People, c.1870s–1990s* (Edinburgh: Edinburgh University Press, 1999), 49.
45. Schmidt, *Peasants, Traders and Wives,* 26.
46. "Spirit Mediums, Healers, Churches and Cult Places, Manicaland, Inyanga," S3276/1, NAZ.
47. "Spirit Mediums, Healers, Churches and Cult Places, Manicaland, Inyanga," S3276/1, NAZ.
48. Superintendent of Natives, Umtali, to Principal, American Methodist Episcopal Church, Umtali, 9 October 1918, NUA2/1/12, NAZ.
49. Superintendent of Natives, Umtali, to Principal, American Methodist Episcopal Church, Umtali, 9 October 1918, NUA2/1/12, NAZ.
50. Native Commissioner, Rusape, to Chief Native Commissioner, 6 September 1901, N3/1/10, NAZ.
51. Native Commissioner, Rusape, to Chief Native Commissioner, 6 September 1901, N3/1/10, NAZ.

52. Native Commissioner, Umtali, to Canon Hallward, 20 May 1913, NUA2/1/11, NAZ.
53. Jon F. Holleman, "Some Shona Tribes of Southern Rhodesia," in *Seven Tribes of Central Africa,* ed. Elizabeth Colson and Max Gluckman (Manchester: Manchester University Press, 1951), 378.
54. Holleman, 378.
55. Native Commissioner, Umtali, to Chief Native Commissioner, 27 April 1904, NUA2/1/5, NAZ.
56. Native Commissioner, Umtali, to Chief Native Commissioner, 27 April 1904, NUA2/1/5, NAZ.
57. Bullock, "Can a Native Make a Will?," 104–9.
58. Bazely, "Manyika Law and Custom," 110–11.
59. Bazely, 112.
60. This resulted from the fact that if a man died in his old age, his children would be by then married and already living in their own homesteads away from the father's homestead. The practice seemed to have been widespread in southern and eastern Africa. Sally Falk Moore found a similar practice among the Chagga of Kilimanjaro in Tanzania. See Sally Falk Moore, *Social Facts and Fabrications: Customary Law on Kilimanjaro, 1880–1980* (Cambridge: Cambridge University Press, 1986), 83.
61. William P. Murphy and Caroline Bledsloe, "Kinship and Territory in the History of a Kpelle Chiefdom (Liberia)," in *The African Frontier: The Reproduction of Traditional Societies,* ed. Igor Kopytoff (Bloomington: Indiana University Press, 1987), 123.
62. Murphy and Bledsloe, "Kinship and Territory," 127–28; Liazzat J. K. Bonate, "The Ascendance of Angoche: The Politics of Kinship and Territory in Nineteenth Century Northern Mozambique," *Lusotopie* 10 (2003): 115–40.
63. Schmidt, *Peasants, Traders and Wives,* 17.
64. Annual Report, Native Commissioner, Umtali, N9/1/3, NAZ.
65. Annual Report, Native Commissioner, Umtali, N9/1/3, NAZ.
66. Annual Report, Native Commissioner, Umtali, N9/1/4, NAZ.
67. Annual Report, Native Commissioner, Goromonzi, N9/1/24, NAZ.
68. Annual Report, Native Commissioner, Inyanga, N9/1/24, NAZ.
69. See, e.g., Richard Hodder-Williams, *White Farmers in Rhodesia, 1890–1965: A History of Marandellas District* (London: Macmillan, 1983), 24.
70. Terence O. Ranger, *Peasant Consciousness and Guerrilla War in Zimbabwe: A Comparative Study* (London: James Currey, 1985).
71. Annual Report, Native Commissioner, Inyanga, N9/1/12, NAZ.
72. Annual Report, Native Commissioner, Inyanga, N9/1/16, NAZ.
73. Annual Report, Native Commissioner, Umtali, N9/1/24, NAZ.
74. Annual Report, Native Commissioner, Umtali, N9/1/24, NAZ.
75. The quotation is from Ian R. Phimister, "Commodity Relations and Class Formation in the Zimbabwean Countryside," *Journal of Peasant Studies* 13, no. 4 (1986): 254. See also Ian R. Phimister, *An Economic and Social History*

of Zimbabwe, 1890–1948: Capital Accumulation and Class Struggle (London: Longman, 1988), 64–80.

76. Phimister, "Commodity Relations," 250.
77. Phimister, 250.
78. Native commissioners estimated the number of people in their districts by multiplying the number of people on their tax registers by 3.5, arguing that this figure represented the average number of children and wives per each taxpayer's household. These estimates may, therefore, have a big margin of error. For the problems with this methodology and the demographic data in general, see David N. Beach, "Zimbabwean Demography: Early Colonial Data," *Zambezia* 17, no. 1 (1990): 31–53.
79. Annual Report, Native Commissioner, Inyanga, N9/1/19, NAZ.
80. Annual Report, Native Commissioner, Goromonzi, N9/1/22, NAZ.
81. Annual Report, Native Commissioner, Marandellas, N9/1/22, NAZ.
82. Annual Report, Native Commissioner, Umtali, N9/1/22, NAZ.
83. Annual Report, Native Commissioner, Marandellas, N9/1/16, NAZ.
84. Annual Report, Native Commissioner, Goromonzi, N9/1/19, NAZ.
85. Annual Report, Native Commissioner, Makoni, N9/1/19, NAZ.
86. Annual Report, Native Commissioner, Goromonzi, N9/1/14, N9/1/15, N9/1/16, NAZ. For completely different reasons, though, oral informants also claimed that Africans preferred to cultivate hillsides. See, e.g., interview between Joseph Jakarasi and *mbuya* Chikonzo, 19 April 2014; Makutu Taonezvi, AOH 80, NAZ; Jera Chanji, AOH 84, NAZ.
87. Annual Report, Native Commissioner, Goromonzi, N9/1/13, NAZ.
88. Annual Report, Native Commissioner, Goromonzi, N9/1/20, NAZ.
89. Annual Report, Native Commissioner, Goromonzi, N9/1/17, NAZ.
90. David Kamusoko, AOH 79, NAZ.
91. Makutu Taonezvi, AOH 80, NAZ.
92. Annual Report, Native Commissioner, Makoni, N9/1/12, NAZ.
93. See, e.g., Schmidt, *Peasants, Traders and Wives.*
94. Annual Report, Native Commissioner, Goromonzi, N9/1/12, NAZ.
95. Annual Report, Native Commissioner, Makoni, N9/1/12, NAZ.
96. Interview with *mbuya* Chikonzo, 25 April 2014.
97. They often ended up in the jaws of missionary paternalism and patriarchy. See Schmidt, *Peasants, Traders and Wives.*

CHAPTER 5: CHANGES IN THE LAW

1. Review of Reports of Native Commissioners in District III, Superintendent of Natives, Umtali, N9/1/21, NAZ.
2. Reports for the districts of Salisbury, Marandellas, Makonu, Inyanga, and Umtali in N9/1/22, N9/1/23, N9/1/24, N9/1/25, and S235/501, all in NAZ.
3. Annual Reports, 1920, Native Commissioner for Salisbury, N9/1/23, NAZ.
4. H. H. Simonds, Assistant Native Commissioner for Wedza, to Native Commissioner for Marandellas, 23 October 1923, S1561/33, NAZ.

5. Annual Reports, 1925, Native Commissioner for Marandellas, S235/203, NAZ.
6. Jocelyn Alexander, *The Unsettled Land: State-Making and the Politics of Land in Zimbabwe, 1893–2003* (Oxford, UK: James Currey, 2006), 22; Murray C. Steele, "The Foundations of a 'Native' Policy in Southern Rhodesia, 1923–1933" (PhD diss., Simon Fraser University, 1972), 10–11, 80–82.
7. Martin Chanock, *Law, Custom and Social Order: The Colonial Experience in Malawi and Zambia* (Cambridge: Cambridge University Press, 1985); Mahmood Mamdani, *Citizen and Subject: Contemporary Africa and the Legacy of Late Colonialism* (Princeton: Princeton University Press, 1996).
8. Alexander, *Unsettled Land,* 22.
9. Annual Reports, 1923, Native Commissioner, Charter District, S235/501, NAZ.
10. Native Commissioner, Marandellas, to Chief Native Commissioner, 21 August 1929, S138/41, NAZ; Steele, "Foundations of 'Native' Policy," 333–34.
11. Native Commissioner, Marandellas, to Chief Native Commissioner, 21 August 1929, S138/41, NAZ; Steele, "Foundations of 'Native' Policy," 84.
12. Chief Native Commissioner to Native Commissioner, Marandellas, 21August 1930, S138/41, NAZ.
13. See Allison Shutt, "The Natives Are Getting Out of Hand: Legislating Manners, Insolence and Contemptuous Behaviour in Southern Rhodesia, 1910–1963," *Journal of Southern African Studies* 33, no. 3 (2007): 653–72; Allison K. Shutt, *Manners Make a Nation: Racial Etiquette in Southern Rhodesia, 1910–1963* (Rochester: Rochester University Press, 2015), 21–50.
14. Native Commissioner, Marandellas, to Chief Native Commissioner, 18 August 1930, S138/41, NAZ.
15. See, e.g., Lan, *Guns and Rain: Guerrillas and Spirit Mediums in Zimbabwe* (London: James Currey, 1985), 72–111.
16. Native Commissioner, Marandellas, to Chief Native Commissioner, 18 August 1930, S138/41, NAZ.
17. I borrow the phrase from Steven Feierman, *Peasant Intellectuals: Anthropology and History in Tanzania* (Madison: University of Wisconsin Press, 1990). See also Admire Mseba, "Environmental Phenomena, Colonial Injustices, and Vernacular Discourse in Early Colonial Zimbabwe, 1895–c.1935," in *Environment, Power and Justice: Southern African Histories,* ed. Graeme Wynn, Jane Caruthers, and Nancy J. Jacobs (Athens: Ohio University Press, 2022), 193–220.
18. Native Commissioner, Marandellas, to Chief Native Commissioner, 18 August 1930, S138/41, NAZ.
19. Steele, "Foundations of 'Native' Policy," 49; Native Commissioner, Marandellas, to Chief Native Commissioner, 21 August 1929, S138/41, NAZ; Chief Native Commissioner to Major Chomley, 22 December 1930, S138/41, NAZ.
20. Steele, "Foundations of 'Native' Policy," 49.
21. Steele, 76.

22. The quotation is from Steele, 77. See also Alexander, *Unsettled Land,* 22.
23. Native Commissioner, Marandellas, to Chief Native Commissioner, 21 August 1929, S138/41, NAZ.
24. Chief Native Commissioner to Native Commissioner, Marandellas, 27 June 1928, S138/41, NAZ.
25. Native Commissioner, Marandellas, to Chief Native Commissioner, 21 August 1929, S138/41, NAZ.
26. Steele, "Foundations of 'Native' Policy," 141.
27. Steele, 141.
28. Chief Native Commissioner to Native Commissioner, Marandellas, 24 July 1930, S138/41, NAZ. Chief Svosve had fined the complainants ten to fourteen cattle. In the case of Mauskwa, Chief Svosve demanded that he should "work for a month for . . . [him]—breaking up new lands—as a 'bandit,' i.e., a prisoner, without pay."
29. Native Commissioner, Marandellas, to Chief Native Commissioner, 18 August 1930, S138/41, NAZ.
30. Assistant Native Commissioner, Wedza, to Native Commissioner, Marandellas, 11 August 1930, S138/41, NAZ.
31. Native Commissioner, Marandellas, to Chief Native Commissioner, 18 August 1930, S138/41, NAZ.
32. Native Commissioner, Marandellas, to Chief Native Commissioner, 18 August 1930, S138/41, NAZ.
33. Chief Native Commissioner to Native Commissioner, Marandellas, 21 August 1930, S138/41, NAZ.
34. Chief Native Commissioner to Native Commissioner, Marandellas, 21 August 1930, S138/41, NAZ.
35. Chief Native Commissioner to Native Commissioner, Marandellas, 21 August 1930, S138/41, NAZ.
36. Minister of Native Affairs to Attorney General, 26 August 1930, S138/41, NAZ.
37. Attorney General to Prime Minister, 29 August 1930, S138/41, NAZ.
38. Chief Native Commissioner to Native Commissioner, Marandellas, 15 September 1930, S138/41, NAZ.
39. Steele, "Foundations of 'Native' Policy," 83.
40. Murray Steele suggests that in the 1920s and early 1930s, major ideological differences could be seen between experienced native commissioners who had been with the Native Affairs Department for a long time and the newer ones who had cut their teeth in other colonies, particularly Natal. Fritz Posselt might have been an exception to this. Steele, "Foundations of 'Native' Policy," 83–84.
41. Native Commissioner, Marandellas, to Chief Native Commissioner, 14 November 1931, S1561/59, NAZ.
42. Mseba, "Environmental Phenomena," 193–220. See also James L. Giblin, *A History of the Excluded: Making Family a Refuge from the State in Twentieth*

Century Tanzania (Athens: Ohio University Press, 2005); James L. Giblin, "Vampires and History," *African Studies Review* 44, no. 1 (2001): 86–87.

43. Assistant Native Commissioner, Wedza, to Native Commissioner, Marandellas, 11 August 1930, S138/41, NAZ.
44. Christopher Kasege's Statement, S138/41, NAZ.
45. Christopher Kasege's Statement, S138/41, NAZ.
46. Native Commissioner, Marandellas, to Chief Native Commissioner, 21 August 1929, S138/41, NAZ.
47. James C. Scott, *Seeing Like a State: How Certain Schemes to Improve the Human Condition Have Failed* (New Haven, CT: Yale University Press, 1998).
48. Donald S. Moore, *Suffering for Territory: Race, Place and Power in Zimbabwe* (Durham, NC: Duke University Press, 2005).
49. Steele, "Foundations of 'Native' Policy," 86–87.
50. For a discussion of this point and its weaknesses, see Alexander, *Unsettled Land,* 23.
51. Steele, "Foundations of 'Native' Policy," 86.
52. Steele, 86.
53. Native Law and Courts Bill, S1561/59, NAZ.
54. Solicitor General, Notes on Native Courts Bill (no date), S1561/59, NAZ.
55. Steele, "Foundations of 'Native' Policy," 75.
56. Native Commissioner, Inyanga, to Chief Native Commissioner, 30 July 1933, S1542/C16/1, NAZ.
57. Native Commissioner, Inyanga, to Chief Native Commissioner, 30 July 1933, S1542/C16/1, NAZ.
58. See discussion in chapter 2.
59. See discussion in chapter 2. See also [Jason Takafa] Machiwenyika, "History and Customs of the Manyika," Lesson 89, MA 14/1/1, NAZ; David N. Beach, "Oral Tradition in Eastern Zimbabwe: The Work of Jason Takafa Machiwenyika, c1889–1924," paper presented at Words and Voices: Critical Practices of Orality in Africa and African Studies conference (Bellagio, Italy, February 24–28, 1997), 15.
60. The colonial state had begun to undermine African agriculture well before this point through land dispossessions and, beginning in 1908, an explicit policy of promoting white settler agriculture. But in parts of the colony, African agriculture was quite resilient. See, e.g., Victor E. M. Machingaidze, "The Development of Settler Capitalist Agriculture in Southern Rhodesia with Particular Reference to the Role of the State, 1908–1939" (DPhil thesis, University of London, 1980); Robin Palmer, *Land and Racial Domination in Rhodesia* (Berkeley: University of California Press, 1977); Robin Palmer, "The Agricultural History of Rhodesia," in *The Roots of Rural Poverty in Central and Southern Africa,* ed. Robin Palmer and Neil Parsons (Berkeley: University of California Press, 1977), 221–54; Steele, "Foundations of 'Native' Policy," 10; Terence O. Ranger, *Peasant Consciousness and Guerrilla War in Zimbabwe: A Comparative Study* (London: James Currey, 1985).

61. Steele, "Foundations of 'Native' Policy," 304; JoAnn McGregor, "Conservation, Control and Ecological Change: The Politics and Ecology of Colonial Conservation in Shurugwi, Zimbabwe," *Environment and History* 1, no. 3 (1995): 257–79; Moore, *Suffering for Territory*.
62. Alexander, *Unsettled Land*, 23–26. This paragraph draws on Alexander's work. See also Eira Kramer, "The Clash of Economies: Early Centralization Efforts in Colonial Zimbabwe, 1929–1935," *Zambezia* 25, no. 1 (1998): 83–98; Steele, "Foundations of 'Native' Policy."
63. I am alluding to the idea of legibility in the sense that it is discussed by James C. Scott. See Scott, *Seeing Like a State*. See also Victor Machingaidze, "Agrarian Change from Above: The Southern Rhodesia Native Land Husbandry Act and African Response," *International Journal of African Historical Studies* 24, no. 3 (1991): 557–88; Alexander, *Unsettled Land;* Moore, *Suffering for Territory;* William A. Munro, *The Moral Economy of the State: Conservation, Community Development and State-Making in Zimbabwe* (Athens: Ohio University Center for International Studies, 1998).
64. Gwatidzo Panyanyiwa, AOH 89, NAZ. See also Jera Chanji, AOH 84, NAZ.
65. See Victor Muchineripi Gwande, *Manufacturing in Colonial Zimbabwe, 1890–1979: Interest Group Politics, Protectionism and the State* (Woodbridge, UK: James Currey, 2022).
66. Quoted in Machingaidze, "Agrarian Change from Above," 567.
67. Machingaidze, 567.
68. Native Commissioner, Umtali, to Provincial Native Commissioner, Umtali, 23 March 1949, S1012/27, NAZ.
69. Ian R. Phimister, "Rethinking the Reserves: Southern Rhodesia's Land Husbandry Act Reviewed," *Journal of Southern African Studies* 19, no. 2 (1993): 225–39.
70. For the stated goal of native demonstration work in the reserves, see Assistant Native Commissioner, Wedza, to Native Commissioner, Marandellas, 23 October 1923, S1561/33, NAZ; Native Commissioner, Marandellas, to Superintendent of Natives, Salisbury, 24 October 1923, S1561/33, NAZ; Superintendent of Natives, Umtali, to Chief Native Commissioner, 23 October 1923, S1561/33, NAZ. For the rising concerns about environmental degradation in the reserves in the 1930s, see William Beinart, "Soil Erosion, Conservationism and Ideas about Development: A Southern African Exploration, 1900–1960," *Journal of Southern African Studies* 11, no. 1 (1984): 52–83; Ian R. Phimister, "Discourse and the Discipline of Historical Context: Conservationism and Ideas about Development in Southern Rhodesia, 1930–1950," *Journal of Southern African Studies* 12, no. 2 (1986): 263–75; Machingaidze, "Agrarian Change from Above"; David Anderson, "Depression, Dust Bowl, Demography and Drought: The Colonial State and Conservation in East Africa in the 1930s," *African Affairs* 83, no. 332 (1984): 321–43.
71. For the role played by these officials, see the extensive correspondence in S2384/K5843/3236, Native Township, Chihota; and S2588/1977, Correspondence, Land: 1931–1957, Inyanga, vol. 2.

72. Michael Drinkwater, *The State and Agrarian Change in Zimbabwe's Communal Areas* (Houndsmills, UK: Macmillan, 1991).
73. Alexander, *Unsettled Land,* 24; Mbofana Philip Willie George, AOH 70, NAZ. Mbofana was among the early African demonstrators to be trained at Domboshava Government Training School and was deployed to Chihota Reserve in 1933.
74. See, e.g., Pius S. Nyambara, "A History of Land Acquisition in Gokwe, Northwestern Zimbabwe, 1945–1997" (PhD diss., Northwestern University, 1999); McGregor, "Conservation."
75. Interview between *mbuya* Chikonzo and Joseph Jakarasi, 19 April 2014.
76. Phimister, "Rethinking the Reserves."
77. Interview with *mbuya* Chikonzo, 25 April 2014; interview between *mbuya* Chikonzo and Joseph Jakarasi, 19 April 2014.
78. Interview with *mbuya* Chikonzo, 25 April 2014.
79. See Phimister, "Rethinking the Reserves"; Moore, *Suffering for Territory,* 117.
80. Quoted in Ranger, *Peasant Consciousness,* 153.
81. Ranger, *Peasant Consciousness,* 153.
82. Moore, *Suffering for Territory,* 117.
83. Interview with *mbuya* Shava and *mbuya* Mashizha, 26 June 2013.
84. Terence Ranger, *Writing Revolt: An Engagement with African Nationalism, 1957–1967* (Harare: Weaver Press, 2013), 33. For disparities elsewhere in Zimbabwe, see also Nyambara, "History of Land Acquisition."
85. Nyambara, "History of Land Acquisition," 3.
86. Nyambara, 3.
87. Admos Chimhowu and Philip Woodhouse, "Forbidden but Not Suppressed: A 'Vernacular' Land Market in Svosve Communal Lands, Zimbabwe," *Africa: Journal of the International African Institute* 80, no. 1 (2010): 23–24.
88. Jon F. Holleman, *Shona Customary Law with Particular Reference to Kinship, Marriage, the Family and Estate* (London: Oxford University Press, 1952), 320.
89. E. D. Alvord, "Observations Re: Col Curbutt's Views," date-stamped 1 June 1937, S1542/R9, NAZ.
90. Report of an Ad Hoc Committee on Marandellas District, 12 November 1946, S2384/K5843/3236, NAZ.
91. Director of Native Agriculture to Provincial Native Commissioner, 25 March 1947, S2384/K5843/3236, NAZ.
92. Director of Native Agriculture to Provincial Native Commissioner, 25 March 1947, S2384/K5843/3236, NAZ.
93. Acting Director of Native Agriculture to Chief Native Commissioner, 10 December 1946, S2384/K5843/3236, NAZ.
94. Native Commissioner, Marandellas, quoted in Jennifer A. Elliot, "Soil Erosion and Conservation in Zimbabwe: Political Economy and the Environment" (PhD diss., Loughborough University of Technology, 1989), 88.
95. Holleman, *Chief, Council and Commissioner,* 335.

96. Holleman, 335. As a member of this commission, Holleman was largely responsible for putting the commission's final report together. The report forms the core of his book.
97. See, e.g., Nyambara, "History of Land Acquisition"; Mark Nyandoro, "Zimbabwe's Land Struggles and Land Rights in Historical Perspective: The Case of Gokwe-Sanyati Irrigation (1950–2000)," *Historia* 57, no. 2 (2012): 336.
98. Ngwabi Bhebe, *Benjamin Burombo: African Politics in Zimbabwe* (Harare: College Press, 1989); Ranger, *Peasant Consciousness;* Machingaidze, "Agrarian Change from Above"; Nyambara, "History of Land Acquisition," 102; interview between Trymore Jena and Joseph Jakarasi, 20 April 2014.
99. "Agricultural Demonstration Work in Chihota Reserve" (no date), date-stamped 9 September 1947, S2384/K5843/3236, NAZ.
100. Chikore's reminiscences from group interview with Madzivanyika Bvudzijena, Taonezvi Mazivei, and Simon Zhuwarara, AOH 81, NAZ.
101. Interview between Joseph Jakarasi and John Mupfumi Tigere and Edmund Ndoro, 23 July 2014.
102. Interview between Joseph Jakarasi and John Mupfumi Tigere and Edmund Ndoro, 23 July 2014. Chief Mangwende, who is mentioned in the song, vigorously resisted the NLHA in the Mangwende Reserve in Mrewa District to the north of Goromonzi District. The colonial state dethroned and banished him to Seke Reserve. It set a commission to look into the resistance. See "Report of the Commission of Inquiry into Alleged Discontent in the Mangwende Reserve" (Mangwende Reserve Commission), 1961. See also Holleman, *Chief, Council and Commissioner.*
103. Holleman, *Chief, Council and Commissioner,* 206.
104. Holleman, 206.
105. Holleman, 206.
106. Peter Delius, *A Lion amongst the Cattle: Reconstruction and Resistance in the Northern Transvaal* (Portsmouth, NH: Heinemann, 1996).
107. The ensuing discussion of the failed conservation measures in the Marange Reserves draws on Admire Mseba, "'Cattle Culling and All That Stuff': Modernity, Mobilization and the Everyday Language of Environmental Change in Northeastern Zimbabwe," in *Transplanting Modernity? New Histories of Poverty, Development and the Environment,* ed. Jenny Leigh Smith and Tom Robertson (Pittsburgh: Pittsburgh University Press, 2023), 81–83.
108. Solomon George Majokwe Chipfatsura Maranke Gandidzamwa to Native Commissioner for Umtali, 12 February 1952, S1012/AGRI3–11, NAZ.
109. Native Commissioner for Umtali to Provincial Native Commissioner for Manicaland, 4 April 1952; Land Development Officer to Native Commissioner for Umtali, 16 March 1953; both in S1012/AGRI3–11, NAZ.
110. Kate B. Showers, *Imperial Gullies: Soil Erosion and Conservation in Lesotho* (Athens: Ohio University Press, 2005).
111. Exemplified by Ngwabi Bhebe, *Benjamin Burombo;* Ranger, *Peasant Consciousness.*

112. Native Commissioner for Umtali to Provincial Native Commissioner, Manicaland, 4 April 1952, S1012/AGRI3–11, NAZ.
113. Land Development Officer to Native Commissioner for Umtali, 29 March 1952, S1012/AGRI3–11, NAZ.
114. District Land Development Officer to Assistant Native Commissioner, Wedza, 14 February 1945, S2384/K5843/3236, NAZ.
115. For a study that reveals the benefits of thinking outside the box of statist narratives, see Giblin, *History of the Excluded.*
116. Native Commissioner, Marandellas, to Director of Native Development, 8 October 1944, S2384/K5843/3236, NAZ. Although many scholars have argued that the policy of centralization was a failure, individual farmers claimed that when they adopted the methods taught by demonstrators, especially the use of manure, their yields improved. See, e.g., Madzivanyika Bvudzijena, Taonezvi Mazivei, and Simon Zhuwarara, AOH 81, NAZ; Makutu Taonezvi, AOH 80, NAZ.
117. Interview between Joseph Jakarasi and Trymore Jena, 19 January 2014.
118. Quoted in Holleman, *Chief, Council and Commissioner,* 260. Emphasis in original. See also Gloria Passmore, "Historical Rationale of the Policy of Community Development in the African Rural Areas of Rhodesia," *Zambezia* 2, no. 1 (1971): 67.
119. Alexander, *Unsettled Land,* 83–104.
120. Alexander, 83–104; Munro, *Moral Economy.*

CHAPTER 6: ACCESSING LAND AND CONTESTING AUTHORITY OUTSIDE THE RESERVES OF NORTHEASTERN ZIMBABWE

1. Native Commissioner, Inyanga, to Chief Native Commissioner, 5 December 1908, NUC2/1/3, NAZ.
2. "Return Respecting Adult Males in the Umtali Circuit, i.e., Umtali, Melsetter, Rusape and Inyanga," 29 April 1912, NUA2/1/10, NAZ.
3. Terence O. Ranger, *Peasant Consciousness and Guerrilla Warfare in Zimbabwe: A Comparative Study* (London: James Currey, 1985).
4. Ranger, 33.
5. Quoted in Robin Palmer, *Land and Racial Domination in Rhodesia* (Berkeley: University of California Press, 1977), 266. T. B. Hulley, the native commissioner in question, began his tenure in Umtali in June 1896. See Services of Officers, Thomas Benjamin Hulley, NUA2/1/8, NAZ.
6. Palmer, *Land and Racial Domination,* 257.
7. Native Commissioner, Inyanga (other details missing), 1 August 1908, NUC2/1/3, NAZ.
8. Native Commissioner, Makoni, to Superintendent of Natives, Umtali, 21 May 1912, N3/16/1, NAZ.
9. See, e.g., the descriptions of the localities by the native commissioner for Umtali. Report, Native Commissioner, Umtali, 4 May 1914, NUA2/1/11, NAZ.
10. Native Commissioner, Inyanga, to Superintendent of Natives, Umtali, 4 August 1916, NUC2/1/6, NAZ.

11. Native Commissioner, Inyanga, to Superintendent of Natives, Umtali, 4 August 1916, NUC2/1/6, NAZ.
12. For Matabeleland, see Jocelyn Alexander, JoAnn McGregor, and Terence Ranger, *Violence and Memory: One Hundred Years in the "Dark Forests" of Matebeleland* (Portsmouth, NH: Heinemann, 2000); Terence O. Ranger, *Voices from the Rocks: Nature, Culture and History in the Matopos Hills of Zimbabwe* (Oxford, UK: James Currey, 1999).
13. Annual Report, Native Commissioner, N9/1/13, NAZ.
14. Native Commissioner, Inyanga, to Civil Commissioner, Umtali, 8 September 1905, NUC2/2/1, NAZ.
15. Native Commissioner, Umtali, to Chief Native Commissioner, 15 January 1909, NUA2/1/8, NAZ.
16. Max Angelbeck to Native Commissioner, Umtali, 1 June 1903, NUA1/1/2, NAZ. See also John K. Rennie, "White Farmers, Black Tenants and Landlord Legislation: Southern Rhodesia, 1890–1930," *Journal of Southern African Studies* 5, no. 1 (1978): 86–98.
17. Rennie, "White Farmers, Black Tenants," 86–98.
18. Report titled "Native Nomenclature," 19 April 1912, NUA2/1/10, NAZ.
19. Majubane, "African Names of Native and District Commissioners," *Native Affairs Department Annual* 11, no. 2 (1975): 254.
20. Majubane, "African Names."
21. The imperial government made this point clear by outlawing forced labor, one of the major grievances that sparked the 1896–97 risings.
22. Extract from Exhibit "A" Rex v Mukutsha, NUA2/1/8, NAZ.
23. Superintendent of Natives, Umtali, to O.C. "D" Troop, BSAP, 31 December 1908, NUA2/1/8, NAZ.
24. Superintendent of Natives, Umtali, to O.C. "D" Troop, BSAP, 31 December 1908, NUA2/1/8, NAZ.
25. Superintendent of Natives, Umtali, to O.C. "D" Troop, Umtali, 5 January 1909, NUA2/1/8, NAZ.
26. Native Commissioner, Umtali, to A. H. Chaser, 11 August 1904, NUA2/1/5, NAZ.
27. Assistant Native Commissioner, Umtali, to Holand, 7 June 1909, NUA2/1/8, NAZ.
28. Native Commissioner, Inyanga, to Superintendent of Natives, Umtali, 31 August 1916, NUC2/1/6, NAZ.
29. Native Commissioner, Umtali, to Manager, Premier Estate, 29 October 1917, NUA2/1/12, NAZ.
30. Native Commissioner, Umtali, to A. H. Chaser, 11 August 1904, NUA2/1/5, NAZ.
31. Superintendent of Natives, Umtali, to Business Manager, Rezende Mines, 2 July 1917, NUA2/1/12, NAZ.
32. For connections between ideas of civilization and the rule of law, see Mahmood Mamdani, *Citizen and Subject: Contemporary Africa and the Legacy of Late Colonialism* (Princeton: Princeton University Press, 1996), 115.

33. Mathew W. White to Native Commissioner, Umtali, 16 November 1900, NUA1/1/1, NAZ.
34. Assistant Native Commissioner, Umtali, to Chief Native Commissioner, 12 December 1900, NUA1/1/1, NAZ.
35. Native Commissioner, Umtali, to C. Weissenborn, 24 March 1904, NUA2/1/5, NAZ.
36. Native Commissioner, Umtali, to C. Weissenborn, 19 April 1904, NUA2/1/5, NAZ.
37. Native Commissioner, Inyanga, to Chief Native Commissioner, 26 March 1907, NUC2/1/2, NAZ.
38. Native Commissioner, Umtali, to Chief Native Commissioner, 15 April 1904, NUA2/1/5, NAZ.
39. Assistant Native Commissioner, Inyanga, to White, 19 December 1900, NUA2/1/4, NAZ.
40. Superintendent of Natives, Umtali, to Chief Native Commissioner, 22 October 1908, NUA2/1/8, NAZ.
41. Superintendent of Natives, Umtali, to Chief Native Commissioner, 22 October 1908, NUA2/1/8, NAZ.
42. Superintendent of Natives, Umtali, to Chief Native Commissioner, 2 January 1914, NUA2/1/11, NAZ.
43. Superintendent of Natives, Umtali, to Chief Native Commissioner, 2 January 1914, NUA2/1/11, NAZ.
44. Pius S. Nyambara, "'That Place Was Wonderful!' African Tenants on Rhodesdale Estate, Colonial Zimbabwe, *c.*1900 to 1952," *International Journal of African Historical Studies* 38, no. 2 (2005): 269.
45. Annual Report, Native Commissioner, Umtali, N9/1/13, NAZ. Under section 13 of the Private Locations Ordinance (1908), settler landowners could have more than forty adult male Africans on their farms provided they did not demand rent or labor in lieu of rent from the tenants but would, instead, employ them at prevailing wages on the market. Farms where such arrangements existed were the exempted farms.
46. See, for example, Assistant Native Commissioner, Umtali, to J. W. Gray, 1 April 1912, NUA2/1/10, NAZ; Assistant Native Commissioner, Umtali, to J. W. Gray, 3 April 1912, NUA2/1/10, NAZ.
47. Superintendent of Natives, Umtali, to V. A. Gross, 13 March 1914, NUA2/1/11, NAZ.
48. Letter to Superintendent of Natives, Umtali (other details missing), S156/10/1, NAZ.
49. Letter to Superintendent of Natives, Umtali (other details missing), S156/10/1, NAZ.
50. Native Commissioner, Inyanga, to Acting Chief Native Commissioner, 6 January 1905, NUC2/3/1, NAZ.
51. Native Commissioner, Inyanga, to Acting Chief Native Commissioner, 5 January 1905, NUC2/3/1, NAZ.

52. Native Commissioner, Inyanga, to Acting Chief Native Commissioner, 5 January 1905, NUC2/3/1, NAZ.
53. Palmer, *Land and Racial Domination,* 257.
54. Native Commissioner, Inyanga, to L. L. Ewing, 13 October 1910, NUC2/1/4, NAZ.
55. Native Commissioner, Inyanga, to Chief Native Commissioner, 9 December 1904, NUC2/3/1, NAZ. The native commissioner pointed out that Chief Chikomba's old homestead had been two to three miles west of the border in Southern Rhodesia.
56. Native Commissioner, Umtali, to Chief Native Commissioner, 1 October 1906, NUA2/1/6, NAZ.
57. Letter from Superintendent of Natives, Umtali, to Chief Native Commissioner (no date), NUA2/1/12, NAZ.
58. Native Commissioner, Inyanga, to Superintendent of Natives, Umtali, 4 August 1916, NUC2/1/6, NAZ.
59. See the discussion of the Vhimba (in Chimanimani to the south of Mutare) and Gogoi borderlands of Southern Rhodesia and Portuguese East Africa by David M. Hughes. Hughes shows that while land alienation on the Zimbabwean side occurred early in the colonial period, the threat of land dispossession in Gogoi emerged as a result of the actions of South African timber companies in the 1990s. David McDermott Hughes, *From Enslavement to Environmentalism: Politics on a Southern African Frontier* (Seattle: University of Washington Press, 2006).
60. Native Commissioner, Umtali, to Chief Native Commissioner, 1 October 1906, NUA2/1/6, NAZ.
61. Monthly Report, March 1909, Native Commissioner, Inyanga, NUC2/1/3, NAZ.
62. Native Commissioner, Inyanga, to Superintendent of Natives, Umtali, 12 November 1909, NUC2/1/3, NAZ.
63. Many Africans may have exploited the practice of *kuronzera* to conceal their wealth. See Ngwabi Bhebe, *Benjamin Burombo: African Politics in Zimbabwe* (Harare: College Press, 1989).
64. Native Commissioner, Inyanga, to Superintendent of Natives, Umtali, 12 November 1909, NUC2/1/3, NAZ.
65. Mamdani, *Citizen and Subject.* See also Mahmood Mamdani, *Define and Rule: Native as Political Identity* (Cambridge, MA: Harvard University Press, 2012).
66. Mamdani, *Citizen and Subject.*
67. Native Commissioner, Rusape, to Superintendent of Natives, Umtali, 21 May 1912, N3/16/1, NAZ.
68. Native Commissioner, Rusape, to Superintendent of Natives, Umtali, 21 May 1912, N3/16/1, NAZ.
69. Chief Native Commissioner to Secretary, Department of Administrator, 16 August 1922, N3/16/1, NAZ.

70. Chief Native Commissioner to Secretary, Department of Administrator, 16 August 1922, N3/16/1, NAZ.
71. For cases elsewhere in the colony, see L2/2/5, Ancestral Graves for Natives. See also Joost Fontein, *Remaking Mutirikwi: Landscape, Water and Belonging in Southern Zimbabwe* (Woodbridge, UK: James Currey, 2015), esp. 139–68.
72. Native Commissioner, Makoni, to Chief Native Commissioner, 8 May 1934, S1542/C16/2, NAZ.
73. Chief Chipunza to Chief Native Commissioner, 8 April 1934, S1542/C16/2, NAZ. Chief Chipunza dictated the contents of the letter to an African minister at St. Faith Mission; see Native Commissioner, Makoni, to Chief Native Commissioner, 8 May 1934, S1542/C16/2, NAZ.
74. Native Commissioner, Inyanga, to Superintendent of Natives, Umtali (no date), NUC1/4/1, NAZ.
75. Special Land Commission Report, 28 August 1931, S1542/L4, NAZ.
76. Special Land Commission Report, 28 August 1931, S1542/L4, NAZ.
77. Special Land Commission Report, 28 August 1931, S1542/L4, NAZ.
78. Annual Reports, Native Commissioner, Inyanga, S235/520, NAZ.
79. Eric Worby, "Discipline without Oppression: Sequence, Timing and Marginality in Southern Rhodesia's Postwar Development Regime," *Journal of African History* 41, no. 1 (2000): 101–25; Jocelyn Alexander, "Technical Development and the Human Factor: Sciences of Development in Rhodesia's Native Affairs Department," in *Science and Society in Southern Africa,* ed. Saul Dubow (Manchester: Manchester University Press, 2000), 222–37.
80. Palmer, *Land and Racial Domination;* Henry V. Moyana, *The Political Economy of Land in Zimbabwe* (Gweru: Mambo Press, 2002).
81. Chief Native Commissioner to Secretary to the Premier, 26 March 1931, S1542/L4, NAZ.
82. Special Land Committee Report, 28 August 1931, S1542/L4, NAZ.
83. Memorandum from Native Commissioner, Umtali (other details missing), 13 January 1937, S1542/L4, NAZ.
84. Native Commissioner, Umtali, to Chief Native Commissioner, 29 September 1938, S1542/L4, NAZ. For the historical developments involving Chief Tendai Mutasa, the Portuguese, and the British at the time of the scramble for the European Zimbabwe plateau, see Admire Mseba, "Late Precolonial Struggles, European Expansion, and the Making of Colonial Authority in Northeastern Zimbabwe, ca. 1840 to 1903," *International Journal of African Historical Studies* 51, no. 2 (2018): 243–62; David N. Beach, "The Origins of Mozambique and Zimbabwe: Paiva de Andrada, the Companhia de Moçambique and African Diplomacy, 1881–91" (History Seminar Paper no. 89, Department of History, University of Zimbabwe, 1992); A. S. Nyamatore, "Mutasa, the British South Africa Company and the African Portuguese Syndicate: The Fight for Manyika in the 1890s" (Henderson Seminar Paper no. 41, Department of History, University of Zimbabwe, 1978); Hoyini H. K. Bhila, *Trade and Politics in a Shona Kingdom: The Manyika and Their*

Portuguese and African Neighbours (London: Longman, 1983); Philip Warhurst, *Anglo-Portuguese Relations in South-Central Africa, 1890–1900* (London: Longman, 1962).

85. Memorandum from Native Commissioner, Umtali (other details missing), 13 January 1937, S1542/L4, NAZ.
86. Ian R. Phimister, "Discourse and the Discipline of Historical Context: Conservationism and Ideas about Development in Southern Rhodesia, 1930–1950," *Journal of Southern African Studies* 12, no. 2 (1986): 263–75.
87. This was part of a much wider debate about African land use and holding practices. See, e.g., Nyambara, "That Place Was Wonderful"; Barry N. Floyd, "Changing Patterns of African Land Use in Southern Rhodesia" (PhD diss., Syracuse University, 1959).
88. Undersecretary, Department of Lands, to Chief Native Commissioner, 4 December 1937, S1542/R3, NAZ.
89. Memorandum on Conservation of Natural Resources on Land Occupied by Natives, S1188/3, NAZ.
90. Memorandum on Conservation of Natural Resources on Land Occupied by Natives, S1188/3, NAZ.
91. See Nyambara, "That Place Was Wonderful."
92. Pius S. Nyambara, "A History of Land Acquisition in Gokwe, Northwestern Zimbabwe, 1945–1997" (PhD diss., Northwestern University, 1999); Nyambara, "That Place Was Wonderful"; Ranger, *Voices from the Rocks;* Alexander, McGregor, and Ranger, *Violence and Memory.*
93. Priest-in-Charge, St. David's Bonda Mission, to Chief Native Commissioner, 4 April 1951, S2588/1977, NAZ.
94. Interview between Joseph Jakarasi and John Mupfumi Tigere and Edmund Ndoro, 23 July 2014.
95. Minutes of Meeting of Committee Appointed in Terms of Chief Native Commissioner's Minute no. F2666 of 19 April 1949, 19 May 1949, S1012/3, NAZ.
96. Ad Hoc Committee on Marandellas District Report, 12 November 1946, S2384/K5843/3236, NAZ.
97. Director of Native Agriculture to Provincial Native Commissioner, 25 March 1947, S2384/K5843/3236, NAZ.
98. Report on Zimunya (no date), S1012/3, NAZ. Although the report does not have a date, it was produced after the committee visited the reserve on 9 May 1949. See Minutes of Meeting of Committee Appointed in Terms of Chief Native Commissioner's Minute no. F2666 of 19 April 1949, 19 May 1949, S1012/3, NAZ.
99. Minutes of Meeting with Muponda, Mupotedzi, Ragu, Chimbodza, Manhanda, Head Messenger Patrick and Native Commissioner for Inyanga (date is missing, but a note accompanying the minutes is date-stamped 29 August 1952), S2985/LAN/1, NAZ.
100. Minutes of Meeting with Muponda, Mupotedzi, Ragu, Chimbodza, Manhanda, Head Messenger Patrick and Native Commissioner for Inyanga

(date is missing, but a note accompanying the minutes is date-stamped 29 August 1952), S2985/LAN/1, NAZ.

POSTSCRIPT

1. Shadreck Chirikure et al., "No Big Brother Here: Heterarchy, Shona Political Succession and the Relationship between Great Zimbabwe and Khami, Southern Africa," *Cambridge Archaeological Journal* 28, no. 1 (2017): 45–66.
2. George Hamandishe Karekwaivanane, *The Struggle over State Power in Zimbabwe: Law and Politics since 1950* (Cambridge: Cambridge University Press, 2017), 47–80.
3. Terence O. Ranger, *Peasant Consciousness and Guerrilla War in Zimbabwe: A Comparative Study* (London: James Currey, 1985); Terence O. Ranger, *Voices from the Rocks: Nature, Culture and History in the Matopos Hills of Zimbabwe* (Oxford, UK: James Currey, 1999).
4. Donald S. Moore, *Suffering for Territory: Race, Place and Power in Zimbabwe* (Durham, NC: Duke University Press, 2005).
5. Ben Cousins and Steven Robins, "Institutions for Land Redistribution and Management: The Zimbabwean Experience," *South African Sociological Review* 6, no. 2 (1994): 33.
6. Edward A. Dougherty, "Zimcord Conference Documentation," *African Issues* 11, no. 3–4 (1981): 53.
7. Cousins and Robins, "Institutions for Land Redistribution," 32.
8. In 1982, the government set a target of resettling 162,000 families on 10 million hectares of land. Cousins and Robins, 33.
9. Cousins and Robins, 34.
10. Sam Moyo, "The Political Economy of Land Acquisition and Redistribution in Zimbabwe, 1990–1999," *Journal of Southern African Studies* 26, no. 1 (2000): 5.
11. Moyo, 9.
12. The main objection to the constitution was because it gave excessive powers to the president.
13. Ian Scoones et al., *Zimbabwe's Land Reform: Myths and Realities* (Woodbridge, UK: James Currey, 2010), 7.
14. Cousins and Robins, "Institutions for Land Redistribution," 33. See also Allison Goebel, *Gender and Land Reform: The Zimbabwean Experience* (Montreal: McGill-Queen's University Press, 2005).
15. Moyo, "Political Economy," 21.
16. Joseph Hanlon, Jeannette Manjengwa, and Theresa Smart, *Zimbabwe Takes Back Its Land* (Boulder, CO: Kumarian Press, 2013), 160.
17. Prosper B. Matondi, *Zimbabwe's Fast Track Land Reform* (London: Zed Books, 2012), 185.
18. Lloyd M. Sachikonye, "The Situation of Commercial Farm Workers in Zimbabwe after Land Reform," report prepared for the Farm Community Trust of Zimbabwe (FCTZ), Harare, 2003; Lloyd M. Sachikonye, "Land Reform for Poverty Reduction? Social Exclusion and Farm Workers in Zimbabwe,"

paper prepared for Staying Poor: Chronic Poverty and Development Policy conference, organized by the IDMP, Manchester University, April 2003; Blair Rutherford, "Conditional Belonging: Farm Workers and the Cultural Politics of Recognition in Zimbabwe," *Development and Change* 39, no. 1 (2008): 73–99.

19. Sabelo J. Ndlovu-Gatsheni, *Do "Zimbabweans" Exist? Trajectories of Nationalism, National Identity Formation and Crisis in a Postcolonial State* (New York: Peter Lang, 2009), 264–76.
20. See the discussions in Mahmood Mamdani, *Citizen and Subject: Contemporary Africa and the Legacy of Late Colonialism* (Princeton: Princeton University Press, 1996); Mahmood Mamdani, *When Victims Became Killers: Colonialism, Nativism, and the Genocide in Rwanda* (Princeton: Princeton University Press, 2001).
21. James Muzondidya, quoted in Ndlovu-Gatsheni, *Do "Zimbabweans" Exist?*, 178. See also James Muzondidya, "'Zimbabwe for Zimbabweans': Invisible Subject Minorities and the Quest for Justice and Reconciliation in Postcolonial Zimbabwe," in *Zimbabwe: Injustice and Political Reconciliation*, ed. Brian Raftopoulos and Tyrone Savage (Cape Town: Institute for Justice and Reconciliation, 2004), 213–35.
22. Joseph Mujere, *Land, Migration and Belonging: A History of the Basotho in Southern Rhodesia, c. 1890–1960s* (Woodbridge, UK: James Currey, 2019), 75–98.
23. Quoted in Ndlovu-Gatsheni, *Do "Zimbabweans" Exist?*, 264.
24. Staff Reporter, "Zanu PF Accused of Tribalism," *Daily News*, 14 October 2002, http://www.zimbabwesituation.com/old/oct15_2002.html.
25. Mamdani, *Citizen and Subject*; Mamdani, *When Victims Became Killers*.
26. Quoted in Ndlovu-Gatsheni, *Do "Zimbabweans" Exist?*, 277.
27. Communal Land Act, chapter 20:04, https://faolex.fao.org/docs/pdf/zim2771.pdf (accessed 18 April 2023).
28. Mamdani, *When Victims Became Killers*.
29. Staff Reporter, "Zanu PF Accused of Tribalism."
30. Pius S. Nyambara, "A History of Land Acquisition in Gokwe, Northwestern Zimbabwe, 1945–1997" (PhD diss., Northwestern University, Evanston, IL, 1999).
31. Marja J. Spierenburg, *Strangers, Spirits and Land Reforms: Conflicts about Land in Dande, Northern Zimbabwe* (Leiden: Brill, 2005).
32. Jocelyn Alexander, *The Unsettled Land: State-Making and the Politics of Land in Zimbabwe, 1893–2003* (Oxford, UK: James Currey, 2006); Karekwaivanane, *Struggle over State Power*; William A. Munro, *The Moral Economy of the State: Conservation, Community Development and State-Making in Zimbabwe* (Athens: Ohio University Center for International Studies, 1998), 157–58.
33. Karekwaivanane, *Struggle over State Power*.
34. See, e.g., Cousins and Robins, "Institutions for Land Redistribution"; Alexander, *Unsettled Land*; Michael Drinkwater, *The State and Agrarian Change in Zimbabwe's Communal Areas* (Houndsmills, UK: Macmillan, 1991).

35. See, e.g., Nyambara, "History of Land Acquisition." See also Alexander, *Unsettled Land.*
36. Zimbabwe Land Acquisition Act, chapter 20:10 (2004).
37. Mbiba Lloyd, "Police Boot Out Villagers to Make Way for Grace," *Daily News,* 8 January 2015, http://www.dailynews.co.zw/articles/2015/01/08/police-boot-out-villagers-to-make-way-for-grace; Ndebele Hazel, "Manzou Evictions: State to Move In Wildlife," *Zimbabwe Independent,* 16 January 2015, http://www.theindependent.co.zw/2015/01/16/manzou-evictions-state-move-wildlife/; Staff Writer, "Chinotimba Invades 300ha Farm," *Daily News,* 8 January 2015, https://dailynews.co.zw/chinotimba-invades-300ha-farm/; Veritas, "Bill Watch 19-2021—Revisiting the Chlonga Story," https://www.veritaszim.net/node/4881 (accessed 1 December 2022); Zimbabwe Human Rights Association, "For the People of Chilonga, the Right to Land Remains Elusive," https://kubatana.net/2021/04/01/for-the-people-of-chilonga-the-right-to-land-remains-elusive/ (accessed 1 December 2022); VOA Zimbabwe, "Over 13000 Zimbabwe Villages Face Eviction in Area Set Aside for Cattle Feed Production," 7 March 2021, https://www.voazimbabwe.com/a/zimbabwe-farmers-eviction-chiredzi/5804754.html#; Zenda Cyril, "Fresh Land Grabs in Zimbabwe Kick Villagers off Ancestral Lands," FairPlanet, 29 April 2021, https://www.fairplanet.org/story/fresh-land-grabs-in-zimbabwe-kick-villagers-off-ancestral-lands/.

Bibliography

ARCHIVAL SOURCES

Jesuit Archives Harare

Box 196, St. Triashill

Makoni District Archives

Makoni District Council Files, PER/Chiduku

National Archives of Zimbabwe (NAZ)

A1/6, Administrator's In-Letters
D3, Criminal Cases
L2, Lands Department
MA14/1/1-2, [Jason Takafa] Machiwenyika, "History and Customs of the Manyika" (unpublished mss. in English and in Chishona/Chimanyika)
N3, Native Department Correspondence and Reports
N9/1, Native Commissioners' Annual Reports
NUA1, Native Commissioner and Superintendent of Natives, Umtali, In-Letters
NUA2, Native Commissioner and Superintendent of Natives, Umtali, Out-Letters
NUC1, Native Commissioner and Assistant Magistrate, Inyanga, In-Letters
NUC2, Native Commissioner and Assistant Magistrate, Inyanga, Out-Letters
S, Prime Minister's Office, Post 1923
SE1/1/1, Frederick Courteney Selous (1851–1917) Papers
ZAH1/1, Land (Morris Carter) Commission

ORAL INTERVIEWS

Charova, interviewed by Admire Mseba, 28 June 2013
Chikonamombe, interviewed by Admire Mseba, 11 March 2017
Mbuya Chikonzo, interviewed by Joseph Jakarasi, 19 April 2014; interviewed by Admire Mseba, 25 April 2014
Steven Dzimano, interviewed by Primrose Nyamhute, 13 October 2020

Stella Dzivira, interviewed by Primrose Nyamhute, 12 October 2020
Gatsi elders, interviewed by Admire Mseba, 11 March 2017; interviewed by Esther Chipashu, n.d.
Mbuya Gededza, interviewed by Admire Mseba, 29 June 2013
Sophia Gondokondo, interviewed by Primrose Nyamhute, 18 October 2020
Sara Guta, interviewed by Primrose Nyamhute, 16 October 2020.
Tendai Hamunakwadi, interviewed by Primrose Nyamhute, 19 October 2020
Trymore Jena, interviewed by Joseph Jakarasi, 20 April 2014
Makanya, interviewed by Admire Mseba, 29 June 2013
Charles Mandikonza, interviewed by Primrose Nyamhute, 14 October 2020
Rosemary Mandikonza, interviewed by Primrose Nyamhute, 14 October 2020
George Mandikwaza, interviewed by Primrose Nyamhute, 9 October 2020
Samuel Mandikwaza, interviewed by Primrose Nyamhute, 9 October 2020
Peter Mandisonza, interviewed by Primrose Nyamhute, 19 October 2020
Hatinakwaye Manyaira, interviewed by Primrose Nyamhute, 13 October 2020
Majorie Mapfurira, interviewed by Primrose Nyamhute, 6 October 2020
Mbuya Mashizha, interviewed by Admire Mseba, 26 June 2013
Tsitsi Matowanyika, interviewed by Primrose Nyamhute, 10 October 2020
Sophia Mhande, interviewed by Primrose Nyamhute, 16 October 2020
Elizabeth Mironga, interviewed by Primrose Nyamhute, 10 October 2020
Tonderai Murengami, interviewed by Primrose Nyamhute, 11 October 2020
Mutsago, interviewed by Admire Mseba, 28 June 2013
Mutsago clan elders, interviewed by George Bishi, 29 June 2013
Phillipa Mutsakara, interviewed by Primrose Nyamhute, 12 October 2020
Mutyawasara, interviewed by Admire Mseba, 10 March 2017
Peter Mwanaa, interviewed by Primrose Nyamhute, 11 October 2020
Tendayi Mwonzoro, interviewed by Primrose Nyamhute, 4 October 2020
Tsitsi Mwonzoro, interviewed by Primrose Nyamhute, 4 October 2020
Sylvester Nyagota, interviewed by Primrose Nyamhute, 17 October 2020
Fungayi Nyambuya, interviewed by Primrose Nyamhute, 9 October 2020
Julius Nyamugafata, interviewed by Primrose Nyamhute, 15 October 2020
Webster Nyamugafata, interviewed by Primrose Nyamhute, 15 October 2020
Sekai Sadzai, interviewed by Primrose Nyamhute, 15 October 2020
David Sakarombe, interviewed by Primrose Nyamhute, 15 October 2020
SaMuponda, interviewed by Admire Mseba, 24 June 2013 and 1 July 2013
Sylvia Satuku, interviewed by Primrose Nyamhute, 18 October 2020
Taurai Satuku, interviewed by Primrose Nyamhute, 18 October 2020
Mbuya Shava, interviewed by Admire Mseba, 26 June 2013
Simboti, interviewed by Admire Mseba, 8 March 2017
Soko, interviewed by Admire Mseba, 8 and 9 March 2017
Svongore, interviewed by Admire Mseba, 28 June 2013
Toto Tangwena, interviewed by Admire Mseba, 10 March 2017
John Mupfumi Tigere and Edmund Ndoro, interviewed by Joseph Jakarasi, 23 July 2014

Interviews in the National Archives of Zimbabwe's Oral History Collection

AOH 14, Aaron Jacha; AOH 31, Kapiro Chisvo; AOH 34, Chikwaka Chief Marufu; AOH 37, Rwambiwa Chari; AOH 39, Nhira Nzvere Chinhoyi; AOH 70, Mbofana Philip Willie George; AOH 73, Chief Chinamhora, Muchenje; AOH 79, David Kamusoko; AOH 80, Makutu Taonezvi; AOH 81, Madzivanyika Bvudzijena, Taonezvi Mazivei, and Simon Zhuwarara; AOH 84, Jera Chanji; AOH 89, Gwatidzo Panyanyiwa

ONLINE DICTIONARIES

Kalanga Online Talking Dictionary. http://talkingdictionary.swarthmore.edu/kalanga/.

Nambya Online Talking Dictionary. http://talkingdictionary.swarthmore.edu/nambya/.

Ndau Online Talking Dictionary. http://talkingdictionary.swarthmore.edu/ndau/?lang=en.

SECONDARY SOURCES

Abraham, Donald P. "The Principality of Maungwe: Its History and Traditions." *Native Affairs Department Annual* 28 (1951): 56–83.

Alexander, Jocelyn. "The Historiography of Land in Zimbabwe: Strengths, Silences and Questions." *Safundi: The Journal of South African and American Studies* 8, no. 2 (2007): 183–98.

———. "Technical Development and the Human Factor: Sciences of Development in Rhodesia's Native Affairs Department." In *Science and Society in Southern Africa*, edited by Saul Dubow, 222–37. Manchester: Manchester University Press, 2000.

———. *The Unsettled Land: State-Making and the Politics of Land in Zimbabwe, 1893–2003*. Oxford, UK: James Currey, 2006.

Alexander, Jocelyn, JoAnn McGregor, and Terence Ranger. *Violence and Memory: One Hundred Years in the "Dark Forests" of Matebeleland*. Portsmouth, NH: Heinemann, 2000.

Anderson, David. "Depression, Dust Bowl, Demography and Drought: The Colonial State and Conservation in East Africa in the 1930s." *African Affairs* 83, no. 332 (1984): 321–43.

Anonymous. "Chorographic Description of the Kingdom of Manhica, Its Customs and Laws." In Beach and de Noronha, "The Shona and the Portuguese," vol. 2, 1–12.

Arrighi, Giovani. *The Political Economy of Rhodesia*. The Hague: Mouton, 1967.

Austin, Gareth. *Labour, Land and Capital in Ghana: From Slavery to Free Labour in Asante, 1807–1956*. Rochester: Rochester University Press, 2005.

Baines, Thomas. *The Gold Regions of South Eastern Africa*. London: Edward Stanford, 1877.

Barbosa, Duarte. "Extracts from a Book Written by Duarte Barbosa, 1516." In Theal, *Records of South-Eastern Africa,* vol. 1, 92–99.

Barnes, Bertram H. *A Vocabulary of the Dialects of Mashonaland in New Orthography.* London: Sheldon Press, 1932.

Barnes, Herbert. *Nyanja-English Vocabulary.* London: Society for Promoting Christian Knowledge, 1902.

Barnes, Teresa. *"We Women Worked So Hard": Gender, Urbanization and Social Reproduction in Colonial Harare, Zimbabwe, 1930–1956.* Portsmouth, NH: Heinemann, 1992.

Bastin, Yvonne, and Thilo Schadeberg, eds. Bantu Lexical Reconstruction 3. Truven, Belgium: Musée Royale de l'Afrique Centrale. https://www.africamuseum.be/en/research/discover/human_sciences/culture_society/blr/bantou_history.

Baxter, T. W., and A. da Silva Rego, eds. *Documents on the Portuguese in Mozambique and Central Africa.* 8 vols. Salisbury: National Archives of Rhodesia, 1975.

Bazely, W. S. "Manyika Headwomen." *Native Affairs Department Annual* 17 (1940): 3–5.

———. "Manyika Law and Custom Regarding Inheritance of Wives and Property and the Guardianship of Children." *Native Affairs Department Annual* 7 (1929): 110–12.

Beach, David N. "'Chimurenga': The Shona Rising of 1896–7." *Journal of African History* 20, no. 3 (1979): 395–420.

———. "Cognitive Archaeology and Imaginary History at Great Zimbabwe." *Current Anthropology* 39, no. 1 (1998): 47–72.

———. "From Heroism to History: Mapondera and the Northern Shona Plateau, 1840–1904." *History in Africa* 15 (1988): 85–161.

———. "History and Archaeology in Nyanga." Annex in Robert C. Soper, *Nyanga: Ancient Fields, Settlements and Agricultural History in Zimbabwe,* 222–34. London: British Institute in Eastern Africa, 2002.

———. "An Innocent Woman Unjustly Accused? Charwe, Medium of the Nehanda Mhondoro Spirit, and the 1896–97 Central Shona Rising in Zimbabwe." *History in Africa* 25 (1998): 27–54.

———. "Mutapa: An Alternative Approach to the Study of Titles." *Rhodesian History* 6 (1975): 97–99.

———. "Ndebele Raiders and Shona Power." *Journal of African History* 15, no. 4 (1974): 633–51.

———. "Oral Tradition in Eastern Zimbabwe: The Work of Jason Takafa Machiwenyika, c1889–1924." Paper presented at Words and Voices: Critical Practices of Orality in Africa and African Studies conference, Bellagio, Italy, 24–28 February 1997.

———. "The Origins of Mozambique and Zimbabwe: Paiva de Andrada, the Companhia de Moçambique and African Diplomacy, 1881–91." History Seminar Paper no. 89, Department of History, University of Zimbabwe, 1992. Unpublished ms.

———. "'Refugee' Archaeology, Trade and Gold Mining in Nineteenth Century Zimbabwe: Izidoro Correia Pereira's List of 1857." *Zimbabwean Prehistory* 20 (1988): 3–8.
———. "The Rozvi in Search of Their Past." *History in Africa* 10 (1983): 13–34.
———. *The Shona and Their Neighbours.* Oxford, UK: Blackwell, 1994.
———. *The Shona and Zimbabwe, 900–1850: An Outline of Shona History.* Gweru: Mambo Press, 1980.
———. *War and Politics in Zimbabwe, 1840–1900.* Gweru: Mambo Press, 1986.
———. "Zimbabwean Demography: Early Colonial Data." *Zambezia* 17, no. 1 (1990): 31–53.
———. *A Zimbabwean Past: Shona Dynastic Histories and Oral Traditions.* Gweru: Mambo Press, 1994.
Beach, David, Michael F. C. Bourdillon, James Denbow, Martin Hall, Paul Lane, Innocent Pikirayi, and Gilbert Pwiti. "Reviews of *Snakes and Crocodiles: Power and Symbolism in Ancient Zimbabwe* by Thomas N. Huffman." *South African Archaeological Bulletin* 52, no. 166 (1997): 135–43.
Beach, David N., and H. de Noronha, eds. "The Shona and the Portuguese." Vol. 1, 1575–1700; vol. 2, 1700–1890. Unpublished ms., University of Zimbabwe, 1980.
Beinart, William. "Soil Erosion, Conservationism and Ideas about Development: A Southern African Exploration, 1900–1960." *Journal of Southern African Studies* 11, no. 1 (1984): 52–83.
Bernhard, F. O. "Two Types of Iron Smelting Furnaces on Ziwa Farm (Inyanga)." *South African Archaeological Bulletin* 17, no. 68 (1962): 235–36.
Berry, Sara. *Chiefs Know Their Boundaries: Essays on Property, Power, and the Past in Asante, 1896–1996.* Portsmouth, NH: Heinemann, 2001.
———. "Hegemony on a Shoestring: Indirect Rule and Access to Agricultural Land." *Africa* 62, no. 3 (1992): 327–55.
———. *No Condition Is Permanent: The Social Dynamics of Agrarian Change in Sub-Saharan Africa.* Madison: University of Wisconsin Press, 1993.
Bhebe, Ngwabi. *Benjamin Burombo: African Politics in Zimbabwe.* Harare: College Press, 1989.
———. "The Ndebele and Mwari before 1893: A Religious Conquest of the Conquerors by the Vanquished." In Schoffeleers, *Guardians of the Land,* 287–95.
Bhila, Hoyini H. K. "The History and Misspelling of a Shona Term." *Rhodesian History* 5 (1974): 79–80.
———. *Trade and Politics in a Shona Kingdom: The Manyika and Their Portuguese and African Neighbours.* London: Longman, 1983.
Blennerhassett, Rose, and Lucy Sleeman. *Adventure in Mashonaland.* London: Macmillan, 1893.
Bocarro, Antonio. "Decade of the Performances of the Portuguese in the East." In Theal, *Records of South-Eastern Africa,* vol. 3, 342–435.
Bohannan, Paul. "'Land,' 'Tenure' and Land Tenure." In *African Agrarian Systems,* edited by Daniel Biebuyck, 101–15. New York: Oxford University Press, 1963.

Bonate, Liazzat J. K. "The Ascendance of Angoche: The Politics of Kinship and Territory in Nineteenth Century Northern Mozambique." *Lusotopie* 10 (2003): 115–40.

Börjeson, Lowe. "A History under Siege: Intensive Agriculture in the Mbulu Highlands, Tanzania, 19th Century to the Present." PhD thesis, Stockholm University, 2004.

Borland, C. H. "Conflicting Methodologies of Shona Dialect Classification." *South African Journal of African Languages* 4, no. 1 (1984): 1–12.

Bourdillon, Michael F. C. "The Cults of Dzivaguru and Karuva amongst the North Eastern Shona Peoples." In Schoffeleers, *Guardians of the Land,* 235–55.

———. *The Shona Peoples: An Ethnography of the Contemporary Shona, with Special Reference to Their Religion.* Gweru: Mambo Press, 1987.

Brightman, Robert. "Hierarchy and Conflict in Mutual Being." *HAU: Journal of Ethnographic Theory* 3, no. 2 (2013): 259–70.

British South Africa Company. "Reports on the Native Disturbances in Rhodesia, 1896–97." March 1898. Unpublished ms.

Bullock, Charles. "Can a Native Make a Will? Concepts of Testate Succession in Native Law." *Native Affairs Department Annual* 7 (1929): 104–9.

Burke, Edmund E., ed. *The Journals of Karl Mauch, 1869–1872.* Salisbury: National Archives of Rhodesia, 1969.

Candido, Mariana P. *Wealth, Land and Property in Angola: A History of Dispossession, Slavery and Inequality.* Cambridge: Cambridge University Press, 2022.

Chanaiwa, David. "A History of Nhowe before 1900." PhD diss., University of California, Los Angeles, 1971.

Chanock, Martin. *Law, Custom and Social Order: The Colonial Experience in Malawi and Zambia.* Cambridge: Cambridge University Press, 1985.

Charumbira, Ruramisai. *Imagining a Nation: History and Memory in Making Zimbabwe.* Charlottesville: University of Virginia Press, 2015.

———. "Nehanda and Gender Victimhood in the Central Mashonaland 1896–97 Rebellions: Revisiting the Evidence." *History in Africa* 35 (2008): 103–31.

———. "Over Her Dead Body: The Gendered Exercise of Power in a Sixteenth Century Southern African Kingdom." Unpublished ms, n.d.

Chatelain, W. *Pocket Dictionary: Thonga (Shangaan)-English, English-Shangaan.* Lausanne: George Bridel, 1909.

Cheater, Angela P. "The Ideology of 'Communal' Land Tenure in Zimbabwe: Mythogenesis Enacted?" *Africa: Journal of the International African Institute* 60, no. 2 (1990): 188–206.

Chidziva, Joshua. "History of the VaShawasha." *Native Affairs Department Annual* 9, no. 1 (1964): 16–33.

Chimhowu, Admos, and Philip Woodhouse. "Forbidden but Not Suppressed: A 'Vernacular' Land Market in Svosve Communal Lands, Zimbabwe." *Africa: Journal of the International African Institute* 80, no. 1 (2010): 14–35.

Chimhundu, Herbert. "Early Missionaries and the Ethnolinguistic Factor during the Invention of Tribalism in Zimbabwe." *Journal of African History* 33, no. 1 (1992): 87–109.

———. "Some Problems Relating to the Incorporation of Loanwords in the Lexicon." *Zambezia* 7 (1979): 75–91.

Chirawu, Stephen. "The Archaeology of the Ancient Agricultural and Settlement Systems in Nyanga Lowland." MPhil thesis, University of Zimbabwe, 1999.

Chirikure, Shadreck. *Great Zimbabwe: Reclaiming a Confiscated Past.* London: Routledge, 2021.

———. "Iron Production in Iron Age Zimbabwe: Stagnation or Innovation?" PhD thesis, University College London, 2005.

Chirikure, Shadreck, Foreman Bandama, Michelle House, Abigail Moffett, Tawanda Mukwende, and Mark Pollard. "Decisive Evidence for Multidirectional Evolution of Sociopolitical Complexity in Southern Africa." *African Archaeological Review* 33, no. 1 (2016): 75–95.

Chirikure, Shadreck, Munyaradzi Manyanga, A. Mark Pollard, Foreman Bandama, Godfrey Mahachi, and Innocent Pikirayi. "Zimbabwe Culture before Mapungubwe: New Evidence from Mapela Hill, South-Western Zimbabwe." *PLoS One* 9, no. 10 (2014): 1–18.

Chirikure, Shadreck, Tawanda Mukwende, Abigail J. Moffett, Robert T. Nyamushosho, Foreman Bandama, and Michelle House. "No Big Brother Here: Heterarchy, Shona Political Succession and the Relationship between Great Zimbabwe and Khami, Southern Africa." *Cambridge Archaeological Journal* 28, no. 1 (2017): 45–66.

Chirikure, Shadreck, and Innocent Pikirayi. "Inside and Outside the Dry Stone Walls: Revisiting the Material Culture of Great Zimbabwe." *Antiquity* 82 (2008): 976–93.

Chitepo, Herbert W. "Soko Risina Musoro." In *Nduri DzeZimbabwe*, by Herbert Chitepo, Solomon Mutsvairo, Joseph Kumbirai, and Aaron Hodza, 1 -17. Harare: Longman Zimbabwe, 1983.

Cobbing, Julian. "The Absent Priesthood: Another Look at the Rhodesian Risings of 1896–1897." *Journal of African History* 18, no. 1 (1977): 61–84.

Colson, Elizabeth. "The Impact of the Colonial Period on the Definition of Land Rights." In *Colonialism in Africa,* vol. 3, *Profiles of Change: African Society and Colonial Rule,* edited by Victor Turner, 193–215. Cambridge: Cambridge University Press, 1971.

———. "Land Rights and Land Use among the Valley Tonga of the Rhodesian Federation: The Background to the Kariba Resettlement Scheme." In *African Agrarian Systems,* edited by Daniel Biebuyck, 137–56. New York: Oxford University Press, 1963.

———. *Marriage and Family among the Plateau Tonga.* Manchester: Manchester University Press, 1958.

Cousins, Ben, and Steven Robins. "Institutions for Land Redistribution and Management: The Zimbabwean Experience." *South African Sociological Review* 6, no. 2 (1994): 32–55.

Cripps, Arthur S. "African Land Tenure (A Plea for Tolerance)." *Native Affairs Department Annual* 4 (1926): 96–101.

Crowley, Terry, and Claire Bowern. *An Introduction to Historical Linguistics.* 4th ed. Oxford: Oxford University Press, 2010.
da Conceição, Antonio. "Treatise on the Rivers of Cuama." In Beach and de Noronha, "The Shona and the Portuguese," vol. 1.
Dande, Innocent, and Joseph Mujere. "Contested Histories and Contested Land Claims: Traditional Authorities and the Fast Track Land Reform Programme in Zimbabwe, 2000–2017." *Review of African Political Economy* 46 (2019): 86–100.
Daneel, Martinus. *God of the Matopo Hills: An Essay in the Mwari Cult of Rhodesia.* The Hague: Mouton, 1970.
da Silva, Manoel Galvão. "A Journal of Manoel Galvao da Silva's Travels through the Territory of Manica in 1790." Translated by Hoyini H. K. Bhila. *Monumenta: Publicacão dos Monumentos Nacionals de Moçambique* 8 (1972): 79–84.
de Andrade, António Alberto. *Relações de Moçambique Setecentista.* Lisbon: Agencia Geral do Ultramar, Divisão de Publicaçöes e Biblioteca, 1955.
Delius, Peter. *A Lion among the Cattle: Reconstruction and Resistance in the Northern Transvaal.* Portsmouth, NH: Heinemann, 1996.
de Luna, Kathryn M. *Collecting Food, Cultivating People: Subsistence and Society in Central Africa.* New Haven, CT: Yale University Press, 2016.
———. "Collecting Food, Cultivating Persons: Wild Resources Use in Central African Political Culture, c. 1000 B.C.E. to c. 1900 C.E." PhD diss., Northwestern University, 2008.
de Luna, Kathryn M., and Jeffrey B. Fleisher. *Speaking with Substance: Methods of Language and Materials in African History.* Cham, Switzerland: Springer, 2019.
Denbow, James. "A New Look at the Later Prehistory of the Kalahari." *Journal of African History* 27, no. 1 (1986): 10–25.
de Rezende, Pedro Barreto. "Of the State of India." In Theal, *Records of South-Eastern Africa,* vol. 2, 401–26.
de Sousa, Francisco. "Oriente Conquistado a Jesu Christo pelos Padres da Campanhia de Jesua da Provincia de Goa." In Beach and de Noronha, "The Shona and the Portuguese," vol. 1.
do Couto, Diogo. "Chapters XX–XXV of 9th Decada Da Asia." In Baxter and da Silva Rego, *Documents on the Portuguese,* vol. 8, 249–306.
Doke, Clement. *A Comparative Study in Shona Phonetics.* Johannesburg: University of the Witwatersrand Press, 1931.
———. "The Earliest Records of Bantu." *African Studies* 19, no. 1 (1960): 26–32.
Dos Santos, Joao. "Eastern Ethiopia." In Theal, *Records of South-Eastern Africa,* vol. 7, 83–383.
Dougherty, Edward A. "Zimcord Conference Documentation." *African Issues* 11, no. 3–4 (1981): 51–53.
Drinkwater, Michael. *The State and Agrarian Change in Zimbabwe's Communal Areas.* Houndsmills, UK: Macmillan, 1991.

E., T. "The Story of the Origin of the Name 'Makoni.'" *Native Affairs Department Annual* 14 (1937): 76–78.

Eckersley, W. Alfred. "Notes in Eastern Mashonaland." *Geographic Journal* 5, no. 1 (1895): 27–46.

Edwards, William. "Sacred Places." *Native Affairs Department Annual* 6 (1928): 23–27.

Ehret, Christopher. *An African Classical Age: Eastern and Southern Africa in World History.* Charlottesville: University of Virginia Press, 1998.

———. *History and the Testimony of Language.* Berkeley: University of California Press, 2011.

———. "Outlining Southern African History: A Re-evaluation, AD 100–1500." *Ufahamu: A Journal of African Studies* 3, no. 1 (1972): 9–28.

———. *Southern Nilotic History: Linguistic Approaches to the Study of the Past.* Evanston, IL: Northwestern University Press, 1971.

Ehret, Christopher, and Margaret Kinsman. "Shona Dialect Classification and Its Implications for Iron Age History in Southern Africa." *International Journal of African Historical Studies* 14, no. 3 (1981): 401–43.

Elliot, Jennifer A. "Soil Erosion and Conservation in Zimbabwe: Political Economy and the Environment." PhD diss., Loughborough University of Technology, 1989.

Falk Moore, Sally. *Social Facts and Fabrications: "Customary" Law on Kilimanjaro, 1880–1980.* Cambridge: Cambridge University Press, 1986.

Feierman, Steven. *Peasant Intellectuals: Anthropology and History in Tanzania.* Madison: University of Wisconsin Press, 1990.

Floyd, Barry N. "Changing Patterns of African Land Use in Southern Rhodesia." PhD diss., Syracuse University, 1959.

Fontein, Joost. *Remaking Mutirikwi: Landscape, Water and Belonging in Southern Zimbabwe.* Woodbridge, UK: James Currey, 2015.

———. *The Silence of Great Zimbabwe: Contested Landscapes and the Power of Heritage.* New York: UCL Press, 2006.

Fortune, George M. "Linguistics and Prehistory." In *Essays in Shona Dialects,* edited by George Fortune. Harare: University of Zimbabwe, 2004. http://www.edd.uio.no/allex/ibooks/fortune/index.html.

———. "A Rozvi Text with Translation and Notes." *Native Affairs Department Annual* 33 (1956): 67–84.

———. "Who Was Mwari?" *Rhodesian History* 4 (1973): 1–20.

Franklin, H. "'The War of the Tell-Tale' between Chiefs Makoni and Mtasa." *Native Affairs Department Annual* 15 (1938): 39–40.

Froes, Luiz. "Of the Voyage of the Father Dom Gonçalo to the Kingdom of Monomutapa and of His Happy Passing Away." In Theal, *Records of South-Eastern Africa,* vol. 2, 116–28.

Fry, Peter. *Spirits of Protest: Spirit Mediums and the Articulation of Consensus among the Zezuru of Southern Rhodesia (Zimbabwe).* Cambridge: Cambridge University Press, 1976.

Garbett, G. Kingsley. "The Mhondoro—Chiminuku." *Native Affairs Department Annual* 36 (1959): 6–10.

———. "Religious Aspects of Political Succession among the Valley Korekore (N. Shona)." In *The Zambezian Past: Studies in Central African History,* edited by Eric Stokes and Richard Brown, 137–70. Manchester: Manchester University Press, 1966.

Garlake, Peter S. *Great Zimbabwe: Described and Explained.* Harare: Zimbabwe Publishing House, 1985.

———. "Pastoralism and Zimbabwe." *Journal of African History* 19, no. 4 (1978): 479–93.

Gelfand, Michael. "The Mhondoro—Chaminuka." *Native Affairs Department Annual* 36 (1959): 6–10.

Giblin, James L. *A History of the Excluded: Making Family a Refuge from the State in Twentieth Century Tanzania.* Athens: Ohio University Press, 2005.

———. "Vampires and History." *African Studies Review* 44, no. 1 (2001): 86–87.

Goebel, Allison. *Gender and Land Reform: The Zimbabwean Experience.* Montreal: McGill-Queen's University Press, 2005.

Gomes, Fr. Antonio, to Fr. João Marachi. "Voyage Made by Fr. Antonio Gomes of the Society of Jesus, to the Empire of Monomutapa Empire and His Work There for Several Years, January 2, 1648." In Beach and de Noronha, "The Shona and the Portuguese," vol. 1.

Gonzalez, Rhonda M. *Societies, Religion, and History: Central East Tanzanians and the World They Created, c. 200 BCE to 1800 CE.* New York: Columbia University Press, 2009.

Goody, Jack. *Technology, Tradition and the State in Africa.* London: Oxford University Press, 1971.

Grollemund, Rebecca, David Schoenbrun, and Jan Vansina. "Moving Histories: Bantu Language Expansions, Eclectic Economies, and Mobilities." *Journal of African History* 64 (2023): 1–25.

Guthrie, Malcom. *Comparative Bantu: An Introduction to the Comparative Linguistics and Prehistory of the Bantu Languages.* Vol. 4. Hants, UK: Gregg International Publishers, 1970.

Guyer, Jane I. "Wealth in People and Self-Realization in Equatorial Africa." *Man* 28, no. 2 (1993): 243–65.

———. "Wealth in People, Wealth in Things—Introduction." *Journal of African History* 36, no. 1 (1995): 83–90.

Guyer, Jane I., and Samuel M. Eno Belinga. "Wealth in People as Wealth in Knowledge: Accumulation and Composition in Equatorial Africa." *Journal of African History* 36, no. 1 (1995): 91–120.

Gwande, Victor Muchineripi. *Manufacturing in Colonial Zimbabwe, 1890–1979: Interest Group Politics, Protectionism and the State.* Woodbridge, UK: James Currey, 2022.

Hanlon, Joseph, Jeannette Manjengwa, and Teresa Smart. *Zimbabwe Takes Back Its Land.* Boulder, CO: Kumarian Press, 2013.

Hannaford, Mathew J. "The Consequences of Past Climate Change for State Formation and Security in Southern Africa." PhD thesis, University of Sheffield, 2015.
Hannaford, Mathew J., and David J. Nash. "Climate, History, Society over the Last Millennium in Southeast Africa." *Wiley Interdisciplinary Reviews: Climate Change* 7, no. 3 (2016): 370–92.
Hannan, M. *Standard Shona Dictionary*. Rev. ed. Harare: College Press, 2000.
Herbert, Eugenia W. *Iron, Gender and Power: Rituals of Transformation in African Societies*. Bloomington: Indiana University Press, 1993.
Hodder-Williams, Richard. *White Farmers in Rhodesia, 1890–1965: A History of Marandellas District*. London: Macmillan, 1983.
Holleman, Jon F. *Chief, Council and Commissioner: Some Problems of Government in Rhodesia*. Assen: Royal VanGorcum, 1969.
———. *Shona Customary Law with Particular Reference to Kinship, Marriage, the Family and Estate*. London: Oxford University Press, 1952.
———. "Some Shona Tribes of Southern Rhodesia." In *Seven Tribes of Central Africa*, edited by Elizabeth Colson and Max Gluckman, 354–95. Manchester: Manchester University Press, 1951.
Huffman, Thomas N. "Expressive Space in the Zimbabwe Culture." *Man* 194, no. 4 (1984): 593–612.
———. *Handbook to the Iron Age: The Archaeology of Precolonial Farming Societies in Southern Africa*. Scottsville: University of Kwazulu Natal Press, 2007.
———. "Leopard's Kopje and the Nature of the Iron Age in Bantu Africa." *Zimbabwea* 1 (1984): 28–35.
———. "The Origins of Leopard's Kopje: An 11th Century Difaquane." *Arnoldia* 23, no. 8 (1978): 1–23.
———. "Revisiting Great Zimbabwe." *Azania: Archaeological Research in Africa* 45, no. 3 (2010): 321–28.
———. "Snakes and Birds: Expressive Space at Great Zimbabwe." *African Studies* 40, no. 2 (1981): 131–50.
———. *Snakes and Crocodiles: Power and Symbolism in Ancient Zimbabwe*. Johannesburg: Witwatersrand University Press, 1996.
Hughes, David McDermott. *From Enslavement to Environmentalism: Politics on a Southern African Frontier*. Seattle: University of Washington Press, 2006.
Isaacman, Allen. "Madzi-Manga, Mhondoro and the Use of Oral Traditions: A Chapter in Barue Religious and Political History." *Journal of African History* 14, no. 3 (1973): 395–409.
———. *Mozambique, the Africanization of a European Institution: The Zambezi Prazos, 1750–1902*. Madison: University of Wisconsin Press, 1972.
Isaacman, Allen E., and Barbara S. Isaacman. *Slavery and Beyond: The Making of Men and Chikunda Ethnic Identities in the Unstable World of South-Central Africa, 1750–1920*. Portsmouth, NH: Heinemann, 2004.
Jeater, Diana. *Law, Language and Science: The Invention of the "Native" Mind in Southern Rhodesia, 1890–1930*. Portsmouth, NH: Heinemann, 2007.

——. *Marriage, Perversion and Power: The Construction of a Moral Discourse in Southern Rhodesia, 1894–1930.* Oxford, UK: Clarendon Press, 1993.

Jimenez, Raevin. "Rights of Reproduction: Gender, Generation and Political Economic Transformations among Nguni Speakers of Southern Africa, 8th to 19th Century CE." PhD diss., Northwestern University, 2017.

Jonsson, Jimmy. *Early Plant Economy in Zimbabwe.* Uppsala: Societas Archaeologica Upsaliensis, 1998.

Jowett, L. V. "The Hungwe People of the Makoni District." *Native Affairs Department Annual* 11, no. 5 (1968): 54–55.

Junod, Henri Alexander. *Elementary Grammar of the Thonga Shangaan Language.* Shiluvane: Swiss Mission, 1907.

Kaplan, Martha. *Neither Cargo nor Cult: Ritual Politics and the Colonial Imagination in Fiji.* Durham, NC: Duke University Press, 1995.

Karekwaivanane, George Hamandishe. *The Struggle over State Power in Zimbabwe: Law and Politics since 1950.* Cambridge: Cambridge University Press, 2017.

Katsamudanga, Seke. "Environment and Culture: A Study of Prehistoric Settlement Patterns in the Eastern Highlands of Zimbabwe." DPhil thesis, University of Zimbabwe, 2007.

Kay, George. *Rhodesia: A Human Geography.* New York: African Publishing Corporation, 1970.

Kerr, Walter Montagu. *The Far Interior: A Narrative of Travel and Adventure from the Cape of Good Hope across the Zambezi to the Lake Regions of Central Africa.* 2 vols. London: Sampson, Low, Martson, Searle and Rivington, 1887.

Knight-Bruce, George Wyndham Hamilton. *Journals of the Mashonaland Mission, 1888–1892.* London: Society for the Propagation of the Gospel in Foreign Parts, 1892.

——. *Memories of Mashonaland.* London: Edward Arnold, 1895.

Kodesh, Neil. *Beyond the Royal Gaze: Clanship and Public Healing in Buganda.* Charlottesville: University of Virginia Press, 2010.

——. "History from the Healer's Shrine: Genre, Historical Imagination and Early Ganda History." *Comparative Studies in Society and History* 49, no. 3 (2007): 527–52.

Kopytoff, Igor. "The Internal African Frontier: The Making of African Political Culture." In *The African Frontier: The Reproduction of Traditional African Societies,* edited by Igor Kopytoff, 3–84. Bloomington: Indiana University Press, 1987.

Kopytoff, Igor, and Suzzaine Miers. "Introduction: African Slavery as an Institution of Marginality." In *Slavery in Africa: Historical and Anthropological Perspectives,* edited by Suzzaine Miers and Igor Kopytoff, 3–81. Madison: University of Wisconsin Press, 1977.

Kramer, Eira. "The Clash of Economies: Early Centralization Efforts in Colonial Zimbabwe, 1929–1935." *Zambezia* 25, no. 1 (1998): 83–98.

Lan, David. *Guns and Rain: Guerrillas and Spirit Mediums in Zimbabwe.* London: James Currey, 1985.

Landau, Paul. *Popular Politics in the History of South Africa, 1400–1948.* Cambridge: Cambridge University Press, 2010.
Laws, Robert D. *English Nyanja: Dictionary of the Nyanja Language Spoken in British Central Africa.* Edinburgh: James Thin, 1894.
Lentz, Carola. *Land, Mobility, and Belonging in West Africa.* Bloomington: Indiana University Press, 2013.
Lindahl, Anders, and Innocent Pikirayi. "Ceramics and Change: An Overview of Pottery Production Techniques in Northern South Africa and Eastern Zimbabwe during the First and Second Millennium AD." *Archaeological and Anthropological Sciences* 2, no. 3 (2010): 133–49.
Lloyd, Elaine M. "Mbava." *Native Affairs Department Annual* 3 (1925): 62–64.
Louw, C. S. *A Manual of the Chikaranga Language with Grammar, Exercises, Useful Conversational Sentences and Vocabulary.* Bulawayo: Philpott & Collins, 1915.
Lovejoy, Paul E. *Transformations in Slavery: A History of Slavery in Africa.* Cambridge: Cambridge University Press, 2000.
Macdonald, Frederic William. *The Story of Mashonaland and the Missionary Pioneers.* London: Wesleyan Mission House, 1893.
Machingaidze, Victor E. M. "Agrarian Change from Above: The Southern Rhodesia Native Land Husbandry Act and African Response." *International Journal of African Historical Studies* 24, no. 3 (1991): 557–88.
———. "The Development of Settler Capitalist Agriculture in Southern Rhodesia with Particular Reference to the Role of the State, 1908–1939." DPhil thesis, University of London, 1980.
Maggs, Tim. "The Iron Age South of the Zambezi." In *Southern African Prehistory and Paleoenvironments,* edited by Richard G. Klein, 329–60. Rotterdam: A. A. Balkema, 1984.
Majubane. "African Names of Native and District Commissioners." *Native Affairs Department Annual* 11, no. 2 (1975): 253–55.
Mamdani, Mahmood. *Citizen and Subject: Contemporary Africa and the Legacy of Late Colonialism.* Princeton: Princeton University Press, 1996.
———. *Define and Rule: Native as Political Identity.* Cambridge, MA: Harvard University Press, 2012.
———. *When Victims Became Killers: Colonialism, Nativism, and the Genocide in Rwanda.* Princeton: Princeton University Press, 2001.
Manungo, Kenneth D. "The Role Peasants Played in the Zimbabwe War of Liberation with Special Emphasis on Chiweshe." PhD diss., Ohio University, 1991.
Manyanga, Munyaradzi, and Plan Shenjere. "The Archaeology of the Northern Nyanga Lowlands and the Unfolding Farming Community Sequence in Northeastern Zimbabwe." *South African Archaeological Bulletin* 67, no. 196 (2012): 244–55.
Masola, Kumile. *Nau DzabaKalanga / A History of the Kalanga.* Vol. 1. Translated by Petrus Johannes Wentzel. Pretoria: University of South Africa, 1983.
Matondi, Prosper B. *Zimbabwe's Fast Track Land Reform.* London: Zed Books, 2012.

Mavhunga, Clapperton Chakanetsa. *The Mobile Workshop: The Tsetse Fly and African Knowledge.* Cambridge, MA: MIT Press, 2018.

Maxwell, David. *Christians and Chiefs in Zimbabwe: A Social History of the Hwesa People, c.1870s–1990s.* Edinburgh: Edinburgh University Press, 1999.

Mazarire, Gerald Chikozho. "Changing Landscapes and Oral Memory in South Central Zimbabwe: Towards a Historical Geography of Chishanga, c1850–1990." *Journal of Southern African Studies* 29, no. 3 (2003): 701–15.

———. "Defence Consciousness as a Way of Life: The 'Refuge Period' and Karanga Defence Strategy in the 19th Century." Typescript, March 2005.

———. "Defence Consciousness as a Way of Life: The 'Refuge Period' and Karanga Defense Strategies in the 19th Century." *Zimbabwean Prehistory* 25 (2005): 19–26.

———. "The *Gadzingo:* Towards a Karanga Expansion Matrix in 18th- and 19th-Century Southern Zimbabwe." *Critical African Studies* 5, no. 1 (2013): 4–16.

———. "Reflections on Precolonial Zimbabwe, *c.* 850–1880s." In *Becoming Zimbabwe: A History from the Precolonial Period to 2008,* edited by Brian Raftopoulos and Alois S. Mlambo, 1–38. Harare: Weaver Press, 2009.

———. "A Social and Political History of Chishanga: South-Central Zimbabwe, *c.*1750–2000." DPhil thesis, University of Zimbabwe, 2009.

McGaffey, Wyatt. *Chiefs, Priests and Praise-Singers: History, Politics and Land Ownership in Northern Ghana.* Charlottesville: University of Virginia Press, 2013.

McGregor, JoAnn. "Conservation, Control and Ecological Change: The Politics and Ecology of Colonial Conservation in Shurugwi, Zimbabwe." *Environment and History* 1, no. 3 (1995): 257–79.

Miller, Joseph C. "Introduction: Listening for the African Past." In *The African Past Speaks: Essays on Oral Tradition and History,* edited by Joseph Miller, 1–59. Kent: W. M. Dawson and Sons, 1980.

———. *Way of Death: Merchant Capitalism and the Angolan Slave Trade.* Madison: University of Wisconsin Press, 1988.

Mitchel, Peter. *The Archaeology of Southern Africa.* Cambridge: Cambridge University Press, 2002.

Moffett, Abigail Joy, and Shadreck Chirikure. "Exotica in Context: Reconfiguring Prestige, Power and Wealth in the Southern African Iron Age." *Journal of World Prehistory* 29, no. 4 (2016): 337–82.

Monclaro (Father). "Account of the Journey Made by Fathers of the Company of Jesus with Francisco Barreto in the Conquest of Monomotapa in the Year 1569." In Theal, *Records of South-Eastern Africa,* vol. 3, 202–53.

Monclaro, Francisco de. "Narrative by Father Francisco de Monclaro of the Society of Jesus of the Expedition to Monomutapa, Led by Francisco Barreto." In Baxter and da Silva Rego, *Documents on the Portuguese,* vol. 8, 325–429.

Moore, Donald S. *Suffering for Territory: Race, Place and Power in Zimbabwe.* Durham, NC: Duke University Press, 2005.

Moore, Henrietta L., and Meghan Vaughan. *Cutting Down Trees: Gender, Nutrition and Agricultural Change in the Northern Province of Zambia, 1890–1990.* Portsmouth, NH: Heinemann, 1994.

Morris, Ernest W. "'Marondella's District': History of Native Tribes and Chiefs; Information Supplied to the South African Native Affairs Commission, 1903." *Native Affairs Department Annual* 9, no. 4 (1977): 436–42.

Moyana, Henry V. *The Political Economy of Land in Zimbabwe.* Gweru: Mambo Press, 2002.

Moyo, Sam. "The Political Economy of Land Acquisition and Redistribution in Zimbabwe, 1990–1999." *Journal of Southern African Studies* 26, no. 1 (2000): 5–28.

Mseba, Admire. "'Cattle Culling and All That Stuff': Modernity, Mobilization and the Everyday Language of Environmental Change in Northeastern Zimbabwe." In *Transplanting Modernity? New Histories of Poverty, Development and the Environment,* edited by Jenny Leigh Smith and Tom Robertson, 69–85. Pittsburgh: Pittsburgh University Press, 2023.

———. "Environmental Phenomena, Colonial Injustices and Vernacular Discourse in Early Colonial Zimbabwe, 1895–c.1935." In *Environment, Power and Justice: Southern African Histories,* edited by Graeme Wynn, Jane Caruthers, and Nancy J. Jacobs, 193–220. Athens: Ohio University Press, 2022.

———. "Late Precolonial Struggles, European Expansion, and the Making of Colonial Authority in Northeastern Zimbabwe, ca. 1840 to 1903." *International Journal of African Historical Studies* 51, no. 2 (2018): 243–62.

———. "Narratives, Rituals and Political Imaginations: The Social and Political World of the Vashona of North-Eastern Zimbabwe from the 16th to the 19th Centuries." *Journal of Southern African Studies* 46, no. 3 (2020): 435–54.

Mtetwa, Richard M. G. "The Relationship between Gutu Dynasties and the Mwari Cult." *Rhodesian History* 6 (1975): 89–95.

Mudenge, Stanislus Isack G. *A Political History of Munhumutapa, c1400–1902.* Harare: Zimbabwe Publishing House, 1988.

———. "The Role of Foreign Trade in the Rozvi Empire: A Reappraisal." *Journal of African History* 15, no. 3 (1974): 373–91.

———. "The Rozvi Empire and the Feira of Zumbo." PhD thesis, University of London, 1972.

Muhlanga, Samuel (with Elaine M. Lloyd). "In the Early Days." *Native Affairs Department Annual* 4 (1926): 107–10.

Mujere, Joseph. *Land, Migration and Belonging: A History of the Basotho in Southern Rhodesia c. 1890–1960s.* Woodbridge, UK: James Currey, 2019.

———. "The Marumbi Rain Cult: Gender and the Interface between Rain Making and the Politics of Water in Gutu." Paper presented at The Power of Water: Landscape, Water and the State in Southern and Eastern Africa conference, CAS, University of Edinburgh, Scotland, 28–29 March 2007.

Mukabeta, Kevin. "Does Similarity Equal Relationship? An Archaeological Study of Tsindi, a Dzimbabwe Site in North-Eastern Zimbabwe." MPhil thesis, University of Cape Town, 2018.

Munro, William. *The Moral Economy of the State: Conservation, Community Development and State-Making in Zimbabwe.* Athens: Ohio University Center for International Studies, 1998.

Murphy, William P., and Caroline H. Bledsloe. "Kinship and Territory in the History of a Kpelle Chiefdom (Liberia)." In *The African Frontier: The Reproduction of Traditional Societies,* edited by Igor Kopytoff, 123–47. Bloomington: Indiana University Press, 1987.

Musoni, Francis. "Cross-Border Mobility, Violence and Spiritual Healing in Beitbridge District, Zimbabwe." *Journal of Southern African Studies* 42, no. 2 (2016): 317–31.

Muzondidya, James. "'Zimbabwe for Zimbabweans': Invisible Subject Minorities and the Quest for Justice and Reconciliation in Post-colonial Zimbabwe." In *Zimbabwe: Injustice and Political Reconciliation,* edited by Brian Raftopoulos and Tyrone Savage, 213–35. Cape Town: Institute for Justice and Reconciliation, 2004.

[British] Naval Staff Intelligence Department. *Portuguese Nyasaland Vocabularies: Nyanja, Yao, Ronga, Portuguese, Makua, Swahili.* London: Naval Staff Intelligence Department, 1918.

Ndlovu-Gatsheni, Sabelo J. *Do "Zimbabweans" Exist? Trajectories of Nationalism, National Identity Formation and Crisis in a Postcolonial State.* New York: Peter Lang, 2009.

Ndoro, Weber. "Why Decorate Her?" *Zimbabwea* 3 (1991): 60–65.

Newitt, Malyn. Introduction to *Treatise in the Rivers of Cuama* by António da Conceição, xi–xxxix. Edited and translated by Malyn Newitt. Oxford: Oxford University Press, 2009.

Nyamatore, A. S. "Mutasa, The British South Africa Company and the African Portuguese Syndicate: The Fight for Manyika in the 1890s." Henderson Seminar Paper no. 41, Department of History, University of Zimbabwe, 1978.

Nyambara, Pius S[hungudzapera]. "A History of Land Acquisition in Gokwe, Northwestern Zimbabwe, 1945–1997." PhD diss., Northwestern University, 1999.

———. "*Madheruka* and *Shangwe:* Ethnic Identity and the Culture of Modernity in Gokwe, Northwestern Zimbabwe, 1963–1979." *Journal of Africa History* 43, no. 2 (2002): 287–306.

———. "'That Place Was Wonderful!' African Tenants on Rhodesdale Estate, Colonial Zimbabwe, *c.*1900 to 1952." *International Journal of African Historical Studies* 38, no. 2 (2005): 267–99.

Nyandoro, Mark. "Zimbabwe's Land Struggles and Land Rights in Historical Perspective: The Case of Gokwe-Sanyati Irrigation (1950–2000)." *Historia* 57, no. 2 (2012): 298–349.

Ownby, Carolan Postma. "Early Nguni History: The Linguistic Evidence and Its Correlation with Archaeology and Oral Tradition." PhD diss., University of California–Los Angeles, 1985.

Pacheco, Albino Manoel. *A Journey from Tete to Zumbo.* Edited and translated by Malyn Newitt. Oxford: Oxford University Press, 2013.

———. "A Journey from Tete to Zumbo." In Beach and de Noronha, "The Shona and the Portuguese," vol. 2.
Packard, Randall. *Chiefship and Cosmology: An Historical Study of Political Competition.* Bloomington: Indiana University Press, 1981.
Palmer, Robin. "The Agricultural History of Rhodesia." In *The Roots of Rural Poverty in Central and Southern Africa,* edited by Robin Palmer and Neil Parsons, 221–54. Berkeley: University of California Press, 1977.
———. *Land and Racial Domination in Rhodesia.* Berkeley: University of California Press, 1977.
Passmore, Gloria. "Historical Rationale of the Policy of Community Development in the African Rural Areas of Rhodesia." *Zambezia* 2, no. 1 (1971): 61–70.
Peters, Pauline E. "Revisiting the Social Bedrock of Kinship and Descent in the Anthropology of Africa." In *A Companion to the Anthropology of Africa,* edited by Roy Richard Grinker, Steven C. Lubkemann, Christopher B. Steiner, and Euclides Gonçalves, 33–62. Oxford, UK: John Wiley and Sons, 2019.
Phimister, Ian R. "Commodity Relations and Class Formation in the Zimbabwean Countryside." *Journal of Peasant Studies* 13, no. 4 (1986): 240–57.
———. "Discourse and the Discipline of Historical Context: Conservationism and Ideas about Development in Southern Rhodesia, 1930–1950." *Journal of Southern African Studies* 12, no. 2 (1986): 263–75.
———. *An Economic and Social History of Zimbabwe, 1890–1948: Capital Accumulation and Class Struggle.* London: Longman, 1988.
———. "Rethinking the Reserves: Southern Rhodesia's Land Husbandry Act Reviewed." *Journal of Southern African Studies* 19, no. 2 (1993): 225–39.
Pikirayi, Innocent. "Archaeological, Historical and Anthropological Sources on Great Zimbabwe and the Nyanga Archaeological Complex." *Aluka Technical Report* (2008).
———. *The Archaeological Identity of the Mutapa State: Towards an Historical Archaeology of Northern Zimbabwe.* Studies in African Archaeology 6. Uppsala: Department of Archaeology and Ancient History, Uppsala University, 1993.
———. "Stone Architecture and the Development of Power in the Zimbabwe Tradition, AD 1270–1830." *Azania: Archaeological Research in Africa* 48, no. 2 (2013): 282–300.
———. *The Zimbabwe Culture: The Origins and Decline in Southern Zambezian States.* Walnut Creek, CA: AltaMira Press, 2001.
Pikirayi, Innocent, and Shadreck Chirikure. "Debating Great Zimbabwe." *Azania: Archaeological Research in Africa* 46, no. 2 (2011): 221–31.
Pikirayi, Innocent, and Anders Lindahl. "Ceramics, Ethnohistory and Ethnography: Locating the Meaning in Southern African Iron Age Ceramic Assemblages." *African Archaeological Review* 30, no. 4 (2013): 1–19.
Plug, Ina. "Early Iron Age Buffalo Hunters on the Kadzi River, Zimbabwe." *African Archaeological Review* 14, no. 2 (1997): 85–105.
Posselt, Friedrich Wilhelm Traugott. "Chaminuka the Wizard." *Native Affairs Department Annual* 4 (1926): 35–37.

———. *Fact and Fiction.* Bulawayo: Books of Rhodesia, 1935.
Pwiti, Gilbert. *Continuity and Change: An Archaeological Study of Farming Communities in Northern Zimbabwe, AD 500–1700.* Studies in African Archaeology 13. Uppsala: Department of Archaeology and Ancient History, Uppsala University, 1996.
———. "Peasants, Chiefs and Kings: A Model of the Development of Cultural Complexity in Northern Zimbabwe." *Zambezia* 23, no. 1 (1996): 31–52.
Radcliffe-Brown, Alfred R. Introduction to *African Systems of Kinship and Marriage,* edited by Alfred R. Radcliffe-Brown and Daryll Forde, 1–85. New York: Routledge, 2015. First published in 1950.
Ranger, Terence. "The Communal Areas of Zimbabwe." In *Land in African Agrarian Systems,* edited by Thomas J. Bassett and Donald E. Crummey, 354–85. Madison: University of Wisconsin Press, 1993.
———. "Invention of Tradition in Colonial Africa." In *The Invention of Tradition,* edited by Eric J. Hobsbawm and Terence O. Ranger, 211–62. Cambridge: Cambridge University Press, 1983.
———. "The Invention of Tradition Revisited: The Case of Colonial Africa." In *Legitimacy and the State in Twentieth Century Africa,* edited by Terence Ranger and O. Vaughan, 62–111. Houndsmills, UK: Macmillan, 1993.
———. *The Invention of Tribalism in Zimbabwe.* Gweru: Mambo Press, 1985.
———. "The Meaning of Mwari." *Rhodesian History* 5 (1974): 5–17.
———. "Missionaries, Migrants and the Manyika: The Invention of Ethnicity in Zimbabwe." African Studies Seminar Paper, African Studies Institute, University of the Witwatersrand, 1984.
———. *Peasant Consciousness and Guerrilla Warfare in Zimbabwe: A Comparative Study.* London: James Currey, 1985.
———. *Revolt in Southern Rhodesia, 1896–7: A Study in African Resistance.* London: Heinemann, 1967.
———. *Voices from the Rocks: Nature, Culture and History in the Matopos Hills of Zimbabwe.* Bloomington: Indiana University Press, 1999.
———. *Writing Revolt: An Engagement with African Nationalism, 1957–1967.* Harare: Weaver Press, 2013.
Rennie, John K. "From Zimbabwe to a Colonial Chieftaincy: Four Transformations of the Musikavanhu Territorial Cult in Rhodesia." In Schoffeleers, *Guardians of the Land,* 257–85.
———. "White Farmers, Black Tenants and Landlord Legislation: Southern Rhodesia, 1890–1930." *Journal of Southern African Studies* 5, no. 1 (1978): 86–98.
Rutherford, Blair. "Conditional Belonging: Farm Workers and the Cultural Politics of Recognition in Zimbabwe." *Development and Change* 39, no. 1 (2008): 73–99.
Sachikonye, Lloyd M. "Land Reform for Poverty Reduction? Social Exclusion and Farm Workers in Zimbabwe." Paper prepared for Staying Poor: Chronic Poverty and Development Policy conference, organized by the IDMP, Manchester University, April 2003.

———. "The Situation of Commercial Farm Workers in Zimbabwe after Land Reform." Report prepared for the Farm Community Trust of Zimbabwe (FCTZ), Harare, 2003.

Sackeyfro, Naaborko. *The Politics of Chieftaincy: Authority and Property in Colonial Ghana, 1920–1950.* Rochester: University of Rochester Press, 2014.

Sahlins, Marshall. *What Kinship Is—And Is Not.* Chicago: University of Chicago Press, 2013.

Saidi, Christine. *Women's Authority and Society in Early East-Central Africa.* Rochester: University of Rochester Press, 2010.

Schmidt, Elizabeth. *Peasants, Traders and Wives: Shona Women in the History of Zimbabwe, 1870–1939.* Portsmouth, NH: Heinemann, 1992.

Schmidt, Heike. *Colonialism and Violence in Zimbabwe: A History of Suffering.* Suffolk, UK: Boydell & Brewer, 2013.

———. "Healing the Wounds of War: Memories of Violence and the Making of History in Zimbabwe's Most Recent Past." *Journal of Southern African Studies* 33, no. 2 (1997): 301–10.

Schoenbrun, David L. "Early African Pasts: Sources, Interpretations, and Meanings." In *The Oxford Research Encyclopedia of African History.* Oxford: Oxford University Press, 2018: 1-42.

———. *A Green Place, a Good Place: Agrarian Change, Gender and Social Identity in the Great Lakes Region to the 15th Century.* Portsmouth, NH: Heinemann, 1998.

———. *The Historical Reconstruction of Great Lakes Bantu Cultural Vocabulary: Etymologies and Distributions.* Köln: Rüdiger Köppe Press, 1997.

———. "The (In)visible Roots of Bunyoro-Kitara and Buganda in the Lakes Region, AD 800–1300." In *Beyond Chiefdoms: Pathways to Complexity in Africa,* edited by Susan Keech McIntosh. Cambridge: Cambridge University Press, 1999.

Schoffeleers, Mathew J., ed. *Guardians of the Land: Essays on Central African Territorial Cults.* Gweru: Mambo Press, 1979.

———. *River of Blood: The Genesis of a Martyr Cult in Southern Malawi, c. AD 1600.* Madison: University of Wisconsin Press, 1992.

Schoffeleers, Mathew J., and R. Mwanza. "An Organizational Model for Mwari Shrines." In Schoffeleers, *Guardians of the Land,* 297–315.

Scoones, Ian, Nelson Marongwe, Blasio Mavedzenge, Jacob Mahenehene, Felix Murimbarimba, and Chrispen Sukume. *Zimbabwe's Land Reform: Myths and Realities.* Woodbridge, UK: James Currey, 2010.

Scott, James C. *Seeing Like a State: How Certain Schemes to Improve the Human Condition Have Failed.* New Haven, CT: Yale University Press, 1998.

Selous, Frederick Courteney. *A Hunter's Wanderings in Africa: Being a Narrative of Nine Years Spent amongst the Game of the Far Interior of South Africa.* London: Richard Bentley & Son, 1881.

———. *Travel and Adventure in Southeast Africa.* New York: Arno Press, 1967.

Shenjere, Plan. "The Animal Economy of Prehistoric Farming Communities in Manicaland, Eastern Zimbabwe." PhD thesis, University of Dar es Salaam, 2011.

Shetler, Jan Bender. *Imagining Serengeti: A History of Landscape and Memory in Tanzania from Earliest Times to the Present.* Athens: Ohio University Press, 2007.

Showers, Kate B. *Imperial Gullies: Soil Erosion and Conservation in Lesotho.* Athens: Ohio University Press, 2005.

Shropshire, Denys. "The Crocodile Ceremony of the Mutasa Dynasty." *Man* 30 (1930): 6.

———. "The Mifananidzo of the Mutasa Dynasty." *Man* 30 (1930): 4–5.

Shutt, Allison K. *Manners Make a Nation: Racial Etiquette in Southern Rhodesia, 1910–1963.* Rochester: Rochester University Press, 2015.

———. "The Natives Are Getting Out of Hand: Legislating Manners, Insolence and Contemptuous Behaviour in Southern Rhodesia, 1910–1963." *Journal of Southern African Studies* 33, no. 3 (2007): 653–72.

Sinclair, Paul J. *Space, Time and Social Formation: A Territorial Approach to the Archaeology and Anthropology of Zimbabwe and Mozambique, c.0–1700 AD.* Uppsala: Societas Archaeologica Upsaliensis, 1987.

Soper, Robert. *Nyanga: Ancient Fields, Settlements and Agricultural History in Zimbabwe.* London: British Institute in Eastern Africa, 2002.

Spear, Thomas T. *Mountain Farmers: Moral Economies of Land and Agricultural Development in Arusha and Meru.* Berkeley: University of California Press, 1997.

———. "Neo-traditionalism and the Limits of Invention in British Colonial Africa." *Journal of African History* 44, no. 1 (2003): 3–27.

Spierenburg, Marja J. *Strangers, Spirits and Land Reforms: Conflicts about Land in Dande, Northern Zimbabwe.* Leiden: Brill, 2005.

Springer, Helen Emily. *A Handbook of Chikaranga or the Language of Mashonaland.* Cincinnati, OH: Jennings and Graham, 1905.

Stead, W. H. "The Clan Organization and Kinship System of Some Shona Tribes." *African Studies* 5, no. 1 (1946): 1–20.

———. "Concepts and Control in Native Life: Elements of a Sociological Analysis." *Native Affairs Department Annual* 13 (1935): 6–13.

Steele, Murray C. "The Foundations of a 'Native' Policy in Southern Rhodesia, 1923–1933." PhD diss., Simon Fraser University, 1972.

Storry, J. G. "The Settlement and Territorial Expansion of the Mutasa Dynasty." *Rhodesian History* 7 (1976): 13–30.

Summers, Roger. *Inyanga: Prehistoric Settlements in Southern Rhodesia.* Cambridge: Cambridge University Press, 1958.

Theal, George M., ed. *Records of South-Eastern Africa.* 9 vols. Cape Town: C. Struik, 1964. Originally published 1902.

Thokozane, J. "A Short History of Chipunza." *Native Affairs Department Annual* 9, no. 2 (1965): 59–60.

Thompson, James Goldsmith. "The Soils of Rhodesia and Their Classification." PhD thesis, University of Natal, 1965.

Tonkin, Elizabeth. *Narrating Our Pasts: The Social Construction of Oral History.* Cambridge: Cambridge University Press, 1992.

Vail, Leroy, and Langdeg White. "Tribalism in the Political History of Malawi." In *The Creation of Tribalism in Southern Africa,* edited by Langdeg White, 151–92. Berkeley: University of California Press, 1989.

Vansina, Jan. *How Societies Are Born: Governance in West Central Africa before 1600.* Charlottesville: University of Virginia Press, 2004.

———. *Oral Tradition as History.* Madison: University of Wisconsin Press, 1985.

———. *Paths in the Rain Forest: Toward a History of Political Tradition in Equatorial Africa.* Madison: University of Wisconsin Press, 1990.

Warhurst, Philip. *Anglo-Portuguese Relations in South-Central Africa, 1890–1900.* London: Longman, 1962.

Werner, A. "A Vocabulary of the Lomwe Dialect of Makua (Mozambique)." *Journal of the Royal African Society* 1, no. 2 (1902): 236–51.

Widgren, Mats. "Towards an Historical Geography of Intensive Farming in Eastern Africa." In *Islands of Intensive Agriculture in Eastern Africa: Past and Present,* edited by Mats Widgren and John E. G. Sutton, 1–18. Oxford, UK: James Currey, 2004.

Wilder, G. A. *Chindau-English and English-Chindau Vocabulary with Grammatical Notes.* Mt. Silinda: Rhodesian Branch of American Board Mission in South Africa, 1915.

Woodward, H. W. "Handbook of the Makua Language as Spoken in the Archdeacon of Magila, Bonde, Tanganyika Territory, 1915." Typescript.

Worby, Eric. "Discipline without Oppression: Sequence, Timing and Marginality in Southern Rhodesia's Postwar Development Regime." *Journal of African History* 41, no. 1 (2000): 101–25.

———. "Maps, Names and Ethnic Games: The Iconography and Epistemology of Colonial Power in Northwestern Zimbabwe." *Journal of Southern African Studies* 20, no. 3 (1994): 371–92.

Zvarevashe, Ignasiyo M. *Dzinza RaVagovera VaChirumhanzu NaMutasa.* Gweru: Mambo Press, 1998.

Index

Italicized page numbers indicate figures, maps, or tables.

Kolibri 360 GmbH
Ferdinand-Jühlke-Straße 7
99095 Erfurt, Deutschland
produktsicherheit@kolibri360.de